LOCAL SUSTAINABLE URBAN DEVELOPMENT IN A GLOBALIZED WORLD

Local Sustainable Urban Development in a Globalized World

Edited by

LAUREN C. HEBERLE
University of Louisville, USA

and

SUSAN M. OPP
Texas Tech University, USA

ASHGATE

Published by
Ashgate Publishing Limited
Gower House
Croft Road
Aldershot
Hampshire GU11 3HR
England

Ashgate Publishing Company
Suite 420
101 Cherry Street
Burlington, VT 05401-4405
USA

Ashgate website: http://www.ashgate.com

British Library Cataloguing in Publication Data
Local sustainable urban development in a globalized world.
  - (Urban planning and environment)
  1. City planning - Environmental aspects 2. Sustainable development
  I. Heberle, Lauren C. II. Opp, Susan M.
  307.1'216

Library of Congress Cataloging-in-Publication Data
Heberle, Lauren C.
  Local sustainable urban development in a globalized world / by Lauren C. Heberle and Susan M. Opp.
       p. cm. -- (Urban planning and environment)
  Includes index.
  1. City planning--Environmental aspects. 2. Urbanization--Environmental aspects. 3. Sustainable development. I. Opp, Susan M., 1979- II. Title.

  HT166.H397 2008
  307.1'216--dc22

                                                                          2007041405

ISBN 978-0-7546-4994-6

Printed and bound in Great Britain by MPG Books Ltd, Bodmin, Cornwall.

Contents

List of Figures

List of Boxes

List of Tables

Notes on Contributors

Hirofumi Abe is a Professor in the Department of Waste Management, Division of Sustainability of Resources, at the Graduate School of Environmental Science, Okayama University, Japan. He specializes in the evaluation of regional policy and the application of regional input-output models to environmental Issues.

Simone Allin, Dipl.-Ing. Since May 2001, Simone Allin is research associate at the Department of Town Planning (University of Kaiserslautern/Germany). Her professional focus lies on analyzing formal planning procedures and the contents of formal plans considering new requirements in spatial and urban development. Her present research activities concentrate on the spatial impacts of virtualization against the background of different social and technological developments.

Jan Jaap de Boer retired at the end of 2006 from the Ministry of Housing, Spatial Planning and the Environment in the Netherlands after a career that started in the Directorate-general for Spatial Planning and that was followed by jobs in environmental impact assessment and strategic impact assessment and finally local environmental quality in the Directorate-general for Environmental Protection. He studied political sciences and land use planning at the University of Amsterdam.

He is now developing a new career in sculpturing (www.deboersculptures.nl). Email address: postbus@deboersculptures.nl.

Davisi Boontharm, Doctorat en projet architectural et urbain, University Paris 8. She is an Assistant Professor at Department of Architecture, School of Design and Environment, National University of Singapore. Her recent research focuses on commercial space and the evolution of Bangkok from 1782 to 2000.

Karen Cairns, EdD, MPH received her Ed.D. from the University of Louisville in Environmental Education. Currently, she is a retired nurse, free-lance environmental educator, community activist, yoga practitioner and teacher. Her research interests include environmental justice, environmental health, and community participation in environmental decision-making. She can be reached at Karen.cairns@gmail.com.

Tzu-Chia Chang is an Assistant Professor in the Department of Land Management and Development at Chang Jung Christian University in Taiwan, R.O.C. Professor Chang's research interests lie primarily in Land and Public Economics.

Andrea Collins, Research Associate, Cardiff University. Andrea is a based in the ESRC Centre for Business Relationships, Accountability, Sustainability and Society

(BRASS), Cardiff University (UK) and specializes in sustainability indicators, ecological footprinting, environmental decision making and environmental impacts of sport events.

Georgina Echániz Pellicer lives in Mexico City where she is an environmental project manager and consultant for the National Institute of Ecology (INE). Before joining INE, Georgina headed the Technical Secretariat of the Veracruz' Council for Environmental Protection and worked as an educational and environmental advisor for Schlumberger's SEED Water Project in Mexico. Georgina holds a Master of Science degree from the MIT/Media Lab where she worked on emergent educational methodologies based on constructionism and sustainable development applied to developing countries in Latin America and Africa, and she also holds a Bachelor of Law degree. Throughout her career, she has been a legal and environmental advisor for the Center for Environmental Law DASSUR, the Institute of Ecology of Xalapa and Greenpeace Mexico, and she has published technical papers in such diverse areas as environmental regulation development, hazardous materials and waste, landmine monitoring, education for sustainable development and children's role in the future of environmental engineering.

Carlton C. Eley, Environmental Protection Specialist. Carlton Eley works for the US Environmental Protection Agency's (EPA) Office of Policy, Economics, and Innovation in Washington, DC. As a staff member of the Development, Community, and Environment Division, which manages the Smart Growth program, he provides communities and stakeholders with the necessary tools, research, and policy that will assist them in pursuing development options that are good for the environment, community, and economy.

Carlton has a BA in Sociology/Social Work Curriculum from Elizabeth City State University (ECSU) as well as a MS in Urban and Regional Planning from the University of Iowa. In 2003, Carlton participated in the Ian Axford (New Zealand) Fellowship in Public Policy. Jointly administered by the Commonwealth Fund and Fulbright New Zealand, the six month fellowship presented him with the opportunity to learn about New Zealand approaches to achieve smart growth objectives. The report, "Smart Growth Down Under: Taking Steps Toward Sustainable Settlements in New Zealand", was the research product from his fellowship.

Andrew Flynn, Senior Lecturer (Environmental Policy and Planning), Cardiff University. Andrew is based in the School of City and Regional Planning, Cardiff University (UK). His research interests lie in the formulation and implementation of environmental and food policy and of the nature of regulation. His most recent work has been on the regulation of food consumption in Britain and the European Union. His work on food regulation has, in turn, helped to inform his work on environmental regulation, particularly in relation to the role of supply chains and business support networks. Andrew is also Course Director of the MSc in Sustainability, Planning and Environmental Policy.

Robin Ganser is Senior Lecturer in Spatial Planning at Oxford Brookes University. His teaching and research specialties include urban fringe and rural issues, regeneration, brownfield re-use, impact assessment and planning process management. He also works as a planning consultant in these specialist areas.

Katrina M. Harmon is a second-year PhD student at the School of Urban and Public Affairs at the University of Louisville. She received her MPA from the Woodrow Wilson School of Public and International Affairs at Princeton University, where she was a Truman Scholar. She also holds a BA from the University of Colorado – Boulder, where she was a Phi Beta Kappa, Summa Cum laude graduate with majors in International Affairs and French. Her interests include economic development, participatory planning, and comparative urban studies.

Lauren C. Heberle, PhD is an Assistant Professor of Sociology at the University of Louisville and Director of the EPA Region 4 Environmental Finance Center at UofL. Her work focuses on environmental policy, community participation in environmental and land use decisions, community and economic development and social movements especially as they pertain to environmental justice.

Hai-Feng Hu is an Associate Professor in the Department of Business Administration at Wenzao Ursuline College of Languages in Taiwan, R.O.C. Professor Hu's research interests are primarily in land and public economics.

Singh Intrachooto is an architect and Assistant Professor of Building Technology at the Faculty of Architecture at Kasetsart University, Bangkok, Thailand. He is currently its Head of the Department of Building Innovation and Technology. He holds a Doctor of Philosophy degree in Design Technology from Massachusetts Institute of Technology (MIT). His design evolves around sustainable design concepts as his research focuses on identifying patterns of technological innovation in environmentally responsible architecture. Dr. Intrachooto's investigations also include material developments from manufacturing and agricultural by-products as well as waste management in buildings' construction, operation and maintenance. Of particular interest is his focus on bridging academia and industry to leverage technology, education and production approaches to stimulate innovation within the design and architecture industry. Dr. Intrachooto also teaches design at the School of Architecture and Urban Planning at the University of Washington and gives lectures in Japan, Hong Kong and the United States while maintaining his design practice in Thailand with industrial products, residential works, commercial facilities and urban redevelopments.

Lidia Mierzejewska, Doctor of Geography, Assistant Professor in the Faculty of Geographical and Geological Sciences, Adam Mickiewicz University, Poznań, Poland. She is the author of two books and over 20 original research papers (six in English) covering such topics as the natural aspects of the development and operation of cities, sustainable development, contemporary urbanization processes, and the local economy. She gives lectures in the theory of spatial management, landscape ecology, sustainable development, and environmental protection.

Marta Moreno studied Biology for her BA and did a PhD in the Social Psychology and Ecology Departments of the Autónoma University of Madrid, Spain on the subject "Environmental attitudes and ecological behavior of Madrid citizens". She is currently Assistant Professor at the Sociology Departament of the Spanish National Open University (Universidad Nacional de Educación a Distancia, UNED). She lectures on Human Ecology and Environment and Society. Her main research interests are in Urban Ecology and Environmental Health.

Criseida Navarro-Díaz, PhD is an Assistant Professor at the University of Puerto Rico (UPR) and President of CNC, Corp. – Planning and Economic Advisors, a consulting firm based in San Juan, PR. She holds a PhD in Regional Planning and Economic Development from the Massachusetts Institute of Technology along with a Bachelors Degree in Architecture from MIT and a Masters in City Planning from UPR. She has thirteen years of experience in the fields of regional land use planning and economic development. She has been responsible for conducting the planning efforts of four high-tech regions and has studied many others in the United States and its territories. Prior to joining the Faculty at the UPR Graduate School of Planning, Dr. Navarro-Díaz was an Instructor of Regional Sciences and Urban Design courses at MIT. The chapter of her writing that is included in this volume is part of her doctoral dissertation (2005) at MIT which was funded by the US Department of Housing and Urban Development's Doctoral Dissertation Grant.

Yoshiro Ono is a Professor in the Department of Waste Management, Division of Sustainability of Resources, at the Graduate School of Environmental Science, Okayama University, Japan. She specializes in environmental capacity on water quality and waste management.

Susan M. Opp, PhD, received her PhD from the University of Louisville in May 2007. Dr. Opp currently works as an Assistant Professor of Public Administration at Texas Tech University. Dr. Opp is also a Research Associate for the Center for Environmental Policy and Management at the University of Louisville. Dr. Opp's research interests include bureaucratic discretion, brownfield redevelopment, regulatory theory, political control of the bureaucracy, and environmental policy.

David Pijawka is Full Professor in the School of Planning at Arizona State University (ASU). He is also Project Director for the US Agency for International Development TIES program at ASU. Dr. Pijawka also serves as a faculty member of the Global Institute of Sustainability. He was the Director of the PhD program in Environmental Design and Planning in the College of Design, the Director of the Southwest Center for Environmental Research and Policy, and the Interim Director for the School of Planning and Landscape Architecture. He has published several books on sustainability and is recognized for his work in the areas of environmental management, waste and risk assessment, disaster recovery and environmental justice.

Raquel Pinderhughes is Director and Professor of Urban Studies at San Francisco State University where she teaches courses on urban environmental planning and policy. Her work focuses on improving quality of life for urban residents. Her areas of expertise include: sustainable development, sustainable urban infrastructure planning and management, environmental justice, urban agriculture, local food systems, urban poverty, and green collar jobs. She has conducted research on sustainable urban development in Cuba, Brazil, India, and the United States. Her current research focuses on how support for green economic development can bring new opportunities and benefits to low-income people and communities by providing low-income youth and adults with barriers to employment with access to green collar jobs, which she defines as "manual labor jobs in businesses whose primary processes, products and/or services have a beneficial effect on the environment and whose work directly improves environmental quality in some way". Her recent book, Alternative Urban Futures: Planning for Sustainable Development in Cities throughout the World, focuses on how we can design and manage urban infrastructures in ways that prioritize human needs, are less damaging to the natural resource base, and produce less waste. She is also Director of the SFSU/Delancey Street College Program which provides ex-felons and drug addicts with an opportunity to get a BA degree; President of the Board of Directors of the Ecology Center and Rising Sun Energy Center/California Youth Energy Services, has served as Environmental Commissioner for the city of Berkeley; on advisory boards for Urban Habitat, San Francisco's Sustainable City Project, and California's Comparative Risk Project.

Juan Pedro Ruiz was trained in Zoology and Anthropology and obtained a PhD in Ecology at the Complutense and Autónoma Universities in Madrid, Spain. He has focused in Human Ecology, Urban Ecology, Landscape Ecology and Environment and Development in Latin America as lecturing subjects and research interests. In recent years he has conducted extensive applied research in these areas in Venezuela, Cuba and Central America. He works as a Senior Lecturer in the Ecology Department of Autónoma University in Madrid.

Kasama Polakit graduated from the University of Melbourne, Australia in 2004. She is an Assistant Professor in the Department of Urban and Regional Planning, Florida Atlantic University, Ft Lauderdale, USA. She has experience in teaching architecture and urban design in Thailand, Australia, and the US. Her research interests include the relationship between the built environment and the development of social and cultural capital and Asian urbanism.

Jaap van Staalduine is Deputy Director, Local Environmental Quality and Traffic, Department of the Environment at the Ministry of Housing, Spatial Planning and the Environment in The Netherlands. Van Staalduine is especially involved with integrating spatial planning into the environment.

Gerhard Steinebach, Prof. Dr.-Ing. Since 1999, Gerhard Steinebach is head of the Department of Town Planning (University of Kaiserslautern/Germany). His professional focus lies on urban land use planning, pollution control and noise modelling, urban ecology, military and civil conversion and regulation of planning processes. His present research activities concentrate on the work of an interdisciplinary International Research Training Group (IRTG) at the University of Kaiserslautern which analyses the possibilities of visualising large and unstructured data sets within applications in geospatial planning. In addition to this, Gerhard Steinebach is affiliated to the Academy for Spatial Research and Planning, the Council of Municipal Development of the federal government of Rhineland-Palatinate, the Council at the European Academy for the Exploration of the Consequences of Scientific Developments and provides expert opinion for the German Academic Exchange Service (DAAD) and the German Research Foundation (DFG).

Yaourai Suthiranart received her Master of Urban Design and Planning from the University of Pennsylvania and PhD in Urban Planning from the University of Washington, USA. She is currently the Head of Masters Program in Urban and Environmental Planning at Kasetsart University in Bangkok, Thailand. Dr. Suthiranart's research focuses on Transportation systems and planning.

Mamoru Taniguchi is a Professor in the Department of Urban Environment Development, Division of Social Engineering and Environmental Management, at the Graduate School of Environmental Science, Okayama University, Japan, where he specializes in urban environmental planning. In addition, he is a member of the National Land Council, and the Council for Infrastructure in Japan.

Ruth Yabes, PhD is an Associate Professor in the School of Planning at Arizona State University (ASU). She is also a former Director of the Program for Southeast Asian Studies at ASU. Her research interests include participation, community development and international and rural development, especially in Southeast Asia and the Philippines. She is co-editor of the book, *Southeast Asian Urban Environments: Structured and Spontaneous*, with Carla Chifos. Most recently she has conducted research on *zanjera* communal irrigation systems based on common property principles and the impact of a regional government irrigation project on the systems in Ilocos Norte, northern Philippines, as a time-series analysis using original research from the mid-1980s until the present.

Luke Yeung received a Bachelor of Science in Architecture from McGill University and a Master of Architecture from the Massachusetts Institute of Technology. His research work focuses primarily on building and architectural materials from the perspectives of manufacturing, localized production and utilization over their life cycles. As this particular research necessitates collaboration across various academic, professional and industrial fields, he has undertaken subsequent investigations concerning the roles of education, practice and production in contemporary design and architecture. Currently he is a Visiting Lecturer and Researcher in the Faculty of Architecture at Kasetsart University, Bangkok, Thailand.

Acknowledgements

The editors of this book would like to thank the International Urban Planning and Environment Association for establishing a biannual conference which brought together many of the authors included in this book to exchange ideas and further their work in the area of urban sustainable development practices. Special thanks goes to Fae Goodman, who provided essential assistance in getting the manuscript ready for publication. To those authors who contributed to this book we extend our thanks for their patience and ability to work with us across space and technological differences. Also, we thank the Valerie Rose and the staff at Ashgate Publishing for their production assistance and their flexibility in working with us on this project.

Finally, we would like to thank Donald Miller and Gert de Roo who helped us conceptualize the structure and content of the book.

Lauren C. Heberle and Susan M. Opp
University of Louisville, Louisville KY and
Texas Tech University, Lubbock, TX, USA

Introduction

Sustainable Urban Development: Local Strategies as Global Solutions

Lauren C. Heberle

Scientists continue to warn about significant negative consequences to the physical and economic future of the planet if current human production and consumption behaviors continue without change. The World Doomsday Clock was recently set closer to midnight due to renewed proliferation of nuclear weapons capability and unprecedented climate change caused by human behavior. Sir Nicholas Stern's report to the Prime Minister and the Chancellor of the Exchequer of the United Kingdom argues that unchecked climate change will reduce the global gross domestic product by an estimate of 5 percent to 20 percent but that an investment of just 1 percent of the global GDP would dramatically reduce those effects (Stern et al., 2006). Geologist M. King Hubbert predicted in 1956 that US oil production would peak in the early 1970s and that it would require more and more energy to extract what oil was left. Others have predicted that we are now on the downward slope for oil extraction in the Middle East and elsewhere (Deffeyes 2003; Goodstein 2004). In addition to oil consumption, humans continue to exploit other natural resources at an unprecedented rate all over the globe causing innumerable local environmental crises with global impact.

Sustainable urban development has become a powerful framework for developing solutions that improve the quality of life on a local level and can also be an important component of responding to the broader global environmental crises. Across the globe, urban planners have taken up the challenge of designing urban living in ways that leave a smaller ecological footprint. Although many rely upon the definition of sustainable development crafted by the UN's World Commission on Environment and Development in *Our Common Future* in 1987, where it is defined as "development that meets the needs of the present without compromising the ability of future generations to meet their needs" (Bruntland 1987), the operationalization, implementation, and measurement of that definition at the local level remains highly contested and variable. The interaction between locally based actors and agencies with those at regional, national, and international levels frames the debates surrounding sustainable development policies and practices. Thus, implementation of sustainable development practices is subject to a wide variety of external cultural, political and economic pressures at every level.

The authors presented in this book represent leading scholars and practitioners of sustainable development from all across the globe. Using case studies and examples of best practices, many of the authors propose methods for understanding and successfully implementing sustainable practices at the local level in the context of the complex systems of pressures and connections within which planning is conducted. Providing geographical diversity, the collected chapters come from sources that reflect very different levels of income, general population education, cultural norms, legal systems, and governmental structures. With the diversity of authors and chapters in this volume valuable insight, tools, and suggestions can be gleaned for practitioners, scholars, students, and the general public alike.

The editors have selected the chapters to be included in this book based upon the author's contribution to a better understanding of two distinct facets of local sustainability planning initiatives and the potential for making meaningful change: First, the wide range of local planning action alternatives available to planners that may be pursued, in spite of the constraints generated by processes of globalization; Second, the array of public policy options, including planning and sustainability education that could reduce the effect of external pressures in shaping the "possible" local alternatives.

The chapters in this volume presume a willingness of local planners and local authorities to act, but many reflect the limited understanding by local decision-makers of the options available to them. As a result, this volume supports the processes of exploration to discover objectives, strategies, and specific actions that reflect or reinforce local populations' interest in the sustainability of their environments.

The authors address questions about urban development, urban planning, and urban culture as they relate to the global problem of environmental sustainability. We have organized this book to provide a discussion of 1) frameworks for implementing sustainable development in planning, 2) a selection of different methods of definition, measurement, and assessment of sustainable practices and 3) a section that raises questions about cultural, values, norms, education, and citizen participation in sustainable development. Within these three broad areas we include some case studies to provide concrete examples of implementation.

Contextual Frameworks of Sustainable Development

Several chapters address the status of Western countries, particularly the United States, as unequal consumers and waste producers. Structures for implementing sustainable development practices in an urban setting need to consider reframing how planning works at the local level in order to make real and lasting positive change.

Raquel Pinderhughes calls on western city planners and others involved in decision making regarding infrastructure in our urban areas to engage in practices that are already in place all over the world that will lead us closer to sustainable urban development. Importantly, she argues that even as the world struggles with vast inequities, enormous environmental problems, and extreme financial limitations, the technical ability already exist to establish sustainable urban development practices that are not financially burdensome. Urban planners in developed countries such as the United States must be willing to shift their perspectives to ask questions about fairness. They must not only be willing to share technology with developing countries but also look to them for answers about how to provide urban infrastructure in a sustainable manner.

Implementing any kind of planning process within a local, regional or national context requires an organizational structure that can process information effectively and efficiently. This is especially true of sustainable urban development practices, since they presume an interaction between various levels of government agencies. Gerhard Steinebach et al., suggest that sustainable urban development can be best achieved if communication systems between local, regional and national agencies are improved. Communication structures must be in place for institutional actors to build trust, make timely decisions, and see how their local decisions have effects external to local boundaries and regional and national decisions affect local communities.

Smart Growth is a term used in the US to describe a set of planning principles that have the potential to contribute to sustainable development. Smart growth outcomes are practices that are implemented mostly on a local level but have broader regional impacts. These principles are meant to guide US planners and land use decision makers in choosing development goals and strategies that help create more sustainable communities in terms of economic, social and environmental well-being. Carlton Eley highlights Wellington, New Zealand as a best practice example of a locality faced with limited room for expansion and a desire to create a sustainable community and points out connections to the US efforts to support smart growth initiatives.

National guidelines for sustainable development practices are often politically touchy and frequently difficult to implement, let alone monitor. Jaap van Van Staalduine and Jan Jaap de Boer both present descriptions of the efforts that are taking place in the Netherlands intended to help bridge local, regional and national planning efforts. Van Staalduine argues that the national environmental policy has developed in a way that recognizes the relationship between spatial and environmental planning by using their noise abatement law, the soil remediation policy, the City and Environment project, and a fairly new Urban Renewal Investment Budget. These tools allow the local and regional authorities to develop area oriented solutions. De Boer offers us a description of the potential for the transition from a national model implemented by local authorities to a more decentralized model to result in more local and area plans with higher quality land use decisions that are more beneficial to the population and the environment.

A case study of how national structures and frameworks impact local sustainable planning efforts comes from Poland. Lidia Mierzejewska examines the current situation in Poland and in Pozna specifically. She develops a general model of sustainable development for Polish cities that integrates the ecological, economic, social, spatial and institutional spheres of activity and decision making. This framework plays through many definitions of the various kinds of sustainable practices that should be considered when constructing a plan for a city. It calls attention to the idea that, to engage in practices that do not harm or deplete resources of future generations, an interdisciplinary approach to urban planning must be utilized.

Measurement, Definition, and Assessment of Sustainable Development

How does a community decide if a particular practice is efficient or even useful to development? To measure whether sustainable development practices are being implemented, and how well those practices succeed requires identification of the means of measurement, the indicators that best represent principles of sustainable development, and benchmarks for what communities decide is adequate. Hai-Feng Hu et. al explore the concept of efficiency in regard to land use conversion decisions, which have an important impact on the possibility and potential effectiveness of sustainable development. These authors view efficiency as a highly subjective term that is dependent upon the perspective of the individual and his or her understanding of specific utility, upon which efficiency depends. Thus, in understanding efficiency, they call for an examination of utility from the perspective of all agents in a decision and the inclusion of a dynamic element that allows for changes in utility over time. Their analysis leads them to argue that individual utility and efficiency are increased and better, more sustainable decisions are made in situations where impacted persons (i.e. those owning adjacent property to that being considered for conversion) engage directly and voluntarily without government intervention or control.

Katrina Harmon's chapter continues the discussion of measurement. She examines why it is important to standardize or calibrate efforts to broadly define sustainable development across global, national and sub-national levels and set up ways to understand how differences of establishing indicators measured at the local level can impact implementation since they often reflect local values and goals. Localities often come up with lists of indicators based on their values and goals thus there is great variation in whether they dovetail with national and international goals such as those set out by the United Nations in Agenda 21. Her comparison of Seattle and Minneapolis demonstrates the variability within one nation and across two cities that are both considered progressive and prosperous.

Once an organization, government, or agency has established sustainability indicators, it is a complicated task to determine and gather the data necessary to actually measure the chosen indicators. Robin Ganser provides a clear example of this issue in his discussion of how sustainable development indicators related to greenspace protection and land reuse should be measured, what data need to be collected at what unit of analysis, and at what point in the planning process that data might be evaluated and used. His close examination of German and English indicator systems highlights the crucial role that organizational structure and procedures play in shaping how agencies manage to define, measure, and document sustainability targets in development practices.

People need benchmarks and methods of measuring impact and progress toward improvement to document positive sustainable development practices. The concept of an ecological footprint has become a tool of some practitioners both for establishing the need for sustainable development practices and for measuring progress toward sustainability. An ecological footprint is a measure that looks at how much a population or practice consumes in production and determines how much land and water are required to sustain that population or practice. It essentially tells a city, an agency, even an individual, what their lasting effect on the ecological systems around them is, given their everyday practices. The measure is usually in global hectares per capita. This is a useful concept for urban planning and development, since it provides a meaningful metaphor to which people can attach concrete practices and a uniform metric to measure diverse practices. Andrea Collins and Andrew Flynn take a look at how the idea is being measured in Wales with a particular focus on the impact that knowledge about footprinting has had on decision making in Cardiff, the capital city of Wales.

Mamoru Taniguchi et al., present a new measurement method concerning the capacity of a given environment to sustain different population levels. They ask "What numbers can the region support with the resources located within the specific ecosystem?" Their case study includes 87 Japanese local regions and covers a time span of over 330 years. Using rice harvest data by region dating from the pre-modern age, they explore the concept of a sustainable population and how the present population of each region is different from the theoretically calculated sustainable population. The authors develop a multiple-regression model that investigates factors affecting this difference, namely the environmental load in each region. Using this model, variables such as political control, infrastructure, and natural disasters that affect the environmental load are evaluated. The unique feature of this chapter is the incredible span of time for which rice harvest data is available, which provides the authors with the opportunity to test measures of sustainability over the long term.

Impact of Culture, Values, Education, and Participation on Development Processes

Culture, values, education and citizen and community participation are all crucial aspects to take into account when defining, measuring or implementing sustainable urban development policies and practices. It is especially important to be cognizant of the relationship between international efforts, national and regional efforts, and local implementation. How communities interpret what is being asked (or required) of them determines how and whether implantation of sustainable practices occurs and is successful. Marta Moreno and Juan Ruiz argue that this process includes psychological processes that intersect with social, environmental, and behavioral factors. They conducted a survey of drivers in Madrid about their attitudes toward and use of automobile and public transportation in order to assess psychosocial influences in their driving behavior. The drivers presented strong resistance to changing driving patterns, and had a perception that merely changing their individual practices would not make a difference for overall change in city transportation patterns. Thus, the authors argue that current cognitive, social, environmental, and behavioral strategies can not be implemented separately and must be developed as an integrated model that recovers the traditional commons model based on the definition of goals and measures by stakeholders for the management of deteriorating common goals.

Cultural practices are extremely important in considering how to plan sustainable cities, especially in areas where certain practices have been in existence for centuries. Kasama Polakit and Davisi Boontharm examine the role of street and canal vendors in Bangkok in everyday life by investigating their social and spatial practices; how they function in everyday urban life; and how they persist and can be sustained amidst the dynamic of the changing global economy imposing upon Bangkok urban environment. The authors argue that official urban planning and design practices in Thailand can not achieve sustainability in urban development without recognizing the local autonomy of everyday social and economic life of the city's inhabitants.

How people learn about sustainability and their depth of understanding forms the basis for future success of any sustainability program or project. The role of education is crucial at every stage, from the elementary levels all the way through to professional schools, including non-formal community education. Culturally sensitive pedagogy and "hands on" learning methods are appealing to sustainable development models that require community participatory elements. Having an educated population willing to develop urban models of sustainability can bring about innovation.

Georgina Echániz-Pellicer emphasizes the need for education to implement a holistic transformation to cope with current sustainability needs. Taking a constructivist approach to pedagogy, she argues that a participatory learning environment must be introduced at the earliest stage possible and that technological learning material that supports the exploration of sustainable development questions must be taught with a hands-on approach where students apply their skills in a local context. Progressive environmental education should provide an opportunity for people to explore and understand urban environmental issues while addressing them within a meaningful local context. This type of learning leads to the generation of autonomous knowledge, the kind demanded by sustainability planning and essential for cities where people not only are aware of urban environmental facts, but also have the skills that allow them to implement the necessary conditions for promoting urban development while ensuring local environmental conservation.

Singh Intrachooto et al., discuss pedagogy employed in an architectural studio education at Kasetsart University in Thailand, not only to instill an awareness of urban problems but also to question the role of architects in ameliorating the urban dilemma. The studio investigation focuses on the problem of annual flooding. An urban water accumulation prototype was explored for Bangkok's central business district (CBD). Addressing the flooding issue while developing a proposal for a CBD's building complex within densely populated commercial structures has generated a number of novel design concepts and solutions, including water-delaying façades, organic building envelopes, and rainwater catchment systems for urban neighborhoods. The authors propose that integrating an urban problem into architectural studio education allows architects the opportunity to provide innovative solutions that mitigate urban desolation.

As environmental education improves in institutional settings, public involvement in environmental decision making and urban planning is also improved. Karen Cairns reviews the need for public involvement in addressing environmental issues and suggests two key components for involvement: education into citizenship and understanding of the Precautionary Principle which simply means that environmental policy should implement protection practices even in the face of limited scientific proof of cause and effect. Public involvement requires environmental literacy. Surveys have found that the majority of Americans are concerned and have positive attitudes about environmental issues, but lack even a rudimentary understanding of these. One basic misconception for example, concerns the role of science and the impossibility of finding "one right answer" to environmental dilemmas. The key to an involved citizenry may be environmental education which links environmental information with "education into citizenship" or the "how to" of participatory democracy. Understanding the limits of science and the relationship of the Precautionary Principle to making risk-based decisions can decrease frustration and promote issue collaboration across many levels.

How and whether public participation occurs varies across space and time. Power dynamics among participants shape the level and quality of participation in vital environmental problem solving. Ruth Yabes and David Pijawaka examine the role of participation in two locations in central Phoenix, Arizona. One case involves a coalition of three neighborhoods whose residents are dealing with environmental hazards. These residents sought information from university classes in order to articulate to government officials the environmental injustices faced by their community. The second case is located in a poor, African-American populated area which has further deteriorated because of a toxic event. A survey of residents examined participation in the community and the implications of a lack of participation by community members. The first case provides insights into the information necessary for participation programs that are starting up and the importance of partnership building between neighborhoods and universities. In the second case the survey demonstrates that the lack of information on environmental hazards in the absence of a participation program leads to stress, alienation, miscommunication and the inability to manage or resolve conflict.

Economic growth can come into conflict with sustainable development when it does not include attention to social equity. Equal education of a population is crucial to the future economic development of an area as unequal educational experiences can limit the forms of economic growth that an area can experience. More specifically, low educational levels in a community can affect the long-term sustainability of that community in economic, social and environmental terms. Criseida Navarro-Díaz measures the distributional effects of technology-driven economic growth. The author questions empirically whether or not the developments within a community of high-tech activities on their own benefit the entire population in an equitable manner. She argues that in high-tech regions, people with lower educational attainment are at a disadvantage, receive fewer benefits from high-tech investment because of higher regional costs of living and large wage differentials between more and less educated people within those regions. This problem could be addressed by harmonizing technology-based economic growth strategies with education and housing affordability policies and programs. Linking these policy components in a region would enable a community to connect economic sectors, more equitably distribute the benefits that are the result of growth, and improve both the economic and the social sustainability of the development process. An area simply can not function in an economically or socially sustainable manner when there is a large economic gap based on skill levels among the population. This connects to sustainable development in that the unequal distribution of resources, in this case education, can cause communities to fail in their efforts to implement sustainable development initiatives.

How to create sustainable urban development is a global problem that requires local, regional, national and international solutions, thus, as demonstrated by the authors in this book, many approaches to definition, measurement and implementation have developed over time. For urban planning to succeed in fostering sustainable development requires interdisciplinary approaches that reach across political borders and make sense at the local levels of implementation. This also requires traditional planning methods to be challenged and reframed so that they include more participatory methods that involve broad representation of communities, actual and perceived equity across diverse populations, goals that move beyond those of traditional economic development models, new modes of communication and education, new organizational structures within, outside and across governments, and a willingness to think about long range returns rather than short term gains. It is our hope that the authors of this book offer the readers some clear examples and methods of how to think about, implement, and evaluate sustainable development practices in ways that make sense at the local level.

References

Brundtland, G. (1987), *Our Common Future: The World Commission on Environment and Development* (Oxford University Press).

Deffeyes, K.S. (2003), *Hubbert's Peak: The Impending World Oil Shortage* (Princeton University Press, Princeton, NJ).

Goodstein, D.L. (2004), *Out of Gas: The End of the Age of Oil* (W.W. Norton & Company, New York).

Stern, N., et al. (2006), 'Stern Review: The Economics of Climate Change', *HM Treasury*, <http://www.hm-treasury.gov.uk/independent_reviews/stern_review_economics_climate_change/stern_review_report.cfm>, (accessed 3/13/07).

Chapter 1

Alternative Urban Futures: Designing Urban Infrastructures that Prioritize Human Needs, are Less Damaging to the Natural Resource Base, and Produce Less Waste

Raquel Pinderhughes

This chapter addresses the question: how can planners and other urban authorities design and manage urban infrastructure in ways that prioritize human needs, are less damaging to the natural resource base, and produce less waste? The focus is on five urban infrastructure areas: waste, water, energy, transportation, and food systems. Infrastructure refers to "long lived engineered structures, equipment, facilities, and services that are used in economic production and by households which enhance residential and non-residential consumption and production. Infrastructure includes: water systems, solid waste management, drainage and flood protection, roads, mass transit, energy installations, and telecommunications, schools and medical facilities, among other systems" (World Bank 1994).

Infrastructure is an essential element of urban development and a major link between development and the environment. Infrastructure has a dramatic impact on a city's local and regional land and natural resource base, on people's daily lives, on the form and quality of urban development, and on the global ecosystem (Rees 1996; De Roo and Miller 2000; Pinderhughes 2004). Adequate infrastructure includes provisions related to both physical infrastructure, such as water supply, sanitation facilities, drainage, roads, solid waste disposal facilities and land management and social infrastructure, such as education and health care facilities (Drakakis-Smith 1995). Adequate infrastructure services are essential to economic activities, coping with density and population growth, improving living standards, reducing poverty, raising productivity, protecting the environment, and promoting social and environmental equity (Ingram and Kessides 1994; Drakakis-Smith 1995). Well-designed and well-managed investments in urban infrastructure development can reduce adverse environmental and social impacts within a city and its periphery, leading to improvements in the natural resource base, public health, and well-being for urban residents (Choguill 1996). Badly-designed and poorly-managed urban infrastructures contribute to environmental degradation, poverty, and social inequality (Drakakis-Smith 1995; Pinderhughes 2004).

One of the most interesting aspects of urban infrastructure from a global perspective is that, although there are very significant differences between cities and regions and between wealthy and poor nations, most urban infrastructure systems share one overarching feature – they have been designed and managed with little regard for their environmental or social impacts. Throughout the world, urban infrastructure systems designed to deliver water, waste, energy, transportation, and food rely on non-renewable energy sources, utilize water and energy inefficiently and wastefully, are based on ever-increasing inputs of non-renewable energy sources, produce air, water, ground contamination, toxic and hazardous waste, and contribute to social and environmental injustices and inequalities.

The fact that infrastructure services related to water, waste, energy, transportation and food are so unfairly and unevenly distributed between countries and regions exacerbates these problems. The richest fifth of the world's population consume 75 percent of the world's economic product, while the poorest fifth of the world's population consume less than two percent. Approximately one quarter of the world's population living in industrialized countries consume more than 80 percent of the world's non-renewable resources and most of the world's food products, while billions of people around the world are deprived of basic needs (Tinbergen and Hueting 1991; Pinderhughes 2004). Although the United States accounts for less than 5 percent of the world population, the nation consumes more than one third of the world's transportation energy. Contrast this with the entire continent of Africa which uses less than 5 percent of the world's commercial energy. While people living in industrialized nations are using three to seven gallons of water to flush their toilets, people living in the poorest countries of the world struggle to survive on a daily ration equal to less than a bucket of water per family (Tearfund 2001).

People in wealthy, industrialized nations are able to consume the vast majority of the world's natural resources and produce the vast majority of the world's waste at such an enormous scale because chains of production extend throughout the planet and, the social and environmental impacts of these productive and consumptive chains are hidden from their view in low-income communities, rural areas, fenced-off industrial locations, and countries far from their national borders (Ryan and Durning 1997). Since wealthy, industrialized countries import the vast majority of resources they use and export much of their waste, people in industrialized countries benefit from transferring the social and environmental costs of their wasteful production and consumption activities to the poor, developing countries and people that supplied them in the first place (Adriaanse et al., 1997; Puckett et al., 2002).

Although the concept of development refers to processes that are supposed to lead to improvements in the living conditions of people, in practice the development paradigm is associated with planning and economic capacity building strategies that develop infrastructures primarily designed to increase economic growth and profit, not quality of life (Rees 1998; Pinderhughes 2004). One of the greatest tragedies of the development paradigm and its associated planning processes is that six decades of development planning and immense increases in urban and industrial development, economic activity, and economic growth around the world have benefited only a small proportion of the world's population. More than one fifth of the world's population still lack access to safe drinking water and four hundred million people still lack access to sanitation services (United Nations Centre for Human Settlements 1994). Almost two-thirds of the urban populations in Africa, Asia, Latin America, and the Caribbean have no hygienic means of disposing of human waste and an even greater number lack adequate means to dispose of waste water (Human Settlement Programme 2001). Anywhere from 30 percent to 50 percent of urban solid waste in developing countries is left uncollected. Globally, two billion people still have no access to modern energy services and more than one billion people breathe unhealthy air daily. Approximately 1.3 billion people live in areas that do not meet World Health Organization (WHO) standards for airborne dust and smoke. About one billion people live in cities that exceed WHO standards for sulfur dioxide. An estimated three million people die each year from air pollution- two thirds of them are poor people, mostly women and children who die from indoor pollution caused by burning wood and dung (Moosa 2002). In the past four decades, the number of people living in cities in conditions of absolute poverty has continued to increase. Millions of urban residents have incomes so low they cannot fulfill the most basic nutritional and housing requirements. Even after spending the bulk of their income on food, people in poverty suffer from hunger and malnutrition.

Worldwide hegemony of the post WWII development paradigm has meant that despite differences between nations, regions, levels of development, abundance, or scarcity of resources, almost every city in the world now suffers from problems related to dispersed and unbalanced patterns of natural resource and energy consumption, air and water contamination, solid waste accumulation, chaotic growth patterns, traffic congestion, decreasing open space and farmland, environmental degradation, and profound social inequality, poverty, and environmental injustice (Couch 1990; Gossaye 2000; Pinderhughes 2004). In both wealthy and poor nations, and despite differences in levels of industrialization, almost all infrastructure projects related to water, waste, energy, transportation and food systems create environmental and social problems. The negative impacts of toxic exposures from infrastructure projects, such as waste treatment plants, landfills, incinerators, oil refineries, coal plants, freeways, etc., are experienced disproportionately by poor people.

Sustainable Development: Prioritizing Human Needs, Reducing Damage to the Natural Resource Base, Producing Less Waste

The environmental and social problems created by problematic models of urban development, growth, and infrastructure planning are being challenged by advocates of sustainable development. In the last few decades, sustainable development has become the most popular concept and buzzword in contemporary urban planning circles. Yet despite the rhetoric about the need for sustainable development, the vast majority of planners in cities throughout the world continue to support an almost constant replication and expansion of unsustainable economic activities, infrastructure development, and consumption patterns. The vast majority of urban planning practices and procedures continue to foster divisions between economic activities and nature and increasing social inequality within and between groups of people, countries and regions; the result is increasing environmental degradation and social inequality at every level, juxtaposed by increased rhetoric about the need to protect precious environmental resources and reduce poverty through sustainable urban development.

But no matter how passionate the commitment to sustainable development, planners will not be able to move beyond rhetoric until they begin to consistently support and promote alternative paradigms, processes, and appropriate technologies designed to deliver urban infrastructure services in ways that reduce environmental degradation, social inequality, and poverty at a large scale. Fortunately, alternative paradigms and processeses have already been developed.

In the rest of this chapter, I provide a very brief pragmatic summary of some of the most accessible and viable alternative processes and appropriate technologies available to planners and other urban authorities who want to support sustainable urban infrastructure development in the areas of water, waste, energy, transportation and food. The summary provides readers with an understanding of the structural changes that need to occur in order to move away from infrastructures that are environmentally and socially problematic and towards more sustainable forms of urban infrastructure development.

Urban water management

In the area of urban water management, inefficiency and overuse of water in wealthy, industrialized countries must be addressed by decreasing drawdown of the water supply. This can be done by immediately reducing water consumption for agriculture and landscaping, installing grey water systems which capture and reuse water, treating wastewater for reuse using constructed wetlands and living machines, and integrating energy and water efficient processes and technologies into households.

The state of Vermont installed a bioremediation wastewater treatment system that uses a series of tanks containing plants and other organisms to naturally clean wastewater at a highway rest area serving 500,000 people per year. A conventional wastewater treatment system would have cost over a million dollars, compared to the living machine they utilized which cost only $250,000 to install. Sewage is biologically treated and then recycled back into the toilets to be used as flush water. Another advantage was that the living machine can be moved to different locations as needed.

A firm in Budapest, Hungary designed a municipal backup waste treatment system that has the capacity to treat raw sewage generated by urban residents on a floating arboretum gravel barge. This floating greenhouse uses polycarbonate panels set in galvanized steel trusses to hold thousands of plants, bacteria, microorganisms, zooplankton, snails, crabs, and fish in an enclosed sunlit managed environment which breaks down and digests organic pollutants in municipal and industrial wastewater.

In Sumida, Japan, the municipality introduced rainwater management strategies to address water shortages and problems related to flooding. During the wet season, users can rely on community-level rainwater collection systems to provide water for firefighting and other non-drinking uses. During the dry season, rainwater users can connect to the municipal water system. In each of these examples, the community benefits not only through an increase in the fresh water supply, but also through an improved environment.

Developing countries face very different challenges, the most important of which is to develop infrastructures that provide clean water for all urban residents utilizing sustainable water management strategies to deliver adequate and safe water supply.

Urban waste management

In the area of urban waste management, economic activities in prosperous nations must be restructured around a resource recognition approach that is designed to significantly reduce waste in production and distribution processes through reduce, re-use, and recycling processes. Policies which encourage materials exchange, reprocessing, and pollution prevention must be promoted in order to facilitate large and small institutions and businesses to trade, sell, and/or give away unwanted materials to one another in order to use them as raw materials in manufacturing or reuse in their existing form. Reusing metals, paper, glass, plastic, textiles, organic waste, and water will result in reductions in the demand for energy, raw materials, fertilizers, foreign exchange and fresh water sources. The use of plastics must be significantly reduced, particularly in packaging. Planners and other urban authorities must immediately put zero-waste goals, and the strategies needed to get there, into place in their cities. Moving towards zero-waste could be a major source of employment and business creation on the local and national levels (Pinderhughes 2006).

Litigation in the Supreme Court of India resulted in the formation of a committee charged with investigating all aspects of solid waste management in India's largest cities and requiring cities to segregate wet waste (the biodegradable fraction) and treat it appropriately. Small-scale composting programs that developed from the new policies led to community-based waste collection and composting projects, new job opportunities, enhanced environmental awareness, new public-private partnerships, and the utilization of appropriate technologies. One cautionary note: as we encourage recycling and reuse, wealthy nations must be prevented from using the guise of "recycling" to send their toxic and hazardous waste to poor nations who do not have an infrastructure in place to responsibly process these wastes.

Urban energy management

In the area of urban energy management, planners and other urban authorities must move cities towards energy systems that are flexible and adaptable to different regions and needs, emphasize energy efficiency, increase reliance on renewable energy sources, and ensure affordable, consistent access to modern energy sources for all households. The emphasis must be on efficient use of both renewable and conventional energy supplies in all sectors. Cities must begin to use a diversity of energy sources provided by various combinations of renewable power sources (wind, solar-thermal electric and photovoltaic power), hydroelectric, biomass, and geothermal power. Intermittent renewable energy sources like wind and solar technologies can provide as much as one-third of total electricity requirements cost-effectively in most regions without the need for new electrical storage technologies. Studies done in the United States predict that while using only 0.6 percent of the land area in the United States, primarily in North Dakota, Wyoming and Montana, wind power could generate about one-fourth of the total US electricity output. The world's largest wind park, located in Middelgrunden, Denmark, is funded through a creative partnership between users and the public sector that provides energy to over 100,000 households.

Achieving the complimentary goals of energy efficiency and expanding markets for renewable energy technologies will require the passage of new planning and policy initiatives that encourage innovation and investment in renewable energy technologies and, prevent subsidies that allow for artificial reductions in the price of fossil, nuclear, and hydro fuels. Bringing renewable energy to urban households could be another major source of employment and business creation on the local and national levels (Moody-Stuart 2002; Pinderhughes 2006).

The positive impact of alternative forms of energy production can be seen in China, Nepal and India where millions of families rely on bio-mass fuels produced in thousands of biogas digesters. Apart from providing a better and more reliable fuel for cooking, biogas digesters greatly improve public health by reducing respiratory ailments associated with smoke inhalation, improve air quality, reduce ground water pollution, deforestation, soil erosion, and greenhouse gas emissions, and produce higher quality manure from animal dung.

Officials in the country of Yemen, among the poorest nations in the world, have expressed interest in using solar water heaters in major cities. Despite the hot, tropical, sunny weather in the coastal, southern and eastern regions, most of the nation's hot water heaters are fueled by expensive fossil fuels. Using solar heaters would reduce reliance on fossil fuels, reduce emissions, and allow precious national and local funds to be used for much needed infrastructure development and social programs.

Urban transportation management

In the areas of urban transportation and land use, urban planners and policy makers must begin to support land uses that have considerably lower impacts on the integrity of ecosystems. They must promote transportation modalities that use energy sources which are renewable, produce no more emissions and waste than can be accommodated by the planet's restorative ability, and pose fewer problems to public health. Land use planning should focus on supporting urban development at a human scale and providing urban residents with affordable, high quality transportation choices that are viable alternatives to the one passenger automobile. Automobile use must be reduced considerably using public policies and planning initiatives that support the use of mass transit and cycling and discourage use of the private automobile. With regard to the popularity of automobiles, it is essential to develop infrastructures that support alternative fuel sources for light motorized vehicles such as biodiesel, methanol, ethanol, hydrogen, and methane (biogas) derived from biomass; as we proceed we must be attentive to the significant problems associated with growing grains for fuel. It is also critical that we require manufactuerers to make changes to the structure and fuel efficiency of the vehicle itself.

Planners in Abidjan, Cote De Ivoire developed a management plan designed to improve the quality, speed and efficiency of bus transit in the capital. The system uses special bus lanes, new road links, and new bus depots, terminals, bus stops, and footbridges to facilitate movement and pedestrian safety.

In Singapore, planners created incentives for reductions in private auto use through a combination of increased fees and restrictions for car drivers while improving mass transit from residential areas into the central city and for inter-city use.

Planners in Curitiba, Brazil created the now-renowned concentric circled bus-lanes that connect five lines and radiate from the center of the city outward like a spider web. Continual improvements to the system, including on the financial side, have resulted in a high quality, well-used system that pays for itself and generates funding for road and terminal maintenance.

Although use of the private automobile is increasing throughout most of the world, planning to promote safe bicycle use is also increasing and must be supported. The municipal government of Lima, Peru embarked on a 20-year program to encourage bike transport. *Transporte Popular de Vehiculos No Motorizados* promotes infrastructure development, policies and standards, and public education to increase bicycle use and safety. Workbikes are being used by postal services in many parts of Western Europe and by small businesses in Latin America, Africa and Asia. A partnership between the Asian Institute for Transport Development in India and the Institute for Transportation and Development Policy in the United States led to major improvements in the human-powered cycle rickshaw and an easier and safer ride for both drivers and passengers. Using human-powered rickshaws rather than cars or motorized rickshaws for transporting people to and from the Taj Mahal is reducing air emissions that damage local air quality and the building's historical façade.

Urban food systems

In the area of food systems, urban planners have paid almost no attention to urban food systems, community food needs, or to the role that urban agriculture can play in reducing socio-economic and environmental problems in cities. This has led urban planners and policy makers to misunderstand the significance of food as a community issue and the linkages between food production, energy, water use, transportation, and waste management. It has also resulted in missed opportunities to develop community-wide plans for composting food wastes, contributing to soil health, increasing food security, and improving urban food systems (Pothukuchi and Kaufman 2000).

Although it will likely remain a small contributor to urban food production overall, urban agriculture represents a unique land use and provides planners with an opportunity to integrate food concerns into their focus on enhancing the livability of human settlements. The environmental benefits of urban agricultural include ecological restoration, supporting biodiversity, creating nutritious soil from organic waste, and reducing energy in production and transport. The social benefits include providing food and income for low-income households, improving nutrition, addressing urban blight, job creation, local economic development, and supporting local food economies.

Urban officials in many cities in Africa, Asia, Latin America and the Caribbean are slowly recognizing the benefits of supporting urban agriculture. The best current model is found in Havana, Cuba. Although the government's support for urban agriculture emerged in response to an acute food shortage, the benefits in nutrition and public health, job creation, water and waste management, and energy savings have been extensive, resulting in Havana's urban farmers currently producing almost all of the fresh vegetables for the city's residents and between 16 percent–20 percent of the nation's fresh food total in 2005. Infrastructure support included the allocation of urban land plots for farming, providing urban residents with consistent access to fresh water; high quality compost, seeds and saplings; training and sponsoring extension agents to help urban residents grow food on a small scale using organic farming methods; creating laboratories and field testing sites, funding research and development on integrated pest management; providing urban residents with concrete incentives to increase their interest in, commitment to urban agriculture; and developing farmers markets as the principle venue where urban farmers could sell their produce to urban residents.

Conclusion

Moving away from conventional development and planning paradigms based on degrading the world's natural resources, exploiting human labor, and compromising the carrying capacity of the globe and the health of humans and other species, will require major paradigmatic and technological shifts. At the global level, international lending institutions must be pressured to reduce their emphasis on conventional economic growth strategies and significantly increase funding for projects that support basic infrastructures related to the delivery of water, waste, energy, transportation and food services in poor countries utilizing environmentally and socially responsible processes and appropriate technologies. Lending institutions can not continue to utilize the debt service repayments of developing countries to ensure that national and local officials are trapped into accepting the overexploitation of their environmental and human resources and/or structural adjustment in the pursuit of economic growth and urban development. Wealthy nations must stop transferring the social and environmental costs and burdens of production and consumption to poorer nations. Governments must reduce, and ultimately remove, incentives and subsidies that encourage public and private sectors to support urban infrastructure delivery sytems that rely on fossil-fuels, synthetic chemicals, and industrial equipment to deliver clean water, collect and dispose of waste, deliver energy and transportation services, and provide people with food.

In wealthy countries, environmental and social problems stem from the immense scale of resource and energy use, waste output, contamination and pollution, greenhouse gas emissions, and environmental inequities from urban infrastructure projects. Although urban infrastructures in wealthy, industrialized nations successfully provide basic public services to the vast majority of the population, problems emerge because infrastructures related to water, waste, energy, transportation and food systems have been designed and implemented with little or no regard for their environmental and social impacts (*Environment and Urbanization* 1992). Industrialized countries must deliver infrastructure services using processes that reduce resource consumption and waste and, distributing social benefits and burden more equitably.

In poor countries sustainable urban development must focus on development and infrastructure planning related to lack of safe water supply, sanitation and drainage, unreliable and unsafe energy supply, inadequate solid and hazardous waste management, uncontrolled emissions from motor vehicles, factories and low-grade domestic fuels, public health problems linked to congestion and crowding, housing needs, the occupation and degradation of environmentally sensitive lands, lack of food security, and the linkages between these problems (Bartone et al., 1994). This means that planners and other urban authorities will need to develop more infrastructure and utilize additional resources. The challenge is do this without creating or increasing the environmental and social problems that consistently result from conventional urban infrastructure planning practices and technologies.

References

Adriaanse, A., et al. (1993), *Resource Flows: The Material Basis of Industrial Economies* (World Resources Institute).

Bartone, C., et al. (1994), *Toward Environmental Strategies for Cities: Policies Considerations for Urban Environmental Management in Developing Countries*. UNDP/UNCHS (Habitat) World Bank Urban Management Programme (UMP) Discussion Paper Series No. 17 (Washington, DC: The World Bank).

Choguill, C. (1996), 'Ten Steps to Sustainable Infrastructure', *Habitat International*, 20:3, 389–404.

Couch, C. (1990), *Urban Renewal: Theory and Practice* (London: Macmillan Education).

De Roo, G. and Miller, D. (2000), *Compact Cities and Sustainable Urban Development* (London: Ashgate Publishing Company).

Drakakis-Smith, D. (1995), 'Third World Cities: Sustainable Urban Development', *Urban Studies*, 32:4, 32:5, 657–677.

Environment and Urbanization (1992), 'Sustainable Cities: Meeting Needs, Reducing Resource Use and Recycling, Re-use and Reclamation', 4:2.

Goodland, D. and El Sarafy (eds) (1991), *Environmentally Sustainable Economic Development Building on Brundtland*, Environmental Working Paper No. 46 (Environment Department, The World Bank).

Gossaye, A. (2000), 'Inner-city Renewal and Locational Stability of the Poor: A Study of Inner-city Renewal Program in Addis Ababa, Ethopia', in *The Sustainable City: Urban Regeneration and Sustainability* (WIT Press).

Hamm, B. and Muttagi, P. (1998), *Sustainable Development and the Future of Cities* (London: Intermediate Technology Publications).

Human Settlement Programme (2001), *Identifying the Groups Most Vulnerable to Urban Environmental Hazards*, International Institute for the Environment and Development Briefing Paper No. 2 (London).

Ingram, G. and Kessides, C. (1994), 'Infrastructure for Development', *Finance and Development*, 31:3.

Moody-Stuart, M. (2002), 'Our Planet', *United Nations Environment Programme Magazine*, 13:2, 13–14.

Moosa Valli, M. (2002), 'African Renaissance', *United Nations Environment Programme Magazine*, 13:2, 13–14.

Pinderhughes, R. (2004), *Alternative Urban Futures: Planning for Sustainable Development in Cities throughout the World* (Rowman & Littlefield).

Pinderhughes, R. (2006), 'Green Collar Jobs: Work Force Opportunities in the Growing Green Economy', *Race, Poverty & the Environment*, 13:1, Summer 2006.

Pothukuchi, K. and Kaufman, J. (2000), 'The Food System: A Stranger to the Planning Field', *APA Journal*, 66:2.

Puckett, J., et al. (2002), 'Exporting Harm: The High-Tech Trashing of Asia', Basel Action Network, Silicon Valley Toxics Coalition, Toxics Link India, SCOPE, and Greenpeace China.

Rees, W. (1998), *Understanding Sustainable Development*, in Hamm and Muttagi (eds).

Tearfund (2001), *Running on Empty* (Tearfund Christian Charity).

Tinbergen, J. and Hueting, R. (1991), *GNP and Market Prices: Wrong Signals for Sustainable Economic Success that Mask Environmental Destruction*, in Goodland and El Serafy (eds).

United Nations Centre for Human Settlements (Habitat) (1994) Task Manager's Report. Sustainable Human Settlements Development: Implementing Agenda 21.

World Bank (1994), *World Development Report* (Oxford University Press).

Chapter 2

Employing Information and Communication Systems in Planning Processes to Increase Efficiency in Sustainable Urban Development

Gerhard Steinebach, Robin Ganser, and Simone Allin

Necessity of Strategic Planning at the Local Level

The principle of sustainable urban development is incorporated into German planning and environmental law. The 1998 amendment of the German "Baugesetzbuch" (Federal Planning Act) introduced the following principle: "The local land-use plans shall guarantee sustainable urban development and land-use which is in accordance with the public good and social inclusion and they shall contribute to safeguarding a humane environment and to protecting and developing the natural resources" (German Federal Planning Act 1997). Based upon this Act, it is a statutory duty for local planning authorities to integrate the concept of sustainable development into their formal land-use plans.

At the local level a two-tier system of "Flaechennutzungsplan" (FNP) – (area wide preparatory land-use plan) and "Bebauungsplan" (BPlan) – (binding land-use plan) is in place. The FNP covers the entire local government area and contains strategic policies and objectives and a map of general land-use allocations. The BPlan forms the obligatory legal basis for most development. It is drawn up for specific parts of the area or for strategic sites and is required to be consistent with the FNP. The contents of the BPlan are binding for subsequent decisions in the scope of development control.

During the 1990s, most local authorities adopted a pragmatic approach to planning that was characterized by neglecting strategic planning. Rather then perform a comprehensive review of the FNP, and in order to accommodate step-by-step BPlan adoptions, numerous alterations of this area-wide plan and more or less "ad-hoc" planning decisions characterized the local planning practice. As a consequence of these frequent alterations, the FNP lost its strategic function to guide urban development over a plan horizon of approximately 15 years. Due to this situation the most sustainable planning and development options may not be realized. In this context the FNP aims to allocate development to the most sustainable sites that are best suited to specific land-uses and that provide optimized access and links between those uses. This planned settlement structure, including, among other things, open space, strategic green buffer zones, and infrastructure as well as service facilities can be disturbed when individual projects (based on B-Plans) depart from the FNP. This, in turn, can lead to less sustainable development (e.g. through conflicts of neighboring land-uses). It became obvious that this "short-sighted" planning approach, dominated by day-to-day political reflections and decisions, could not adequately address the problems of urban growth, suburbanization, urban decline, and consequential environmental effects. In the light of ongoing structural changes in the economic, social, demographic, and environmental sectors and the statutory requirements to further sustainable development, the need for a strategic planning framework at the local level which offers long-term strategic guidance has been rediscovered (Steinebach/Mueller 2006).[1]

This chapter explores barriers to the effectiveness of strategic land-use planning and consequentially for sustainable urban development. Questions of effectiveness in this context are not limited to the contents of land-use plans; they also arise with respect to the plan making process. The core research questions which are addressed by this chapter focus on the latter, more specifically on the potential and the limitations of Information and Communication Technology (ICT) systems to further speed up and streamline the strategic planning procedures at the local level in order to secure effective long-term guidance by formal plans. The results of a research project at the University of Kaiserslautern, Germany form a central part of the analysis and conceptual ideas which are highlighted in this chapter. The starting points for the argument set out below are the central hypotheses that it should indeed be possible to

a) streamline the management of planning processes by means of ICT; and
b) that this, in turn, should reduce the overall duration of the planning process

And, as a consequence this should lead to more up to date plans which can effectively guide sustainable urban development. This chapter begins with a discussion of the current deficits in the planning system as evidenced by the survey and then moves on to how ICT systems can remedy some of these issues and contribute to more sustainable development.

Deficits in the Planning System – Obstacles for Sustainable Development

Several past research projects have explored the deficits of plan making and implementation under the regime of the current German planning system (Difu 1996, Greiving 1998). A recent project at the University of Kaiserslautern,[2] addressed

---

1   The results of a survey – in the scope of research at the University of Kaiserslautern in which 135 local authorities (63 percent) responded to show clearly that the FNP is considered to be a crucial instrument to deliver sustainable urban development.

2   The Department of Town Planning and the Department of Computer Science at the University of Kaiserslautern, Germany, have initiated the interdisciplinary research project: "Increased efficiency of formal planning processes by means of modern information and communication systems".

some of the problems with this system by analyzing planning procedures and the adopted area-wide FNPs in the scope of a survey covering the entire territory of a Bundesland (state in the federal system) (Difu 1996). This 2003 survey was tailored in accordance with an analysis carried out in 1996 for the whole of Germany to allow comparisons of the results at the state level along with the overall picture at the federal level (Difu 1996).

On the basis of a comprehensive mail survey (Steinebach/Mueller 2006)[3] and statistical analysis, the following conflicts and problems were the subject of a thorough investigation in cooperation with numerous selected local planning authorities: lengthy procedures, outdated plans, deficits of information and communication, scope of consultation deficits, technical and management problems, lack of flexibility, and availability of ICT for strategic planning. Each is discussed in greater detail in the following text.

Lengthy procedures

One of the central findings of the 2003 survey was that the preparation of an FNP is often hampered by overly complex and inefficient planning procedures resulting in a lengthy planning process.

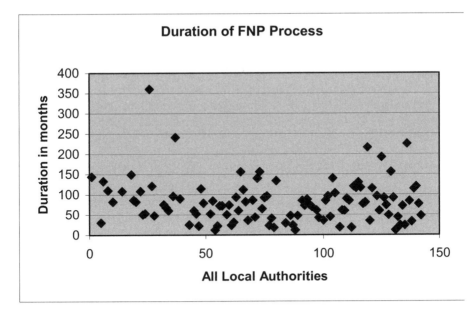

Figure 2.1 Duration of FNP planning process (months)
Source: 2003 Survey.

---

3   The results of this mail survey (performed in 2003) are discussed in Steinebach 2006.

The median of the duration of planning procedures was 75 months or 6.25 years (Steinebach/Mueller 2006). An astonishing duration of 360 months, a full 30 years, marks the maximum in the scope of survey results (Steinebach/Mueller 2006). Given this lengthy process it is not surprising that the views of the participating local authorities reflect some discontent with the current situation. The majority of Local Authorities (82 percent) stated that they would prefer speedier FNP procedures. Seventy-one percent of the Local Authorities judged the duration of processes to be too long (Steinebach/Mueller 2006).

In order to gain a better understanding of where the main delays occur, a more detailed analysis of the different stages of the planning process was carried out. In this context it is significant that the first three phases of the planning process – highlighted in Table 2.1 below – are characterized by an extensive duration.

Table 2.1 Phases of planning process characterized by extensive duration

Phase no.	Planning process phase – material contents
1	general preparatory work
2	preparing preliminary draft
3	soliciting public participation and preparing a draft plan

Source: 2003 Survey.

In addition to identifying the parts of the planning process that suffer the most from delays, it was important to identify the main reasons for these delays. Table 2.2 gives an overview of the main reasons for prolonged procedures identified in the survey responses. The succession of the individual reasons reflects the order of importance that showed up in the analysis of survey results (Steinebach/Mueller 2006).

With a view to improving the existing situation, the above reasons had to be further categorized in terms of two sets of obstacles in the scope of the 2003 study. First, those that were due to, or closely linked to, the planning system and second, those delays that cannot be improved through streamlining the planning system, planning procedures, and relevant legal requirements. As far as the latter is concerned the highest ranking reason for delays: "Slow process of political decision making" is likely to provide a major challenge in the scope of improved and speedier planning processes.

As a consequence of the identified problems and the resulting lengthy procedures, many of the area wide FNPs are outdated and Local Authorities are generally reluctant to engage in a comprehensive plan review. Instead, piecemeal alterations are common – which defeats the purpose of the FNP's strategic function. This problem needs to be addressed in more detail as it is directly linked to the potential of the planning document to encourage and foster sustainable development. As mentioned before, the FNP aims to provide a comprehensive spatial strategy for the entire Local Authority. One of the key tasks in this context is the coordination of urban development and supporting infrastructure (e.g. linking major employment sites with high quality public transport nodes). Another important consideration is to allocate those parts of the area for development which will result in the least environmental damage and to choose locations for individual land-uses or use classes with a goal to minimize disturbance of neighboring land-uses. All of the above can only be guaranteed when B-Plans and individual projects adhere to the framework provided by the FNP.

Table 2.2 Main reasons for prolonged procedures

No.	Reasons stated by local authorities in order of importance
1.	Slow process of political decision making
2.	Complicated consultation of statutory consultees
3.	Problems during early (informal) coordination with strategic tiers of planning
4.	Problems of data collection or adaptation
5.	Problems preparing informal, preliminary planning documents
6.	Complex public participation
7.	Objections from supervisory authority
8.	Deficits in the scope of contracted work
9.	Problems within local planning authority
10.	Consultation with neighbouring local authorities

Source: 2003 Survey.

Outdated plans

The 2003 survey shows that 40 percent of participating local authorities operate with FNPs which were adopted at least 15 years ago. Roughly 8 percent of all FNPs have been in place for 24 years or even longer (Steinebach/Mueller 2006). It has to be noted that the majority of outdated plans were discovered in larger local authorities with a population ranging from 50,000 to over 100,000 and medium-sized local authorities (10,000 to 50,000 inhabitants).[4] Smaller rural authorities proved to have the most up to date FNPs (Steinebach/Mueller 2006).

The 2004 amendments of the Federal Planning Act introduced the statutory requirement for a plan review and comprehensive revision at least once every 15 years (German Federal Planning Act 1997). This, in light of the survey results, means that nearly half of the area wide FNPs have either reached or exceeded their "best before date". With regard to the new legal requirements, a wave of plan reviews is to be expected. The "old" plans remain operational during the process of plan review and drafting the new FNPs. A situation where there is no FNP at all will therefore be avoided.

Regardless of the presence of the old plans, it is still important to reduce the duration of the transitional phase as the drafting of binding B-Plans and, subsequently the determination of project proposals, can be inhibited by the process. On the other

---

4   The largest city in the survey was Mainz with 186,000 inhabitants.

hand, new B-Plans and urban development can complicate the FNP revision as planners are "aiming at a moving target". Both of these situations underline the importance of streamlined planning processes and the need for a shorter duration from the decision on the plan review to the adoption of the finalized FNP. Another important factor in this context is the timely collection and distribution of information in the scope of planning processes. This is explored subsequently.

Information and communication deficits

Due to the necessary multi-agency approach in the scope of plan making involving experts, politicians, statutory consultees, and public participation the process often suffers from communication problems and a consequent loss of information. The principal problem rests within decision-making processes in local government (Steinebach/Mueller 2006). Some of the crucial questions in this context are: How can politicians participate in planning procedures beyond the rather fixed council sessions? Is it possible to initiate a continuous information and communication process? At what stage of the formal planning process should politicians be involved? Is it possible to create a "climate of confidence" between experts and politicians? To what extent and by which means can the information of politicians be improved and further qualified?

Some good practice examples demonstrate that the identified communication deficits can be overcome to a certain extent. The city of Dortmund, for example, introduced an early and wide-ranging involvement of politicians on the basis of a comprehensive communication concept in the scope of drafting FNPs. This approach resulted in achievements in terms of more transparent processes and furthered acceptance across political party boundaries. Closely linked to the question of handling information and communication is the process of public participation and the consultation of statutory and non-statutory consultees.

Deficits in the scope of consultation

A two-stage public participation and consultation process is a statutory requirement for all formal local land-use plans in Germany. The main rationale behind this process is to identify potential problems early in the planning process and to improve the quality of the final planning document. It is surmised that the Local Authorities will benefit from the specific expertise available in different planning agencies.

Unfortunately, it seems to be increasingly difficult to achieve these objectives. As mentioned above (see Table 2.2), central problems of the planning process appear to be vested in consultation procedures. In order to further investigate these specific issues several expert interviews were conducted as a complement to the mail survey. In the scope of this project, Local Authorities bemoaned three main shortcomings and problems associated with consultation.

First and foremost, the Local Authorities pointed out that many of the statutory consultees require an excessively long time to formulate both their statements and their objections. Second, there is an issue of statements being brought forward which are inadequate. This inadequacy means, specifically, that the statements are either insufficient in terms of material content and therefore do not contribute to the enhancement of overall quality, or do not adhere to formal requirements and therefore are legally not a material consideration of the planning process. The third problem Local Authorities bemoaned are statements that are not relevant for the specific plan in question. In many cases, the comments are either not linked to the plan area or they are not related to the realm of land-use planning. In both cases the statements do not make a positive contribution to the quality of the planning document. These problems can be exacerbated by technical problems or complications.

Technical and management problems

Several technical problems which complicate attempts at efficient planning procedures were featured in the 2003 survey. Among these were, for example, incompatible interfaces and loss of data during the exchange of information between different software systems. In addition to these problems, which are clearly related to technical infrastructure, there is a set of diverse management problems which are caused by a lack of standardized processes and proceedings during the FNP review and drafting.

Although the legal requirements set a clear framework for the FNP review and drafting process, the characteristics of land-use planning which are dominated by an iterative methodology, a multitude of involved stakeholders and statutory consultees, and a variety of objectives and targets, do not allow the definition of a single "ideal" line of action. As a result of this, the management of resources, of documents, and of schedules is not standardized. It is therefore difficult to optimize this process and very often mistakes are repeated rather than remedied from review to review. In this context, obviously the long period of time between individual reviews plays a decisive role and prevents the introduction of improved management techniques.

In addition to the aforementioned procedural problems, the contents and the current format of the FNP document are not flexible enough to accommodate changes which become necessary over time.

Lack of flexibility

The 2003 survey showed that the aforementioned lack of flexibility combined with lengthy procedures leads to piecemeal alterations of the adopted FNP documents which in turn hamper sustainable urban development. Some of these alterations are a consequence of new information such as demographic development while others are the result of development proposals which are not compatible with the existing FNP.

The highest number of piecemeal alterations of FNPs, parallel to the adoption of BPlans, takes place in large cities. Here a median of 29 BPlan adoptions, with the necessity of departures from the original FNP resulting in alterations, was observed in the 2003 survey. In medium sized towns six changes were found, while in smaller rural Local Authorities three parallel alterations were detected (Steinebach/Mueller 2006). The main reasons for departures from FNPs and subsequent alterations, again in the order of importance as identified by Local Authorities in the 2003 survey, are:

1. new land-use allocations;
2. environmental protection/environmental compensation;
3. transport infrastructure (of regional or national importance);
4. technical infrastructure;
5. withdrawal of land-use allocations;
6. other reasons (conversions of former defence estate, re-use of previously developed land, change of use in existing buildings, renewable energies, allocations for (light) industrial uses).

The land-use allocations at the top of the list regularly go hand-in-hand with environmental compensation measures, as German planning and environmental law includes strict compensation requirements.

Innovative Application of ICT

In order to test the initial hypotheses, the remaining text takes up the previously identified core problems and explores how the innovative application of ICT during planning processes can contribute to solutions that lead to sustainable development. Particular emphasis is placed upon the possibilities to reduce the overall duration of planning procedures in order to provide more up to date and better quality planning documents which provide a spatial framework for sustainable development.

The adopted approach focuses, on the one hand, on the elimination of problems as well as obstacles. This can primarily be achieved by learning from negative experiences in the past. On the other hand, the approach also focuses on the exploitation of good practice examples in order to extract generally applicable concepts and measures for swift planning procedures and subsequently disseminating the resulting guidelines. Such good practice is highlighted in Figure 2.1, where several Local Authorities managed to draw up FNPs in a reasonable span of time. The shortest planning process which showed up in the survey took merely 12 months to complete. As a basis for all of the above – particularly to back up practical advice for Local Authorities – the current availability and fitness for purpose of ICT systems for strategic planning and potential implementation problems had to be analyzed. The results of this analysis are summarized in the following subsection.

Availability of ICT systems for strategic planning

The market analysis that included visits of international conferences and exhibitions to identify and to compare the available technical solutions established that there are a variety of ICT systems available for tasks in formal planning procedures. These include GIS, workflow systems, and e-government. As an interim result one has to conclude that, with respect to the requirements of the aspired streamlining of FNP procedures, including formal aspects as well as material considerations, satisfactory technical solutions and applications are available. The following products are of key importance: 2D and 3D graphic and construction software specifically tailored for the needs of land-use planning (e.g. ArchiCAD, AutoCAD, AutoVision, SiCAD and Q-CAD as open source application for LINUX). Geographical Information Systems exist in the form of comprehensive data banks and for multi-agency cooperation (Workflow/Intranet) with task-specific software solutions (application modules). Planning management systems exist that are designed to support administrative tasks in planning processes such as scheduling, documentation, management of address databases, and resource calculation . In addition, software solutions particularly for project management of engineering projects are also available.

However, deficits which had to be noted on a regular basis are the following: lack of standardization, quality management, certification, and experience with the systems. The 2003 survey showed that only approximately 25 percent of participating Local Authorities made use of ICT in planning procedures. The main obstacles to the implementation of ICT in planning processes are:

- Ambiguous as well as confusing data and information
- Differing data formats, quality, differing conditions for access and use
- Lacking usability/products driven by technical requirements and not user-friendly
- Incompatibility of systems
- Insufficient integration of GIS and web-solutions (e-government, participation and internet)
- High acquisition and running costs for systems (including time-intensive servicing) and costs for staff training. As measurable positive effects in terms of the efficiency of the new systems could not be established to date, the ratio of expenditure and benefits is bent towards the former.

In addition, strategic implementation of these systems and comprehensive concepts for the introduction of modern ICT systems are lacking. Quality standards and exact definitions of requirements in terms of equipment and usability of new systems very rarely exist or are only just undergoing test in scope of pilot projects.

Towards increased effectiveness of plans and efficiency of plan making

The research project aimed to improve the efficiency of planning procedures by means of information and communication technologies. Early research results indicate that the implementation of ICT in the FNP process can increase effectiveness and reduce the necessary amount of time, particularly during the planning stages which comprise the aspects of: information, communication, participation as well as data and document transfer respectively. These can be found in the first three phases of the planning process (general preparatory work, preparing preliminary draft, consultation/preliminary deposit and preparing the draft – see Table 2.1) and are linked to the main reasons for prolonged procedures which were identified in the 2003 survey (see Table 2.2). As the slow process of political decision-making is very difficult to influence through ICT, the main emphasis of this research is placed upon the improved communication with statutory consultees (the second most important reason for delay).

In order to assess the possibility of improving planning procedures by the introduction of ICT, the three phases mentioned above had to be analyzed in great detail. Therefore, a network plan providing a comprehensive overview of 80 distinct steps (elements) of FNP procedures was devised. This network plan allowed the assessment of linkages between the main reasons for prolonged planning procedures and the three phases identified in the mail survey (see Table 2.1): general preparatory work; preparing preliminary draft; consultation and public participation.

Considering these results and the potential of available ICT solutions, which were explored in the scope of the market analysis, it was possible to identify improvements through the implementation of ICT. Table 2.3 below provides an overview of potential means for enhancement focusing on communication and data as well as document transfer aspects within the individual elements of the FNP process.

Table 2.3 Barriers to swift planning procedures

No.	Reasons stated by local authorities in order of importance	Possible improvement through ICT
1.	Slow process of political decision making	–
2.	Complicated consultation of statutory consultees	internet/e-government
3.	Problems during early (informal) coordination with strategic tiers of planning	internet/e-government
4.	Problems of data collection or adaptation	GIS, web solutions
5.	Problems preparing informal, preliminary planning documents	GIS, CAD, workflow
6.	Complex public participation	internet/e-government
7.	Objections from supervisory authority	internet/e-government
8.	Deficits in the scope of contracted work	GIS, CAD, workflow
9.	Problems within local planning authority	internet/e-government, GIS, CAD, workflow
10.	Consultation with neighbouring local authorities	internet/e-government
	Additional reasons/elements not stated in "Top 10 list"	**Possible improvement through ICT**
11.	Preparation of preliminary draft	GIS, CAD, workflow
12.	Preparation of draft	GIS, CAD, workflow
13.	Modification of draft	GIS, CAD, workflow
14.	Review and updating of planning documents	GIS, CAD, workflow
15.	Monitoring of implementation	RIS, GIS, workflow

Source: Steinebach, Ganser, Allin, 2006.

As previously stated, the slow process of political decision making cannot be readily addressed through ICT. However, the proposed implementation of ICT can contribute to a better knowledge base to help facilitate decision making, particularly with regards to the availability and transparency of the information which guides material considerations in the political process.

A whole set of problems highlighted in Table 2.3 can be influenced by appropriate internet and e-government solutions. This includes the complicated consultation of statutory consultees; the deficits during early (informal) coordination with strategic tiers of planning; the consultation with neighboring local authorities as well as the complex public participation and the possible objections from the supervisory authority.

Standardized participation forms, for example, can help to qualify the statements of the various stakeholders. Additionally, this form of standardization can help to streamline the preliminary structuring and evaluation of the statements.

Regarding public participation, internet discussion forums offer new ways of presenting and conveying plan contents to the public which can make planning outcomes more transparent and more meaningful.

A second set of problems, comprising the significant deficits of data collection or adaptation, can be solved by the use of (online) geographic information systems with database, document management and workflow management solutions.

In addition, geographic information systems, computer aided design programs and workflow management solutions can support the complex stages of preparing informal, preliminary planning documents, preparing the actual draft as well as modifying, reviewing and updating it, respectively. Thereby, the deficits in the scope of contracted work can be addressed. Last but not least, spatial and geographic information systems combined with workflow management systems can be helpful in monitoring the implementation of plan contents. All of the above indicates that ICT solutions can further the topic focus on key material considerations of various spatial planning documents at different levels and also the planning process by supporting preparation, review and monitoring procedures.

The willingness to implement ICT obviously is a central presupposition for any improvements in this area. The mail survey and the close cooperation with Local Authorities showed that there still is widespread apprehension for a strategic application due to a variety of reasons. How can this reluctance be overcome? The next section explores this issue.

Overcoming key problems of acceptance and information deficits

In order to further the implementation of the research findings in planning practice, a comprehensive internet portal has been developed in cooperation with all relevant institutions and stake holders[5] which are involved in the FNP process (the portal has been online since May 2005).

---

5   e.g. Local Authorities, statutory consultees, planning practitioners and researchers and the public. Meanwhile the internet portal is online. For further information see: www. fnpinform.de (only available in German). The portal has been structured according to the

A key aim of the portal is to remedy the reluctance to implement ICT in town planning generally and more specifically in FNP procedures caused by lack of information. The latter seem to be the number one reason for delays to the introduction of ICT simply because Local Authorities are unaware of the real costs and the amount of resources in terms of time and manpower ICT applications require.

The portal features survey results, background information, best-practice examples, legal advice, etc. It will also provide a platform for expert discussions on particular problems and possible benefits thereby furthering the introduction of ICT in Local Authorities and other public bodies.

In this context, the results of an extensive field-test already indicate possible improvements with regard to ICT implementation and, as a result of this, of the effectiveness of plan-making processes. Furthermore, these improvements are of direct relevance for sustainable urban development as the quality and timely adoption of planning documents can be improved.

Conclusions and Outlook

Results of the research highlight that several obstacles for swift planning procedures rest in the necessary multi-agency approach which is characteristic for land-use planning. It is significant that the early stages of the planning process suffer from delays . In addition, specific reasons and elements which are responsible for slowing down the entire FNP process could be identified. Some of the problems cannot be directly remedied as they belong to the sphere of politics. Others, like problems in the scope of statutory consultation, which turned out to be the second greatest obstacle, can potentially be improved.

In this context, the following presuppositions which could be identified through surveys, market research and expert interviews are of core importance:

- Local Authorities do believe that planning procedures are extensively long and they are willing to adopt measures to change this.
- Several technical solutions are available which can readily be introduced in the FNP process and which are geared to avoid time lags and other delays.
- Obstacles to the implementation of ICT caused by information deficits and standardisation problems can be overcome, particularly the latter since they are often linked to organizational issues.
- There are several good practice examples which can provide a benchmark for other Local Authorities.

---

concept of so called "procedural circumstances", which means that – the formal planning process has been dissected into several stages. Within these stages the potential of ICT systems is highlighted with regard to achieving the main planning objectives. The concept derives from the sociological idea of "living circumstances" which describe the biological, psychological, social and economic situation of individuals. The central idea was transferred to "information circum stances" describing the particular need for information of professionals and the public visiting municipal web sites and, finally, "procedural circumstances" which offer a comprehensive and clear description of each stage of the planning process and the material considerations which are relevant for decision making.

The combination of increased flexibility of plan content and swift planning procedures can avoid the central shortcomings of the past: outdated plans and consequent loss of their strategic function to guide development. This, in turn, is a vital presupposition for the determination of planning applications according to a framework which supports the choice of the most sustainable option and is not dominated by day-to-day political preferences.

The 2004 amendments of the German Federal Planning Act specifically promote the introduction of ICT, particularly online consultation procedures. Further research efforts will therefore be focused on this element of the planning process.

It has become clear that ICT implementation in the FNP process must go hand in hand with strategic e-government solutions covering all fields of Local Authority Activities. In this context, consequent technical standardization across all departments is essential. Questions which will need to be addressed in the future include the setting of benchmarks on the basis of best-practice and subsequent definition of quality-indicators for planning procedures which allow an online quality control.

In the United States 50 different systems of local government exist which possess planning powers that are conferred upon them by constitution or enabling act (Cullingworth 2003). Therefore, questions of system and data standardization in the scope of ICT implementation are essential.

As growth management, including concepts such as smart growth, is recognized as an increasingly important strategy for long term economic, social and environmental development, questions of strategic planning gain new momentum. Statutory General Plans and Zoning Ordinances show similarities to the FNP in process and content. Some of the lessons learned in the scope of the research discussed above are therefore transferable and adaptable for the US systems of local government planning.

References

Cullingworth, J. (2003), *Planning in the USA* (New York, Routledge).

Difu (German Institute for Urban Affairs) (eds) (1996), *Die Flachennutzungsplanung – Bestandsaufnahme und Perspektiven fuer die Kommunale Praxis* (Berlin).

German Federal Planning Act (1997), *Abs. 5 Baugesetzbuch* (Federal Ministry for Transport, Construction and Housing).

Greiving, S. (1998), *Bauleitplanung zwischen Rechtsstaalichkeit und Praktikabilitat* (Dortmund).

Steinebach, G and Mueller, P. (2006), 'Dynamisierung von Planverfahren Der Stadtplanung durch Informations – und Kommunikationssysteme', in Steinebach, G. (ed.).

Steinebach, G. (ed.) (2006), *Schriften zur Stadtplanung Vol. 4* (Kaiserslautern).

Chapter 3

Absolutely Positively Wellington: A Model for Smart Growth

Carlton C. Eley

Mō tātou, ā, mō kā uri ā muri ake nei –
For us and our children after us.

Māori Proverb

In the United States (US), the construct of "smart growth" represents the product of a collective synthesis by a coalition of private sector, public sector, and nongovernmental organizations.[1] Known as the Smart Growth Network (SGN), the partner organizations examined the breadth of characteristics of successful communities and developed ten principles for smart growth. These principles illustrate the characteristics of healthy, vibrant, and diverse communities that offer residents choices of how and where to live. Today, the principles have been endorsed and adopted by more than 35 organizations within the SGN, including the American Planning Association, National Trust for Historic Preservation, Urban Land Institute, and the US Environmental Protection Agency.

Although smart growth is not a household term in New Zealand, the principles are transferable, and they speak volumes as to why Wellington is highly celebrated as a city. This chapter presents eight of the ten smart growth principles; explains how they have been met sufficiently in Wellington; and uses the principles to present best practice examples for planning sustainable urban areas.[2] The author participated in the Ian Axford (New Zealand) Fellowship in Public Policy, and the objective of his research was investigation of New Zealand approaches to achieve smart growth objectives.

---

1   http://www.smartgrowth.org/sgn/default.asp.
2   There are actually ten principles for smart growth. Eight are presented in this chapter. The remaining principles are "make development decisions predictable, fair, and cost effective" as well as "encourage community and stakeholder collaboration in development decisions". These principles are just as important as the eight that were profiled in the chapter. However, the author opted to focus the chapter around the principles that lend themselves to an illustration of healthy, vibrant, and diverse communities based on urban form and design.

About Wellington

The national capital of New Zealand, the city of Wellington, is positioned 41° 17.00S (latitude) and 174° 47.00E (longitude). Wellington has transcended simply being the nation's political center. In recent years, the city has flourished as a cultural, recreational, and entertainment hub. Also, the city has acquired a reputation for cinematic production due to the overwhelming success of *The Lord of the Rings* film trilogy.

With a population of 163,824, Wellington is New Zealand's third largest city. Physically, the city conforms to the shape of a natural amphitheatre, buffered by rolling hills west of the city and Wellington Harbour to the east. Because of these signature features, the city is often compared to a similarly situated US city, San Francisco, California.

Wellington has received many accolades in recent years. In 2000, Wellington was named New Zealand's Top Town by *North & South Magazine*. In 2001 and 2003, encouraging results were reported for Wellington in quality of life studies for New Zealand's largest cities.[3] Eight of the ten smart growth principles are used to demonstrate that Wellington is a great city as well as a vibrant and exciting urban center.

1. Take advantage of compact building design

When describing their city, it is common for Wellingtonians to mention the city's compact urban form. The land area of Wellington is approximately 26,625 hectares (103 square miles), yet the area of land classified as urban is approximately 9,324 hectares (36 square miles).[4] Also, the steep and hilly topography of the region has forced most of the city's development to limited low-lying areas near Wellington Harbour, particularly reclaimed land.[5] In fact, a key distinction for the city is that its commercial core wraps in a linear way around the harbor rather than drawing back from it. This unique feature in the city's physical landscape has contributed to a clear sense of public ownership of Wellington's waterfront.

Wellington exhibits a snug urban fabric because much of the central city is composed of small, intensively developed city blocks that are truncated or irregular in shape. The central business district is characterized by concentrated high rise office buildings (10 to 15 stories) and commercial development (Wellington City 2001). The area also hosts a wide range of political, cultural, leisure, and entertainment activities of national and local significance. The built form of the central area has been shaped by this diversity of activities, proximity of the city's port, and the topography of the harbor and hills (Wellington City 2003c). The latter has required

---

3   Auckland City Council, et al. (2003) *Quality of Life in New Zealand's Eight Largest Cities* (Auckland, New Zealand).

4   The land area for the District of Columbia is approximately 15,799 hectares (61 square miles).

5   Once submerged land, some parcels uplifted during the 1855 Wairarapa earthquake but most were the result of filling in areas where there was once seawater.

city planners and designers to creatively use developable space. In some instances, the city has maximized space between detached structures by creating pedestrian plazas that feature a concentrated mix of retail shops.

The city's district plan identifies two broad residential areas. The Inner Residential Area adjoins the central city and is mostly within the inner Town Belt. The Outer Residential Area comprises the remaining suburbs from the inner Town Belt to the boundary of the city's rural area. To foster a city that remains compact, district planning rules encourage more intensive development within existing residential areas (Wellington City 2003c).[6]

2. Create walkable communities

The second popular axiom for describing Wellington is "it's a walkable city." Central Wellington's physical dimensions are 2 kilometers (1.24 miles east to west) by four and one-half kilometers (2.79 miles north to south). As a result, common attractions are within the comfort of a 20 minute walk.

The "Golden Mile" refers to the main retail strip which begins near Parliament and extends to the eastern end of the city's entertainment district (Wellington City 1988). Planning policies for maximizing pedestrian comfort that are common to the Golden Mile include but are not limited to wide footpaths, pavers on footpaths, active ground floors, and consistent setbacks. In some sections office blocks are terraced to maintain sufficient sunlight as well as minimise the effect of wind downdraught at the street level.

Wellington City Council conducted an economic analysis to assess the value-added benefit of pedestrian enhancements to footpaths for business owners along specific streets (Reid 1997). According to the author of the study:

> The enhancement of Wellington's Blair and Allen Streets in the 1990s delivered tangible benefits. The initiative involved new street paving and landscaping; Wellington City Council also assisted with earthquake strengthening of heritage buildings, and facilitated investment planning with local building owners. Value gains have since been evident in rents, capital values and physical indicators such as pedestrian counts and the presence of cafes. An economic assessment of property values suggests that values by the late 1990s were approximately double what they would otherwise have been.

---

6 Because Wellington is commonly referred to as a compact city, it would have been ideal to report the average residential density of the city. However, a challenge that became apparent during the period of study was the lack of robust, reliable, and timely information. According to the Office of the Parliamentary Commissioner for the Environment, one of the consequences of the series of restructurings of central government in the last sixteen years is the loss of national data sets and agency focus for processing information about people and their environment in urban New Zealand (e.g. New Zealand Planning Council or the Ministry for Works). There is little publicly available business or corporate sector data that has a specific urban focus. For example, most of the Wellington District Plan was prepared without empirical data. As a consequence, a challenge confronting Wellington and other district councils across New Zealand is knowing how well planning objectives and outcomes have been achieved.

This is not the first time the City has detected a connection between street augmentation for pedestrians and shopping behaviour. Following the removal of trams and tracks along Wellington's Cuba Street in 1965, the street was closed off to vehicle traffic. When it was noticed that this was an attraction to pedestrian shoppers, the City Council was petitioned to make part of Cuba Street a permanent pedestrian mall. The idea was accepted and Cuba Mall was opened in October 1969. It was the first street in New Zealand to be developed in this way (Wellington City Council 2001b).

Some smart growth advocates suggest pedestrians are the "indicator species" of a smart growth community. According to the 2001 New Zealand census, 13.5 percent of Wellington's working population opted to walk as their means of travel to work. This is higher than any other New Zealand city.

Walking, as the first mode of transport, in Wellington is enhanced by the provision of tools and infrastructure that make the city navigable and legible for pedestrians. Living Streets Aotearoa, a walking advocacy group, and the city partnered to install pedestrian maps throughout the city. In addition to serving as directional aids, the maps identify pedestrian shortcuts (steep steps and pathways) that help walkers traverse the city. In a like manner, Wellington City has erected ornate pedestrian signs throughout the central area which aim to bring art, fun, vibrancy, and a sense of history to the central city.

3. Preserve open space, farmland, natural beauty, and critical environmental areas

The first objective of the Wellington District Plan is "to protect and enhance the natural or "green" areas of the city. This is chiefly all the land beyond the outer town belt, including rural and open space zones, and conservation sites". Historically, the towering green hills encompassing the city were a natural buffer that physically limited the expanse of development. In recent years, the hills of Wellington have been embraced as an asset and a feature worthy of protection.

Wellington policies for protecting open space and recreational areas can be traced to the city's early years. In 1840, the founders of Wellington designated the Town Belt as lying on the first line of hills wrapping around the central city. The Town Belt is approximately 425 hectares in area. To the west of the Town Belt and the city is a complementary bush and grass covered line of ridges known as the Outer Green Belt. The City Council's vision for the Outer Green Belt is for indigenous vegetation to be restored within its boundary and for it to function as a recreational network for citizens and visitors.

Wellington's rural area represents approximately 65 percent of the city's total land area. Extending from the outer boundaries of the city's urban areas to the coast, most of the land is used for pastoral farming, and settlements are small and scattered. Currently, the rural area is home to a small proportion of Wellington's population but increasing demand for rural "lifestyle" blocks is creating pressure for subdivisions and other development. In response, the Wellington District Plan has provisions to control subdivision of land to limit housing (Wellington City 2003c). Further, determinations to subdivide rural land require a change in the District Plan (Wellington City 2001).

Also, Wellington has committed to returning 252 hectares (623 acres) of land to a state reflective of New Zealand prior to human occupation. The Karori Wildlife Sanctuary is the world's first inner city predator-free environment and a safe haven for New Zealand's treasured endangered wildlife. The sanctuary has been referred to as the most ambitious conservation project in the country. The long term vision of the sanctuary is restoration of the flora and fauna once endemic to the area. Situated around two old reservoirs that once supplied Wellington with water and now support a newly created wetland environment, the Sanctuary demonstrates the potential of adaptive reuse of underutilized facilities for ecological restoration.

4. Foster distinctive, attractive communities with a strong sense of place

Quality design is a key factor that reinforces the look and feel within the city that is praised by both citizens and visitors. Wellington City's District Plan 2000 and the Annual Plan 2003/2004 clearly identify quality design as a priority for the city.

The look and feel of Wellington is accented by the impressive display of late nineteenth and early twentieth-century architecture throughout the city. The extent of the heritage fabric varies within the city. For example, the Thorndon neighborhood is tightly packed with wooden houses and cottages that were built by early settlers and serve as reminders of the City's colonial past. Also, specialty shops and restaurants occupy the heritage buildings and contribute to the village atmosphere of this district.

Alternatively, modern office buildings have been seamlessly interwoven with heritage structures in the downtown Central Business District (CBD), and these buildings generally relate well to their neighbors. Although it is too expensive to replicate the craftsmanship, styles, and features of Victorian-era architecture in modern buildings, contemporary downtown buildings honor the late nineteenth and early twentieth-century building tradition through continuity and form that honor the human scale at the street level. This is demonstrated through provision of continuous verandas (on certain routes) that mask the dominance of high-rise structures, setting back office towers from the street, featuring attractive retail frontages and window dressings for shops, as well as limited construction of skyscrapers with a footprint that requires occupation of an entire city block. The result is a modern city skyline that exhibits the essence of a village at the street level.

Wellington has a Built Heritage Policy to conserve the city's heritage footprint. The policy ranges from identifying heritage items to working with owners and developers to facilitate the protection and restoration of heritage assets in appropriate ways. For example, the City Council identifies vintage structures that are earthquake-prone and works with owners to ensure they are strengthened. The city also offers financial and project management assistance as an incentive for building owners to restore their property (Eley 2003).

Because bi-culturalism is central to the New Zealand way of life, the collective identity of Wellington City is derived from Māori and European influences. Wellington has taken progressive steps to honor the rich heritage of New Zealand's indigenous population within the urban fabric. The heritage footprint of Māori is demonstrated in the paving patterns of the Civic Square complex. It is evident in the names of parks and neighbourhoods, such as Te Aro or Pipitea, that honor fortifications or villages that once occupied the same land. In a like manner, district plan consultation with Māori targets resource management as well as recognition of places of traditional importance, thus demonstrating how the area has been historically shaped by Māori settlement. It is widely accepted that much of what is unique to New Zealand is derived from Māori culture. By honoring both cultures, Wellington's sense of place becomes more apparent.

5. Provide a variety of transportation choices

Wellington enjoys the benefits of a transport system that offers citizens the choice of walking, biking, bus, passenger rail, driving, ferry, and in some instances cable car. Research findings from "Quality of Life in New Zealand's Eight Largest Cities 2003" reported means of travel to work for Wellingtonians by mode. The study revealed 49 percent travel by motor vehicle, 14 percent walk, 13 percent use the bus, 3 percent take the train, 2 percent opt to bike, and 20 percent travel by other means.[7] One goal of the City Council is to ensure that travel is safe, convenient and enjoyable regardless of the mode.

Wellington City Council has a strong interest in the successful operation of public transport because it is integral to the functioning of the city. Public transport in Wellington is currently running well with steady improvement in bus services and patronage and modest growth in rail use.[8] Uncertainty over future ownership of rail service has slowed further development of this mode of transportation.[9] Apart from the general impact of road congestion, the biggest issue facing bus services is congestion and delays along the Golden Mile (Wellington City 2004). One approach Wellington took to improve efficiency of bus transport was to provide bus priority lanes. The City Council has asserted this approach appears to be working well to improve bus travel times and service reliability.

The rate of car ownership in Wellington is estimated at 480 vehicles for every 1,000 people in the city, one of the highest car ownership rates in the world (Wellington City 2004). Alternatively, when compared to New Zealand's eight largest cities, Wellington has the lowest percentage of employees who travel to work by motor vehicle. While acknowledging car travel is a major transport mode for

---

7   Statistical findings were rounded to the nearest whole number. Wellingtonians who reported "travel by other means" includes citizens who indicated they work from home.

8   From Wellington, commuter rail transport extends as far as Masterton, 100 kilometers (approximately 62 miles) north of the nation's capital.

9   New Zealand's rail service and rail network were purchased by Tranz Rail, a private company, in 1993. Ten years later, Tranz Rail, the provider of urban passenger rail service in the Wellington Region, entered negotiations for selling their company. Delays in transferring the company to a new owner had the potential to affect infrastructure development and continuity of service. Eventually, Tranz Rail was taken over by Toll Holdings and renamed Toll Rail in 2003. On June 30, 2004, the New Zealand government purchased the national rail network from Toll Rail. Today, the Government owns and operates the network infrastructure via the New Zealand Railways Corporation, with Toll continuing to provide rail services and having exclusive access to the majority of the rail network.

many, Wellington realizes it must deconstruct the built-in bias towards the ease of vehicle-oriented travel (Wellington City 2003a).

For example, the May 2004 Transport Strategy for the city acknowledges that the City Council vision for transport is under girded by the principle of an integrated system where different modes complement each other and produce a comprehensive transport system that maximizes the benefits of each (Transport Strategy 5). Wellington also hired Jan Gehl, a Danish urban design expert, to research improvements for: strengthening public transport; encouraging a higher priority for pedestrians in the city center in general; and fostering a bicycle culture (City to Waterfront 46). Finally, Wellington City Council is a signatory to the New Zealand Urban Design Protocol which calls for a change in the way New Zealanders think about their towns and cities, including transport options.

6. Strengthen and direct development towards existing communities

In general, New Zealand cities are experiencing trends in demography similar to large US cities. Internal migration trends reveal population increases for New Zealand's largest cities. Couples are waiting longer to marry and bear children. New Zealand's household sizes are shrinking, and the nation's ageing population is increasing. The shift is evident in changing lifestyle preferences and needs (Housing New Zealand Corporation 2004).[10] In acknowledging these shifts, Wellington has responded to increasing demand for convenient, diverse, and vibrant communities.

Wellington effectively demonstrates that higher density development and improved quality of life are not mutually exclusive goals. Wellington's success in meeting its intensification objectives is evident in the sentiment of the city's citizens. The proposition of intensifying development in Wellington does not evoke the same type of panic response that is common for citizens in many US cities.[11] Wellingtonians understand that their quality of life benefits – walkable communities, housing choice, transportation choice, community fiscal health, higher sense of safety and comfort, and environmental protection – are inextricably linked to policies for containment and intensification that are reinforced by sound strategies for design.

An advantage of directing growth back to existing communities is maximization of investments (facilities, roads, water/sewer, etc.) as opposed to expending capital to replicate infrastructure and services. Courtenay Place is the eastern terminus of Wellington's Golden Mile and serves as an example of how directing investment to already developed areas pays off. While it is currently known as the city's entertainment precinct, ten years ago, the area primarily consisted of service-oriented businesses and warehouses. Also, the city's produce market, housed by many of the buildings occupying Blair and Allen Streets, was a popular attraction within the precinct until it moved in the early 1990s. Some of the buildings became vacant when the markets moved, and this added to a general state of decline that was already present in Courtenay Place. The City Council and the Historic Places Trust

---

10 By New Zealand standards, Wellington has a disproportionate number of young adults (25 to 35 years old) who are educated/well traveled/slightly affluent.

11 Commonly referred to as "Not In My Backyard" or NIMBY.

recognized the significance of the buildings and encouraged their retention. Today, Blair and Allen Streets have been restored, and their buildings are an important part of Courtenay Place (Wellington City Council 2001).

In a similar vein, the Courtenay Place precinct has been transformed in large part because of the in-migration back to the city. Currently, Courtenay Place features a mix of retail stores, shops, office/commercial space, restaurants, and apartments. In step with the city's policies to protect its heritage assets, the refurbishment of the Embassy Theatre, for *The Return of the King* world premier, was probably the most important restoration to take place in the precinct.

7. Create a range of housing opportunities and choices

Urban living in Wellington is not limited to apartments. Varying housing styles can be found within the city's inner and outer residential areas. The spectrum of housing options includes flats, apartment blocks, duplexes, nineteenth-century cottages, and modern single family residences.

In Wellington's residential areas, including Thorndon, Mt. Victoria, and Aro Valley, there are several neighborhoods with distinctive character due to the presence of older structures, particularly homes constructed during the Victorian Era. The City Council considers such areas to be important to Wellington's identity and the city has provisions to protect them. The restrictions include design guides, controls on multi-unit housing in some neighborhoods, and rules restricting the demolition of pre-1930 buildings in select first-tier suburbs, namely Thorndon and Mt. Victoria (Wellington City 2003c).

Wellington understands that multi-unit housing developments are an effective way to use land in the city's more developed areas. Still, housing of this type can adversely affect residential amenities, especially if it is significantly different from an area's established housing style. To ensure quality multi-unit housing, the city's district plan requires all new developments to be assessed against the relevant design guide to ensure certain design principles are followed, without dictating the development's appearance (Wellington City 2003c). For example, Wellington's Oriental Bay features varying residential alternatives including traditional homes and mid-rise apartments. This is possible because the Oriental Bay Design Guide is flexible enough to allow medium to high-rise residential development while insisting that such development not compromise the character of the area.

Further, Wellington accommodated the demand for quality apartments for almost a decade. According to city officials, growth in the number of apartments has added vibrancy to central Wellington (Johnson 2004). Fifteen years ago, it was common for Wellington's streets to be active by day with civil servants who retreated to their homes in the evening and left the city inert. In recent years, Wellington has fostered a livable downtown by being supportive of residential uses like apartments above street-level retail. Such approaches have enabled the downtown to remain active beyond traditional business hours of operation, and they have complemented existing systems of informal surveillance.

8. *Mixed land use*

Currently, the Resource Management Act (RMA) is New Zealand's main environmental legislation.[12] The RMA does not regulate land use. Instead, it focuses on managing the *effects* of land uses. Mixed land use is permitted unless it is demonstrated that the effects of an alternative land use can not be avoided, remedied, or mitigated.[13] While it is inconclusive whether a connection can be drawn between the increase of mixed use development in Wellington and the passage of the RMA, many New Zealand planning researchers and practitioners would agree that the RMA, when properly applied and implemented, grants local authorities a level of flexibility that could not be obtained under the former Town and Country Planning Act.

The Wellington District Plan acknowledges that the city's residential areas owe much to the many non-residential activities and community services that take place within them such as schools, shops, churches, service stations, childcare facilities, medical centers, and the like. Mixed land use is encouraged by the City's planning policies provided it is appropriately located and compatible with residential amenity. The District Plan also contains live/work provisions since telecommuting is a permitted activity. Working from home is considered to be an effective strategy to reduce travel and save energy (Wellington City 2003c).

Adaptability is a key aim of Wellington's policies. As a result, a wide range of activities and uses are permitted right in the Central area. Since the city is not treated as a static environment, flexibility allows building owners and developers to respond to readily changing market needs or other influences such as new technologies (Wellington City 2003a).

Opportunities for Improvement

There is much to celebrate about Wellington. At the same time, there is room for improvement by planning for sustainable suburbs, upgrading transportation options, and increasing affordable housing.

Reinventing suburbs

While the inner city effectively demonstrates the benefits of mixed land use, clustered development, or directing growth back to existing communities, it is important to also reflect these qualities in the middle and outer-tier suburbs that encompass Wellington. The benefits of reinventing a suburb are best demonstrated through the Runanga (tribal authority) of Waiwhetu in Lower Hutt. Over the past 20 years, the Iwi (tribal)

---

12 The Resource Management Act of 1991 replaced the Town and Country Planning Act of 1977.

13 A conclusion drawn by the author while in New Zealand is the RMA is not "smart growth" legislation – in the sense of being consistent with the objectives of smart growth as subscribed by the US E.P.A. This acknowledgement does not detract from the merits of the law. It merely acknowledges that the law was not designed for this intent.

authority has taken progressive steps to improve the mix of services and to make the community self sustaining. Māori and non-Māori benefit from the provision of services such as the Waiwhetu Medical Centre, kohanga reo (Māori language pre-school), Atiawa Toa FM radio station, Tamaiti Whangai Centre of Learning, and a gymnasium. Moreover, these services improve the sense of community within this neighborhood (Practice Profile 2003).[14] This model for development, reinvestment, and empowerment merits support and should be replicated.

Transport upgrades

Wellington understands public transport is integral to the successful functioning of the city. Structural enhancements are in order for the modernization of passenger rail stops. Enhancements should be made to reduce the exposure of patrons to natural elements and to create an environment that is less intimidating as passengers wait for trains at night.

Alternative improvements are in order for buses. Prior to August 2004, New Zealand's sulfur limits for highway diesel exceeded the limits in Australia and the United States at 3,000 parts per million (ppm). Fortunately, New Zealand's production of "Third World" quality diesel fuel is at an end because current regulations dictate sulfur levels should not exceed 500 ppm. While New Zealand should be applauded for this advancement, public transport bus fleets that service the city of Wellington should be upgraded to include vehicles that are fuel hybrids or run on natural gas. The New Zealand State of the Environment Report notes that in cities, air pollution from motor vehicles can be worse if dispersion is inhibited by the "street canyon" effect (Ministry for the Environment 1997). Depending on weather conditions or the time of day, this effect is noticeable on Vivian Street, Lambton Quay, and Tinakori Road in Wellington. While buses are not the only contributor, further steps should be taken to reduce emission from the diesel buses that are used for public transport.

Reducing the housing divide

Providing quality housing for people of all income levels is an integral component of any smart growth strategy. Unfortunately, in Wellington as in much of New Zealand, housing prices are currently at record levels in relation to average wages and rents. The rapid rise of house prices not only affects disenfranchised parties: many young New Zealanders (in their 20s and 30s) have delayed home ownership because they are currently priced out of the market. Aggravating this trend is the limited supply or decline of government-subsidized housing since Central government vacated its role as a provider of such housing in 1991. In some instances, local governments assumed a limited role in the provision of affordable housing. In brief, Wellington housing policies must work towards the creation of an economically inclusive society.

---

14 http://www.rnzcgp.org.nz/colled/Waiwhetu.php.

Conclusions

New Zealand's indigenous population, the Māori, are known as the Tangata Whenua (People of the Land), and they see themselves as stewards of the natural environment. According to Māori culture, land represents an endowment that is handed down to present generations, and it is the obligation of current generations to pass it on to their progeny in as good a condition as they receive it. Here lies the basis for sustainability.

The international planning community is inclined to agree there is a need for a sustainable urban form, and the world is replete with examples for harvesting lessons learned and best practices. In the US, smart growth represents a sustainable approach that is gaining traction. As a point of clarification, smart growth should not be confused as a surrogate for, or as synonymous with, sustainable development. Smart growth represents one means to a sustainable end.

Although smart growth is not a household term in New Zealand, the principles are transferable, and the synergies of smart growth are evident in Wellington, the nation's capital. Wellington's status as New Zealand's "Top Town" is no accident. While Wellington has the benefit of natural boundaries (hills and the harbor) to contain development, the City owes its recent accolades to the deliberate efforts of local leaders (elected and laypersons) as well as practitioners (planners, urban designers, and developers) who continually nurture and develop the competitive advantages offered by the City.

Maintaining the status of "Top Town" will require looking beyond the physical attributes of Wellington. It will be equally important to understand how the City's policies and practices have delivered a quality of life that is highly sought after in Aotearoa (the original, Māori name for New Zealand which means "land of the long white cloud"). Wellington is a distinctive destination because of several factors:

- Town and green belt polices that establish clear edges for the city;
- Planning policies that foster sustainability, accessibility, security, cohesiveness, vibrancy, and flexibility;
- Heritage polices that preserve the city's historic footprint; and
- Design policies that focus primarily on the way a structure is integrated into its surroundings through the quality of the design and not the architectural attributes of a structure.

In Wellington, New Zealand, as in the United States, achieving smart growth requires leaders who will introduce alternatives to conventional development patterns and have the fortitude to advance their vision because it is the right thing to do. It requires practitioners who can apply innovative approaches and possess a passion for fostering a new reality for their community. It also requires citizens who celebrate the character of their city and understand that quality of life extends beyond the perimeter of one's personal property and is inextricably linked to the condition of one's community. In short, it requires rising above "social cascades" that are based on perpetuating the status quo or limiting choice for lifestyle options that best meet the consumer's needs.

In conclusion, "Absolutely Positively Wellington" is more than a clever, local brand. It is a statement that reflects Wellington's transformation into a livable, world-class city.

References

Department of Prime Minister and Cabinet (2003), *Sustainable Development for New Zealand Programme of Action* (Wellington: Department of Prime Minister and Cabinet).

Eley, C. (2003), *Smart Growth Down Under: Taking Steps Towards Sustainable Settlements in New Zealand* (Wellington, New Zealand: Fulbright New Zealand).

Housing New Zealand Corporation (2004), *Building The Future: Towards A New Zealand Housing Strategy* (Wellington: Housing New Zealand Corporation).

Johnson, A. (2004), 'Downtown Living is Still on the Up and Up', *The Dominion Post*, June 5, 2004, available at <http://www.stuff.co.nz/stuff/dominionpost/>.

Ministry for the Environment (1997), *The State of the Environment* (Wellington, New Zealand: Ministry for the Environment).

Parliamentary Commissioner for the Environment (1998), *The Cities and Their People. New Zealand's Urban Environment* (Wellington: Parliamentary Commissioner for the Environment).

The Royal New Zealand College of General Practitioners (2003), *Practice Profile*, available at <http://www.rnzcgp.org.nz/colled/Waiwhetu.php>.

US Environmental Protection Agency (2001), *Our Built and Natural Environments* (Washington, DC: US Environmental Protection Agency).

Wellington City (1988), *Courtenay Precinct Zone Design Guide* (Wellington: City of Wellington).

Wellington City (2001), *District Plan* (Wellington, New Zealand: City of Wellington).

Wellington City (2003a), *Central City Urban Design Strategy Principles* (Wellington, New Zealand: City of Wellington).

Wellington City (2003b), *Council Plan 2003/2004* (Wellington, New Zealand: City of Wellington).

Wellington City (2003c), *Understanding the District Plan* (Wellington, New Zealand: City of Wellington).

Wellington City (2004), *Draft Transport Strategy* (Wellington: City of Wellington).

Wellington City Council (2001a), *Blair and Allen Streets* (Wellington: City of Wellington).

Wellington City Council (2001b), *Cuba Mall* (Wellington: City of Wellington).

Wellington City Council (2003), *Townbelt*, available at <http://www.wcc.govt.nz/recreation/gardens/index.html#townbelt>.

Whitman, C. (2002), *Speech Notes*, New Partners for Smart Growth Conference, San Diego.

Chapter 4

Environmental Quality and Land Use Plans, a New Development in the Netherlands

Jan Jaap de Boer

The Dutch National Environmental Plan 4 of 2001

The Dutch National Environmental Policy Plan 4 (NEPP4) has introduced a new approach to integrate environmental quality in local land use plans. The environmental sector will focus on the qualities, possibilities, problems and challenges of local areas instead of concentrating on supplying general environmental standards and norms concerning the environmental quality for the country as a whole. This new approach is one of the results of the current government's general policy to decentralize to the local and regional level. It means that local context can be taken into consideration more than it had previously.

In this chapter the development of this new approach is presented. Focusing on the quality of an area instead of the usual more generic approach of environmental quality changes the role of the environmental policy sector. These changes and the relation with other policy fields such as landuse, will also be discussed.

The NEPP 4 of 2001 states that the local level is in a better position to improve the local environmental quality than the national level. This includes a recognition that the quality of an area includes more elements than the environment alone. An integrated approach to the quality of an area is necessary. In some cases the environmental quality will not be the prime concern of the people living in the area. Crime or unemployment as social issues could be more important. All these elements are a part of the quality of life in an area as it is experienced by the inhabitants and users of that area. This has consequences for the way the environmental sector has to approach the quality aspects of an area: less general but concentrating on the specifics of the area. Interestingly, some local and regional authorities have already developed methods and processes for such a specific and integrated approach to areas. These methods and processes have provided the basis for the further development of this approach.

The Quality of an Area as Focus

The starting point in the new approach is that the required quality of an area will be primarily defined by the land use functions of that area: housing requires a different environmental quality than offices, industry or traffic. When an area is dominated by one function the necessary quality can be easily established but with a mix of functions, as is usually the case in inner cities, it is more difficult because of the different requirements and standards applicable to these functions. This shows the strong link with the landuse policy sector. The definition of "area" is rather loose: it may be a neighboorhood or a larger area such as a new urban development. Usually it will be the area that the local government decides to (re)develop.

Differences in environmental quality between areas do exist – as a matter of fact or even as a result of policies. There are, for instance, differences in pollution levels caused by the amount of traffic passing an area or by the industry in or nearby the area. The density of area is also an important factor: suburban housing (low density) is different from the innercity housing (high density).

There is not a complete free choice for the local government of the quality level: the Ministry of the Environment sets the minimum environmental quality level to protect the health of the people and the state of the nature. A higher quality level is however the goal of this policy change by the NEPP4.

The choice for the area approach means that the problems, challenges and possibilities of that area are in the center of the policy development. That is the difference with the usual general approach to local environmental quality in the environmental policy by using only the national standards. The environmental policy sector has to analyze the area by first identifying the existing environmental problems and quality goals in the area and secondly by assessing the quality problems and goals of other policy sectors and agencies. The next step is what are the expected and planned developments in the area, for instance in the field of landuse? This analysis will give an integral view of the area seen from the different angles and will also show the priorities of the policy sectors and agencies and of the users of the area. Public participation in this approach is important as the quality as experienced by the users of the area will play a leading role in the policy development.

An Example

Living in a city center will be noisier than in suburban areas because of the higher levels of traffic and high density of activities. At the same time in the city center one will have easier access to shops, services and public transport. Suburban housing has a better access to (quiet and high quality) green spaces but will, generally speaking, lack services like a shop around the corner. Both areas can have in total a high quality of life that consists of different levels on different elements: one area having high noise levels but having more services nearby while the other area has low noise levels but green spaces available. Of course such description depends on the actual situation. Many American cities are totally different from the West European ones where innercities are usually a mix of landuse functions.

Not One, but Different Levels of Qualities

As discussed earlier the quality of an area consists of different elements with different levels of quality. One of the discussions associated with this approach is about compensation: that the higher noise level is offset by the better access to services. This is a tricky discussion. Maybe it is better to stay out of the compensation discussion as it is very difficult to determine how much noise is compensated by what level of services. It is better to speak of a different set of qualities.

It would be possible to frame this compensation and different levels of quality of life in terms of environmental justice. Do some groups have a higher environmental burden than others? That difference could turn into a political issue if the "suffering" group is living in conditions with a cumulation of problems. In the Dutch situation this question was never raised. One of the reasons is the concept of the minimum environmental quality that is used in the new approach. In all areas at least the same minimum environmental quality is guaranteed to protect the health and well being of the people. Public participation is also an important element giving the area access to the policy development.

The minimum environmental quality are the levels of the limit values set in the regulations for noise, air and water. These levels are the standards which are already applied in the Netherlands. This project did not try to formulate a minimum level for other non-environmental quality aspects.

A New Role for the Environmental Sector

In the area approach there is a direct confrontation with the other policy sectors and interests, such as landowners, developers, land use planners and economic interests. The environmental interests are not always strongly represented in the decision making processes. Minimum environmental quality is backed by standards based on regulation. However, if one would like to realize a higher environmental quality, then other things, such as creating support, combining interests and demonstrating the (financial or even political) value of a higher standard becomes important. If for example, the project developer is only interested in short term moneymaking, then the chances for the environmental interest to command a higher standard than the minimum quality will be pretty slim. In that case developers and local governments tend to build as many buildings as possible allowed by the applicable standards, that is the minimum environmental quality. Countervailing powers coming from the (general) public or environmental NGO's are then necessary to fight for the higher quality. This means that the decision making structure, processes and actors are important to ensure a proper balance in the discussion of the quality goals.

The area oriented approach has challenges for the usual way of policy making in the environmental sector: it becomes like drafting an environmental policy plan for a specific area instead of the usual generic policy plan. That requires knowledge of the problems, challenges and developments in that area, not only on the environmental aspects but also on the land use, traffic or even economic and social aspects. General standards are in the background. The challenge is to establish together with other policy sectors and agencies a higher integral quality of the area. So the environmental policy sector has to be aware that it is not alone in dealing with an area but has to cooperate with other agencies. That requires a clear view of their own environmental interests and policy goals, and at the same time a open mind to the other aspects and policy sectors. A blank or unprepared approach to the integration is certainly not fruitful.

For the policy goals, the environmental sector has also to go back to the national or regional goals and translate these to goals specific for the area. That sets the environmental policy agenda for the area. Then the confrontation with the other policy sectors and agencies starts: is fulfilling the environmental quality goals possible at the same time as the goals of the other sectors and agencies? Is the economic development compatible with a high air quality at the same time? Or is this impossible with the projected economic development or with the expected traffic development? If so, what are the minimum standards for environmental protection that will maintain the well being of the people living in the area? The new approach requires an opening up of the policy making process in the environmental policy sector and agencies.

Goals of the New Approach

The NEPP4 has two goals with this new approach. The first goal is to realize through this approach a higher environmental quality than would be possible by central standard setting, which could never take fully into account the specifics of the concrete area. At the same time the NEPP realizes the danger of a degraded quality level if there would be no safeguarding of health and nature. That is the reason to maintain, at the national level, minimum environmental quality standards.

The other goal is the integration of all relevant policy sectors and agencies such that they work together to solve the problems of the area in question. The next question is of course: what do the other policy sectors or agencies do? Are they working in the same integrated way? In reality, others sectors and agencies are limited in their ability to work in this way. They seem not always forced, or do not feel the need to cooperate in an integrated approach of the area. Some policy sectors have power and do not depend upon the help of others to realize their goals in an area. The cooperation with the landuse agency at the national level in the development of the new approach illustrates this quite clearly: although part of the same ministry and also addressing spatial quality, the agency had no interest in this development. At the local level, better cooperation between the policy sectors was found.

The Development of the Approach

The new approach is developed in a joint project with the organizations of the Dutch local communities, provinces and waterboards. The new approach and its guidance document is developed on the basis of local methods and guidelines. Several local communities and regional authorities have in recent years developed their own methods and processes with more or less integrated approaches to areas. Under this influence, the developed method is much more open and flexible than was originally proposed in the NEPP4. The project has resulted in a guideline manual. A trial period of two years to develop practical applications and methods and to test the new approach began at the end of 2003. The applications are supported by a project bureau housed at the organization of local authorities. The first results are promising but the application will probably be limited to situations with a complex quality problem, highly mixed functions and certain active political settings. For more simple situations, such as areas with one main land use function, the new approach does not add value in comparision with the old approach by applying the standards.

Conclusions

The area approach is a new way of linking environmental quality to development and land use planning by using the common concern for the level of quality of an area as a focus. The area approach is an integrated way of dealing with an area by connecting all relevant policy sectors and agencies. That requires an opening of the environmental sector to the concerns of other policy sectors and agencies. For the environment, it also means a recognition that there are different aspects of the quality of an area that are linked together and should not be dealt with separately. It also illustrates that areas may have, for good reasons and to the satisfaction of the users and people living in that area, different levels of quality on different aspects. Finally this approach brings a change in environmental policy making, requiring the sector to work differently with areas and with other sectors and agencies. It may also open new ways to integrate environmental concerns into other policy fields.

References

Author unknown (2004), 'Handreiking milieukwaliteit in de leefomgeving, weken aan gebiedsgericht maatwerk' (Den Haag).
Ministry of Housing, Spatial Planning and the Environment of the Netherlands (2001), 'Het vierde Nationale Milieubeleidsplan, Een wereld en een wil: werken an duurzaamheid' (NEPP4 chapter 11), available at: <http://international.vrom. nl/pagina.html?id=7377>.
Ruimte Milieu (2006), available at: www.ruimtexmilieu.nl.
Vereniging van Nederlandse Gemeenten (2006), available at: <www.vng.nl/smartsite. dws?ID=21885&ch=DEF>.

Chapter 5

From a Standard-Oriented to an Integral Quality-Oriented Approach

Jaap van Staalduine

Historical Background in the Netherlands

In the beginning: A multitude of laws and regulations

In the 1960s environmental protection in the Netherlands was governed effectively by just two acts: the Nuclear Energy Act and the Nuisance Act. The Nuclear Act encompasses rules that are mainly concerned with radioactive radiation while the Nuisance Act creates a complex system of licences for activities by business or private persons believed to be likely to cause a nuisance (for example: noise, air pollution, odor, etc) in their immediate vicinity. However, at the end of that decade the government decided to draft specific legislation for the various forms of environmental pollution that exists. This approach was expected to produce a set of effective tools faster than any attempt to formulate an overall environmental protection act would.

The environmental burden in urban areas is covered by legislation on noise pollution, soil conservation, air quality, external safety, and environmental impact assessments. Regulations include provisions for environmental quality standards. These standards serve as the limiting values to be applied by the lower governments in their urban planning and anti-pollution policies, for the incidental formulation of "directional" standards (guiding values, preference values or target values), and for instructions on practical implementation.

In 1993 the Environmental Management Act was adopted by the Dutch government to improve the coherence between the various sector-oriented environmental laws. This Act is a general environmental framework that also contains general licensing rules. Some existing laws were incorporated into the Environmental Management Act, such as the Waste Substances Act, which then ceased to exist in independent form. The environmental impact assessment system, which had been formalized in 1986, was also included in the Act. The intention was for all currently existing separate environmental laws to be assimilated into the Environmental Management Act in due time.

Environmental policy plans

In the 1980s the status of environmental policy planning grew as a result of the need for coherence in overall environmental policy and because it was deemed desirable for interested parties and the public at large to be given an opportunity to participate in the formulation of that policy. The national and provincial authorities are still under an obligation to publish regular environmental policy plans covering all relevant environmental themes. The larger municipalities have also established a tradition of developing municipal environmental policy plans although such plans are not mandatory.

Tension between environmental concerns and spatial planning

To start with, there is a great difference between the formal systems of environmental planning and spatial planning.

Spatial planning is "bottom up" in the Netherlands. There are three tiers of government (the national state, 12 provinces, and approximately 500 municipalities) each with a plan. In the Netherlands the local land-use plan is crucial in the spatial planning system because it is the only land-use plan that is legally binding. Provincial and national plans are not legally binding in principle. The local land use plan, made by the municipality, has to be approved by the province. The provinces also make their own plan(s) for their territory in order to have a framework for the approval of the local land use plans. When there is a national interest, the minister of spatial planning can intervene in the process.

In general the Netherlands' spatial planning system is characterized by a high degree of cooperation and consensus-seeking between all parties involved. The formal system for environmental planning in the Netherlands is quite different. There is a legislation oriented part, in which environmental quality requirements are set by the central government. Target groups (industry, agriculture etc.) have to take their own responsibility for environmental planning, based upon national environmental policy. All the provinces have an environmental program and some licensing and enforcement responsibilities.

Municipalities are not required by law to make an environmental plan but do have licensing and enforcement responsibility in environmental policy. They also have to apply the environmental quality requirements in local land use plans. Until recently it was not possible to deviate from those national standards. In the past, environmental policy regularly clashed with spatial planning policy, due to the sector-oriented structure of environmental legislation, the emphasis on formulating separate environmental quality standards, and the lack of uniform regulations to achieve those standards. Occasionally, there were also fundamental contradictions between spatial quality requirements (accessibility, visibility, functional concentration, etc.) and environmental quality requirements (tranquillity, safety, and the need for a healthy and clean environment).

Initially, environmental quality concerns played a very small role in spatial planning. These environmental quality concerns were often not recognized until the moment the spatial planning process was concluded. This late recognition often resulted in drastic and costly alterations to the spatial policy plans, the cancellation of certain sections, or in the resignation to the fact that crucial environmental quality requirements could not be met. In the big cities the urban development process sometimes ended in a deadlock due to the presumed conflict between the goals of spatial planning and those of environmental policy: functional concentration versus compliance with minimum environmental quality requirements.

Experiments

During the 1990s, recognition of the tension between spatial and local environmental planning triggered experiments aimed at improving the relationship between them. In that effort, 11 "Spatial Planning – Environmental Management" areas were created. These areas have been referred to as the "ROM" areas. ROM is the Dutch acronym for Spatial Planning and Environmental Management. The ROM policy was directed at promoting environmental quality by combining environmental and spatial measures within each area. Additionally, another project, City and Environment, was initiated in 1993 that specifically targeted the cities. This project involved the designation of 25 experimental areas where, under the primary responsibility of the local authorities, an integrated and local approach was to produce a living environment of the highest quality as well as ensure an economic and efficient use of space. The City and Environment Project was introduced in areas where the friction between (compact) spatial planning and environmental quality requirements was particularly strong. The City and Environment (Experiments) Act provided for derogation, under certain conditions, from environmental and other laws and regulations when it was deemed necessary to achieve an economic and efficient use of space and to create an optimal living environment.

Towards a solution

The experiences gained in ROM areas and the City and Environment Project experiments lead to the same conclusion: in virtually all cases, recognition of both environmental and spatial planning concerns from the earliest stages of the spatial planning process make it possible, within existing laws and regulations, to optimize the living environment as well as the economic and efficient utilization of space. As of the summer of 2003 only two out of a total of 25 municipalities within the City and Environment Project experiments have applied for (and obtained) a derogation from the national government to prevent stagnation in the planning process. In the other experimental areas such derogations have so far proved unnecessary. A third request for derogation is currently being prepared at the time of the writing of this chapter.

Experiences with area-oriented policy have led to adjustments in existing legislation. The separate sector-oriented environmental regulations were adapted to allow for further balanced decision-making at the local level. For example, the Noise Abatement Act has been amended to shift the responsibility for derogations from preferred limiting values, up to the maximum limiting value, from the provincial to the local authorities. In the case of soil decontamination, the old rule that contaminated soil must be cleaned up to the level that all functions can be resumed has been scrapped in favor of a function-oriented soil decontamination policy. The intensity of the required decontamination operation varies according to the functional use of the soil concerned, as is determined by the local authorities.

Increasing Influence from Brussels

In the past, European legislation had very little influence on local environmental policy with respect to the quality-of-living environment in the individual EU Member States. European environmental rules were primarily aimed at emissions standards, licensing requirements, and products. Brussels did design an environmental impact assessment system, which has been of great significance for local environmental policy, industrial and other projects, and decision-making in the field of infrastructure.

Recently, Brussels extended the scope of its regulations to include local environmental themes such as noise pollution and air quality. However, the Noise Abatement Directive and the Air Quality Directive are very different types of directives. Under the European Noise Abatement Directive, governments and road managers are obliged to draw up an action plan to improve noise conditions every two years and to stage a public debate on the issue. Each Member State must submit its action plan to Brussels. It is up to the Member States themselves, however, to decide what levels of noise pollution are considered to be problematic. In contrast, the European Air Quality Directive does contain a European air quality standard. According to this directive, the lower government levels must list the areas that will be unable to meet that standard by 2010 and must draw up action plans containing measures to eliminate the excess pollution. Once again, each Member State must submit its action plan to Brussels.

These two directives are clearly different with respect of their ambitions regarding the setting of standards, but also with respect to the target groups and the terms set for compliance. Each directive provides for sector-oriented regulations concerning a specific environmental quality requirement. However, those requirements converge at the local level and call for an integrated approach, all the more since the critical levels for both air quality and noise pollution are primarily determined by road traffic. Only an integrated approach of this nature will facilitate the desired kind of interplay between spatial planning, traffic policy, and environmental policy.

Towards Combined Budgets

Pollution abatement measures

In formulating environmental policy for urban areas, policymakers used to distinguish between existing and new situations. The former called for anti-pollution measures, whereas the latter called for a policy to avoid bottlenecks and serious environmental burdens. Indeed, the aim was to achieve high environmental quality standards.

Extensive legislation plus accompanying financial tools have been created to promote pollution abatement in existing situations. For urban areas the most relevant budgets are those concerning noise and soil. Expected air quality bottlenecks will have to be eliminated in the near future.

Noise pollution abatement measures

The noise pollution abatement budget focuses on the national government's pollution control obligation to implement the necessary measures for the protection of homes that, in a given reference year (in this case 1986), suffered excessive external noise levels. Those measures may involve façade insulation as well as acoustic screens around infrastructure. In addition, experiments are performed to test new methods, such as the use of low-noise asphalt. The most relevant noise pollution abatement measures in urban areas are those concerning façade insulation, which, until a few years ago, were covered by a separate subsidy scheme. The scheme only provided for façade insulation; alternative measures that reduced the effective noise level, such as urban redevelopment or the diversion of roads, could not be funded under this scheme.

Soil decontamination

The soil decontamination budget is an investment budget that aims to eliminate health risks and social stagnation (which occurs when areas cannot be developed or redeveloped due to the risks posed by contamination). The strategic use of the budget is intended to ensure that 75 percent is co-financed by market parties. The total volume of contaminated soil in the Netherlands is immense. Calculations based on the budgets available and on current market dynamics have shown that it would take several decades to clean up all the soil that needed it. This means that priorities will have to be set. Until a number of years ago such priorities were set with reference to national criteria against which individual projects could be tested. This meant that some projects which, from an environmental perspective, were not sufficiently urgent were shelved, in spite of positive spatial dynamics, while projects that received priority status were sometimes carried out at higher costs because they were located in areas with much fewer market dynamics.

Need for combination of budgets

It made much more sense, therefore, to combine the noise abatement and soil decontamination budgets for urban areas with other national funds aimed at urban renewal and new housing construction, preferably for long-term programs. This combination of funds was important to municipalities because it enabled them to set their own priorities and channel the various flows of funds, within the constraints of established environmental quality requirements and applicable regulations. It was also important to the national government, because in this way the funds available could be deployed more efficiently. Any reduction in external noise levels for homes gained in the urban restructuring process was welcome. Linking soil decontamination to areas characterized by high levels of spatial dynamics meant that the 75 percent target of private funding became much more realistic.

This type of concentration, and the associated increase in the autonomy and effectiveness of municipal policy was consistent with the urban policy introduced by the Dutch cabinet at the end of the 1990s. The aim of that policy was to place final responsibility for urban issues with the municipalities themselves, and to provide them with the associated legal and financial means.

In 1999, the Urban Renewal Act came into force. Under this Act a number of urban housing construction subsidy schemes (urban renewal, retirement housing, etc.) are combined with subsidy schemes for industrial estates, for green space projects in cities, and for safeguarding environmental quality (soil and noise funds). The Urban Renewal Investment Budget will be made available to the 30 biggest municipalities in the Netherlands under a five-year agreement to achieve a certain output. The environmental component of this comprises the soil decontamination task and the reduction of noise pollution. A part of the Urban Renewal Investment Budget will be channelled to the other municipalities through the provinces.

Air quality

The Netherlands will have to comply with the EU Air Quality Directive by 2010. Measures to eliminate problems along a stretch of a national motorway obviously cannot be solved within the municipal autonomy. But in a number of cases, this directive also covers the quality of the air in city centers, within the reach of local autonomy. The intention is to add this air quality component to the new Urban Renewal Investment Budget agreements for 2005–2009.

Overall perspective

The decision to link urban environmental budgets to a general Urban Investment Budget has proved to be quite fruitful. What is essential under any circumstances is that these environmental budgets are made available to the municipalities in such a way that:

- long-term financial security is provided (which is crucial, given that investments in the spatial environment have a long time span);
- the municipality is enabled to combine planning and execution activities with its other spatial development goals (it should be able to use the available spatial dynamics so as to ensure that state funding is deployed effectively and efficiently); and
- the municipalities can be called to account over compliance with agreed output targets for specific periods.

Combining Environmental and Spatial Planning Policies

In the beginning: Two separate systems

At the municipal level both environmental and spatial requirements determine the quality of the living environment and spatial dynamics. Nevertheless, environmental planning and spatial planning were conceived as separate systems with a number of cross-connections, such as the links mentioned above between the Noise Abatement Act, the land use plan and the environmental impact assessments.

In this way the environment remained a separate concern that spatial planners found difficult to incorporate into their working method and which consequently tended to be regarded as an obstacle. It would only be a slight exaggeration to say that the majority of spatial plans were not tested against environmental quality criteria until the end of the preparatory stage, and if they failed to meet that test the plans were at risk of being delayed; (partially) rejected, or exceeding their budgets, or a combination of all three. Spatial planners also found it difficult to come to grips both with the regulatory differentiation between environmental themes and with the fact that the associated spatial concerns were not always the responsibility of the municipal authorities, but might fall under the competence of another government level, leading to additional uncertainties and procedural delays. One additional consequence was that in dealing with environmental concerns, spatial planners focused solely on compliance with the applicable standards (because compliance meant that the plans could go ahead), while those standards indicate the very limits of what is environmentally acceptable. There was no move whatsoever towards prioritizing environmental quality and achieving better results than the minimum targets set by those standards.

Experiences gained in area-oriented activities (City and Environment, Area-Oriented Environmental Policy Subsidy Scheme, ROM areas) demonstrated that deadlocks could be prevented through the timely involvement of environmental expertise in the spatial planning process. Such a strategy also ensures that attention is focused on the true purpose of spatial planning: to realize the highest possible quality of the living environment for the area concerned.

That observation has strongly increased the emphasis, within environmental policy, on the need to formulate a municipal environmental policy in close connection with spatial planning, and on the need for legislative authorities to take a cautious approach when setting standards. The Spatial Planning Act is currently being amended in such a way that environmental quality requirements can be incorporated into spatial planning processes.

Municipal area-oriented environmental policy, the new approach

The national government sets minimum standards for environmental themes according to the Fourth National Environmental Policy Plan (2001). Those standards may be differentiated according to function and can be based on environmental conditions that must be fulfilled to guarantee the health and safety of the people in the area, on environmental conditions to protect natural areas, on ecological values, or on internationally agreed norms. The minimum standards constitute an absolute lower limit which, in principle, must always be observed. As a result, compensatory measures (pollution abatement) will have to be taken in virtually all existing situations that clash with the minimum standards. The minimum standards can only be deviated from in exceptional cases, when required for the economical and effective use of space and for the optimisation of the overall living environment.

Compliance with the minimum standards, however, only means that in the situation that has been created, safety, health and ecological conditions have been stretched to the limit of acceptability. It by no means indicates that a high-quality living environment has been designed. A high-quality municipal living environment calls for a coherent vision that indicates the desired environmental quality level for each area. After all, in inner city areas different requirements apply as opposed to those in new suburban commuter neighborhoods or rural villages. The national government has refrained from making such a vision compulsory and from prescribing its content. The vision may therefore be published as an environmental policy plan, as a recognizable component of a zoning plan, or as part of the long-term development program that the 30 biggest municipalities in the Netherlands will have to submit to the government to obtain combined funding from the Urban Renewal Investment Budget.

It is unclear what status these desired environmental quality levels will have. The National Environmental Policy Plan mentioned above states that further consideration will have to be devoted to the question of whether the "guiding value", as referred to in the Environmental Management Act, should be used for this purpose. The guiding value is not a limiting value and can be deviated from if sound arguments are put forward. Another option is to incorporate the desired environmental quality requirements into the land use plan. This guarantees transparency in the formal legislative effects; moreover, municipal resolutions of this nature are formally open to appeal, so that the legal rights of the parties involved are safeguarded.

The design for the new Spatial Planning Act

The design of the renewed Spatial Planning Act allows environmental quality requirements with potential spatial consequences to be incorporated into land use plans. Previously this was only possible to a limited extent. The environmental requirements concerned may relate to such aspects as external safety, odour nuisance and public health, as well as to noise pollution.

Exactly which environmental quality requirements are relevant to spatial planning will be specified in orders in council as yet to be published. These will also indicate which standards must or could be incorporated into land use plans.

In the new design environmental and spatial planning will no longer be regarded as separate systems, but as complementary processes: the incorporation of environmental quality requirements into land use plans allows direct testing of the environmental quality of those plans and the acceptability of certain uses of the land and/or of buildings on it. One of the explicit purposes of the land use plan is to promote a high-quality and sustainable living environment by, among other things, laying down appropriate standards. Given that land use plans, with very few exceptions, only cover part of the municipality concerned it is a good idea to ensure that separate plans are based on a municipal environmental policy. That policy may be issued in the form of a council memorandum, the environmental policy plan, a structure vision, etc. This is not provided for under the design of the new Spatial Planning Act.

The shift from a standard-oriented towards a quality-oriented approach

The combination of these policy innovations, i.e. the formulation of an area-oriented environmental vision for each municipality and the incorporation of environmental quality requirements into land use plans, should create the conditions for ensuring that environmental and spatial concerns have an equal share in the spatial planning process. In this way, the desired shift from a standard-oriented towards a quality-oriented approach can be put into practice.

A detailed inclusion of environmental quality requirements in environmental (or other) legislation would eliminate all the scope for establishing additional rules in the land use plans. Exhaustive listing of quality requirements in environmental legislation should therefore be avoided to allow additional local considerations to be reflected in land use plans.

Environmental quality requirements are governed by complex regulations. Some of those requirements cannot automatically be transplanted into land use plans (e.g. group risk within the theme of external safety, which depends entirely on constantly changing local circumstances). The legal basis of the standards is not equally secure for all environmental quality requirements, there may be no uniform definition of certain concepts (for example, the definition of environmentally sensitive designations varies by environmental theme), and the possibilities of derogation from the given standards vary.

In order to ensure the proper balance between land use plans and environmental quality, a more uniform approach should be taken in the technical elaboration of the quality requirements, and irrelevant variations in definitions should be avoided. Moreover, derogations from limiting values and, if applicable, from guiding values should follow the same pattern for all environmental themes. The City and Environment (Interim) Act, which is currently being drafted, provides for a general derogation from limiting values for ammonia and for the themes of noise, external safety, air quality, soil and odour.

Recommendations

The general orientation in environmental planning is shifting from environmental standards towards environmental quality. Certain standards will continue to apply, but the emphasis has shifted towards measures that achieve an optimal living environment far above the minimum permissible standard. With this approach it is conceivable that the benefits from a certain planning design for several environmental themes are such that it would be acceptable for one other environmental theme, under specific conditions and by way of exception, to exceed the limit by a specified margin.

Municipalities will have to draft municipal environmental policies specifying the desired environmental quality levels in relation with spatial functions by district. The best method is then to enshrine those quality levels in the land use plan; the design for the new Spatial Planning Act provides the tools that make this possible.

References

Dutch Ministry of Housing, Spatial Planning and the Environment (1999), 'Environmental Policy of the Netherlands' (The Hague).

Dutch Ministry of Housing, Spatial Planning and the Environment (2001), 'Where There's a Will, There's a World', 4th National Environmental Policy Plan (The Hague).

Dutch Ministry of Housing, Spatial Planning and Environment (2001). 'Making Space, Sharing Space,' 5th National Policy Document on Spatial Planning 2000/2020 (The Hague).

Miller, D. and de Roo, G. (eds) (2004), *Integrating City Planning and Environmental Improvement* (London: Ashgate Publishing).

Chapter 6

Town Planning Models: A Look at Polish Cities and Sustainable Development

Lidia Mierzejewska

Introduction

For many years after the Second World War, the development of Polish towns was largely determined by three processes: 1) an increase in the population, which was especially significant after Poland's wartime losses, 2) economic development, especially industrialization, which was supposed to bring wellbeing and an improvement in the living conditions to the growing population, and 3) spatial expansion, or advancing urbanization of the suburban zone. Today the consequences of this type of development include a chaotic building pattern devoid of any concrete town-planning thought, a devastated natural environment, unemployment, poor environmental conditions, and as a result, deteriorating health of the population and a growing number of street accidents (Pęski 1999). Owing to wrong development assumptions and poor space management, even the landscape in the vicinity of big metropolitan areas has lost its natural character. Town dwellers and even planners and decision-makers have often come to view this state of affairs as normal, although it defies Aristotle's precept that a town should be built in such a way as to make people healthy and happy.

Attention was first drawn to the deteriorating conditions of city life in the Athens Charter of 1933 (Pióro 1962). One cause was claimed to be the incorrect proportion between built-up and open-space areas. Polish town planners of the 1950s believed that, a healthy housing estate could only be devised in the conditions of socialism (Syrkus et al., 1946). A housing development, whose basic element was a block of flats, was supposed to ensure its residents air, sunshine, greenery, land and water, and be in harmony with the surrounding nature. Accordingly, post-war urban development consisted primarily of the building of housing estates with apartment blocks. Such monofunctional structures (dormitory estates) have deformed the spatial structure of many Polish towns. In addition, an excessive concentration of obsolete industries, infrastructural deficiencies and neglect of environmental protections have combined to make urban spatial-functional structures pathological and cause sanitary conditions to deteriorate (Parysek 2005).

An opportunity to overcome the urban crisis appeared in Poland after 1989, with the change of the systemic conditions. When the local government positions were reborn and filled with actual town managers, the managers began to see the need of making urban spatial-functional structures friendly to their users. The adoption of the assumptions of sustainable development, which give special attention to ensuring healthy ecological conditions in addition to focusing on economic and social development, may help them to achieve this aim. The essence of sustainable development is the satisfaction of the needs of present city dwellers without jeopardizing possible aspirations of future generations (Pęski 1999). All local governments in Poland have a statutory duty to implement this model of development under the Constitution of the Polish Republic, the Spatial Development Act, and other legal documents.

Balancing Urban Development

Approaches to the natural environment

Human attitudes towards, and perception of, the natural environment determines the set of solutions available to those wanting to influence the relationship between natural and man made elements and thus the design of a town's spatial-functional structure. Four basic attitudes towards nature have been identified and are those that influence approaches to sustainable planning (Achterberg 1986; Mierzejewska 2001; Mierzejewska and Parysek 2001):

1. a "dominion-over-nature" attitude, an extreme opinion in which nature is merely a resource that humans have the right to use at will to satisfy their needs;
2. a "stewardship" attitude, which sees human's existence as dependent on natural conditions to some extent; nature is a value in itself and hence should be treated with consideration and a sense of responsibility;
3. an environment-oriented attitude, in which humans are perceived as part of a larger ecosystem; hence moral respect for the various life-forms that humans share it with; and
4. a "unity-with-nature" attitude, the other extreme in the classification, represented by proponents of "deep ecology" in whose opinion nature develops autonomously, independent of man, while man is fully dependent on natural processes; hence, nature has an implicit value and man has a moral duty to respect it.

Until the publication in 1968 of U. Thant's Report, the dominion-over-nature approach predominated in the development strategies of most countries, regions and towns of the world. After presenting the situation in various countries, the report points out threats to the natural environment brought about by the very fast, sometimes even uncontrolled, pace of economic growth. This kind of growth tends to lead to overexploitation of the world's resources, degradation of the land, and a serious disturbance of the ecological balance. Scientific and technological progress reinforced people's attempts to both eliminate their dependence on, and take the fullest advantage of nature. The results were in many regions a rapid rate of urbanization, an increase in the volume of traffic, and damage to natural ecosystems.

All of which led to a deterioration in people's living conditions (Bauman 1991). Today this attitude seems to be out of the question. Equally hard to accept would be an arrangement of the living environment leading to human unity with nature, since this attitude negates the sense of progress and human advancement as a species and a cultural being.

In this day and age, with attempts to balance natural, social and economic relations in towns and urbanised areas, the most desirable are the stewardship or nature-oriented approaches. The latter, however, is only applicable to regions developed less intensively than big metropolitan areas.

The systemic nature of the city

City planning, which is in fact a highly organized territorial social system, involves a suitable shaping of relationships between a city's structural and functional elements (Chojnicki 1999). The multitude and diversity of the elements that make up the structure of a city and their various (often clashing) functions gives rise to many conflicts. The conservation of natural resources is at odds with the need to stimulate production and expand the city's built-up area. This land-use competition often leads to elimination of natural elements and excessive concentration of buildings, a process which is detrimental to both the city as a whole and its residents (Chojnicki 1999; Pęski 1999; Mierzejewska 2001).

The character of the interaction between the natural and the socio-economic sphere will determine whether or not a city's development is going to be sustainable. Prioritizing economic development, even if it is no longer industrial -based, is the greatest threat to a healthy relationship between humans and nature in towns (Chojnicki 1999; Parysek 1997; Mierzejewska 2001, and others). However, urban development would not be balanced either if the economy were made to follow strict rules of nature conservation. Thus, because of the complexity of relations within it, keeping a balance in an urban system is no easy task (Leitman 1995; Chojnicki 1988; Mierzejewska 2001).

The city is not an isolated system. Through many links, such as the flow of goods, capital, population and information, it is closely connected with its surrounding area. In addition, it is often dependent on its surrounding region, and grows at a cost to that region (Leitman 1995; Wackernagel and Rees 1996). The city should therefore be seen in a wider context embracing all of its external influences.

Thus, a model of sustainable development constructed for a particular city should accommodate not only its spatial organisation, structure and operation of the urban system, but also its links with the surrounding environment.

Models of sustainable urban development

One can find several models of sustainable urban development in the literature. Haughton (1997) distinguished four models: 1) that of a self-reliant city, 2) a redesigned city, 3) an externally dependent city, and 4) a fair-share city (cf. Table 6.1).

Table 6.1 Models of sustainable urban development

Model	Assumptions	Critical remarks
Self-reliant city	*self-reliance built on*: • use of local environmental resources • satisfaction of local needs by local business • minimisation of unfavourable external influences *emphasis on*: • reduction in city size • greater integration of buildings with nature • more diversified land-use pattern in cities • introduction of the greatest possible number of free spaces and natural elements to cities	• extent of city self-reliance? • huge uneven geographical distribution of resources • cutting cities off from "rest of world" makes no sense
Redesigned city	*restricting excessive consumption and minimising waste stream, e.g. through*: • reduction in city size • organization of efficient urban transport • designing buildings with good thermal isolation that are more able to intercept solar energy	• excessive focus on internal matters of city
Externally dependent city	• including "polluter-pays" principle into market system, • pricing of environmental resources and services so as to discourage excessive resource consumption	• ignoring social effects of market reforms • market reforms are not always geographically neutral
Fair-share city	• reform of environmental management • estimation of environmental capacity of city and its hinterland • export of excess environmental capacity from hinterland to city in return for compensation	• difficulties in estimating city's environmental capacity determining its growth limits and in defining magnitude of flows (of materials and waste) between city and hinterland

Source: Author's compilation on the basis of Haughton (1997).

The model of a self-reliant city emphasises solving the internal problems of cities through the building of a self-reliant local economy. It should run along the following lines: 1) consumption primarily of its own local environmental resources, 2) satisfaction of local needs by local business, 3) minimisation of the amount of waste, 4) minimisation of unfavourable external influences (e.g. by secondary waste recycling), and 5) transition from a human-centred to an environment-oriented attitude (Bookchin 1974). With reference to the spatial structure of the city, this means greater integration of buildings with natural elements, a more diversified land-use pattern, especially on the periphery (e.g. through the elimination of suburban dormitory housing estates), and restoration of open space, especially green areas. The approach described here as self-reliant also appears in Girardet's (1992, 1993) models of urban metabolism, linear and circular. In a linear metabolism, urban growth relies on supplies coming from outside the city and on waste being removed beyond its limits. This is leads to excessive consumption of raw materials and an expanded waste stream, which is certainly far from the idea of sustainable development. This type of metabolism is in opposition to a circular one, which is the type underlying the operation of a self-reliant city (Girardet 1993). While this model of urban development seems attractive enough, there arises the question of the extent to which cities should be self-reliant. Hence, a city's independence is only relative and should be taken to mean self-reliance within specified limits rather than absolute self-reliance. The latter can lead to a city's isolation, which would certainly be neither advantageous nor possible for the city and its residents in the era of globalization (Girardet 1992; Morris 1982 and 1990).

The model of a redesigned city derives from the belief that present-day urban settlement is wasteful of resources, consuming too much energy, water and land, while producing too much sewage and other waste (Morris 1990; Rees and Roseland 1991). In this model, a suitable redesign of a city could restrict the excessive consumption and minimize the waste stream, and thus improve the state of the natural environment both within the city and outside it. One way to achieve this goal is to reduce city size (a compact city), which involves an increase in population density, a reduction in intra-city journeys, and a greater diversity of land use (Breheny 1997). The redesigned city model is associated with that of the self-reliant city, but is more human-centred. Critics argue that it focuses too much on internal matters while neglecting many external factors (e.g. where the resources should come from and where the waste is supposed to be stored (Haughton 1997)).

The model of an externally dependent city works on the assumption that the day-to-day operation of a city requires the supply of resources from outside (water, energy, food, etc.), and the removal of waste to outlying areas. Thus, its development is largely dependent on the surrounding area which has to suffer the city's detrimental effects and often as a result bears measurable costs. Relationships between the city and its surrounding area should rest on more rational principles. For instance, the city should take on full financial responsibility for all the environmental aspects of its operation and the costs of restoring proper quality to elements of its environment. The city should be discouraged from both excessive consumption of resources and putting off costly investment intended to improve the state of the natural environment, both in the city and its surrounding area (World Bank 1991). Critics contend that this approach ignores social effects of the proposed market reforms and point out that charges collected for pollution may not necessarily be directed to areas at the greatest risk of pollution (Haughton 1997).

The model of a fair-share city rests on the assumptions that the city and its surrounding area have each an ecological capacity, and the problem of unbalanced growth emerges when the city starts making use of the ecological capacity of the surrounding area without proper compensatory measures (White and Whitney 1992; Ravetz 1994). Naturally, the city may use the resources of its surroundings but only on condition that this process does not involve any environmental damage to it. However, if such damage should occur, the city is obliged to repair it fully. This fair share model has the advantage of putting a new perspective on the turnover of environmental resources. However, there is a drawback in that it is very difficult to collect, analyze, and interpret the huge amounts of data needed to define the ecological capacities and links between the city and its surroundings. This model, which combines the most useful aspects of the three other city models, offers one of the best ways to improve the relationship between the city and its outlying areas, thus building a more balanced city (Haughton 1997).

It should be noted that some models put more emphasis on external relations rather than those that exist within city limits. It is clear, however, that what crucially affects the chances of sustainable urban development is a city's spatial form. This influence manifests itself primarily in the dependence between the city's spatial structure and the amount of energy it consumes (Pacione 2001; Słodczyk 2002).

In search of the proper spatial form of the city

The twentieth-century urbanization pattern has led to the emergence of a new spatial structure of the city, largely due to the tremendous development of car ownership. Its consequences include an increase in the urban area, separation of functions in particular intra-urban areas, urban sprawl, and lower population density. This, in turn, has created greater transport needs and an increased demand for energy (Słodczyk 2002). This model of a highly dispersed city has chiefly developed in advanced economies. The beginnings of the same tendency can be observed in Polish towns, and the change seems to be accelerating.

An alternative for this type of urban spatial structure is the construction of compact cities mentioned in the self-reliant and redesigned models. The cities are limited in size and are spatially compact with multi-functional districts, which improve accessibility and reduce the demand for fuel. Proponents of compact cities emphasise advantages such as reduced unit costs of infrastructure, the building of a mass transit system, a more efficient waste management system, and improved accessibility to social services such as health care and education. A compact city also generates fewer external links and exerts weaker pressure on the nearby farmland, thus stimulating the processes of redevelopment and rehabilitation of downtown areas (Hall 2001). At the same time, however, in the city itself this leads to an increase in building density and pressure on building-free areas, including green space. Further more, an excessive population density may limit access to particular functions and produce transport overload, and as a result, may lead to deterioration in the urban population's living conditions. This opinion is put forward by proponents of a dispersed city. Among the things they emphasize are the beneficial effect that home gardens have on the city's ecosystem and the possibility of installing equipment driven by solar energy (e.g. to produce electricity or heat water). Another argument for this type of spatial urban structure is cultural expectations, because a major ambition of most families is to have a single-family house with a garden in a suburban quarter (Carley and Spapens 2000).

In view of the above, the city on the surest road to sustainable development will be a compact one with a polycentric spatial structure developed along fair-share lines, and one that reduces its external links and is careful to maintain proper ecological relations with its surroundings.

Sustainable Development in Poland

Until 1989, the post-war period in Poland was one of natural technocratism, or excessive exploitation and destruction of natural resources not counterbalanced by even elementary conservation measures (Kozłowski 2002). The gradually declining resistance of the natural environment accelerated the rate of devastation, so that many areas came to the brink of ecological disaster. The proof is the establishment in 1985 of 27 ecologically endangered areas. These areas suffered from "a total breakdown of the natural equilibrium manifesting itself in the loss of resistance, elimination of the processes of self-purification and regeneration of biological systems, greater health hazards, and a higher incidence of environment-generated diseases" (Kassenberg, Rolewicz 1985). The areas included practically all big cities and their peripheries.

The collapse of the totalitarian regime in Poland and the country's switch to a market economy initiated a systemic transformation reflected in the adoption of a pro-ecological development position. As a result of these changes, along with cultural changes and new laws, Poland became an undisputed leader of Central and Eastern Europe in the implementation of sustainable development. It also took active part in the Rio de Janeiro Earth Summit, where it signed all the final documents. In addition, the Spatial Development Act passed in 1994 stipulated that eco-development and spatial order should be the underlying principles of all physical planning, and in 1997 sustainable development became a constitutional principle in Poland. Unfortunately, since the mid-1990s, one can observe a slow departure from the assumptions of ecological policy due to both global trends and the new challenges Poland had to face as a result of the systemic transformation. The challenges followed chiefly from the restructuring of the economy, which produced unemployment (a phenomenon practically unknown under socialism) and other social problems. Economic problems, the impoverishment of a substantial sector of society, the weakness of the state budget and local governments, as well as lack of a pro-ecological policy brought about a decline in society's interest in environmental protection. Another probable cause of this state of affairs was an incorrect understanding of sustainable development (also on the part of authorities of various levels). Its definition in Polish legislation only mentions the satisfaction of basic needs, not an improvement in the quality of life, and puts great emphasis on the importance of natural capital while treating the other kinds of capital (economic and social) in rather general terms (Piontek 2002).

In view of the above, it seems that the building of a sustainable development model for the Polish city requires international experience: taking models worked out in other countries and foreign scientific centers and adapting them to the Polish socio-economic and natural conditions.

A General Sustainable Development Model for Polish Cities

To build a sustainable development model for Polish cities, it is necessary to consider all the dimensions of this type of development as well as the various methods of implementation. Successful sustainable development integrates five areas of human life: ecological, social, economic, spatial, and institutional. How each of these spheres is viewed sets the stage for defining problems and the solutions proposed to solve problems associated with sustainable development.

Within the ecology of a city, it is necessary to improve environmental conditions in the city through such measures as care for the quality of its natural elements, special protection of areas of high natural value, and a reduction in its energy consumption. These targets can be achieved through various kinds of investments in environmental protection, a search for renewable sources of energy, thermal isolation of buildings, promoting mass and bike transport, etc. Another important issue is preserving proper proportions between open space and built-up areas, which will allow an improvement in the city's living conditions and in the operation of its ecological systems (Mierzejewska 2001, 2004). Owing to the variety of functions that greenery and open spaces play in urban areas (ecological, social, economic, technological, didactic, etc.), it is desirable for building-free places to constitute no less than 30 percent of a city's area (Odum 1971). However, the proportion of open spaces is not the only consideration here; equally important is their arrangement to ensure the city proper air circulation. In this respect, among the more advantageous patterns of greenery seems to be the green wedge system.

The basic aim of the social development of Polish cities at present is a struggle against mounting unemployment and rising poverty of an ever growing group of people. Efforts should be made to provide equal public access to schools, childcare, healthcare, shops, and services, and to ensure social, personal and public safety.

Social aims cannot be achieved without economic growth, which at present should be oriented toward stimulating the development of small and medium-sized trading and service businesses. As experience shows, small and medium-sized enterprises are among the most effective economic units. Their establishment is a manifestation of a growing level of entrepreneurship, especially those forms that do not require great financial inputs. This is especially important in Poland where there is a general shortage of investment capital. In small and medium-sized businesses it is relatively easy to implement new technologies and hence to make manufacturing more flexible. There are also many service establishments naturally fitting this size category, e.g. a hairdresser's or a beautician's. In Poland this is the only way to change the economic structure and increase the role of those services that were generally underdeveloped before 1989. Industrial activity, in turn, should only be pursued using the best available manufacturing technologies (BAT) which are either neutral to, or only slightly affect the quality of, the urban environment. One consideration here is the limitation of the detrimental effect on the environment; another is improvement in the competitiveness of enterprises active in Poland.

Because spatial order is an extremely important element of sustainable development of towns, the Physical Planning Act considers it a planning principle. The observed order is largely a consequence of a town's history and the changeability of spatial policy. However, it is also a heritage of the previous regime. Today, it seems that the favoured urban layouts should be selectively compact and meet biological and health criteria, as well as socio-economic requirements, which should lead to an improvement in the sanitary and ecological conditions of the various parts of the city (Pęski 1999).

Solid institutional structure involves the setting up of agencies and institutions dealing with the socio-economic and spatial development of the city and its operation. It should be emphasised at this point, however, that city authorities are often too apt to treat city limits as the limits of their responsibility, and are not always concerned about the external effects of the decisions they make (Beatley 1991; Ravetz 1994). Also, local authorities are not always aware that there are environmental problems impossible to solve within city limits. It should be remembered, therefore, that a town can only develop when it has established proper relations with its surrounding region.

In order to deal with problems inherited from the previous regime and those brought about by the present transformation of the system, Polish towns need a policy of sustainable development centred primarily on social and ecological development. This is not only a need, but also a constitutional duty reiterated in Polish legal acts. Generally, sustainable development is usually seen in ecological terms while not much attention is given to its social and economic aspects. Naturally, balancing the economic and the social system has an ecological aspect because in the case of the economy, it concerns its environmental impact, and in the case of the social system, ecological awareness. The growth of ecological awareness and the level of knowledge represented by a local community are those factors that ensure a city its balanced development (Mierzejewska 2004). Ecological awareness of society is still not great, and it is not rare for a person to treat the environment differently as a resident than as an economic agent.

The Sustainable Development of Poznań: A Preliminary Assessment

Poznań ranks fifth among Polish cities in terms of population: its 261.3km^2 are inhabited by 572,000 people. The city lies in west-central Poland on the river Warta and is the capital of Wielkopolska, one of the most economically advanced regions of the country. The city authorities are greatly concerned for its advancement, as evidenced by numerous development plans, projects and strategies. However, we must ask whether those programmes lead to the sustainable development of the city.

Table 6.2 Assessment of congruence between the effects of Poznań's development policy and the sustainable development model

Aspects	Effects of policy congruous with aims of sustainable development	Effects of policy incongruous with aims of sustainable development
Ecological	• reduction in air pollution • thermal renovation of buildings • construction of bike routes • extension of sewerage system • construction of Central Treatment Plant • introduction of selective waste collection • construction of biogas-fuelled power plant and treatment plant on municipal landfill site • construction of parks on block-of-flat estates	• no comprehensive measures to reduce noise • low competitiveness of mass transport • no sewerage system on some estates • poor water quality in standing bodies of water
Economic	• increase in number of economic entities in private sector • growth of small and medium-sized enterprise • dynamic growth of services, including business services • increase in mean monthly wages • construction of Poznań Scientific-Technological Park • establishment of Technology Transfer Centre	• limitation of employment • collapse of many enterprises, especially state-owned
Social	• improved access to health care facilities • increase in number of pharmacies • improved access to higher education	• rise in unemployment rate since 1998 • increase in proportion of unemployed with higher education • increase in crime rate • increase in welfare expenditure • poorer access to nursery schools, kindergartens, and elementary schools
Spatial	• development oriented towards compact city • partial renewal of neglected central city quarters	• earmarking free lots in city centre for investment • construction of objects whose architectural style clashes with city's historic buildings

Source: Author's compilation on the basis of Haughton (1997).

The ecological

The Poznań authorities and residents are aware of the role the natural environment plays in their city's system. The awareness appeared in 1985 when Poznań and its surrounding communes were identified as one of the Ecologically Endangered Districts by the Council of Ministers' Planning Commission. Ten years later, in 1995, the result of another assessment made by the Voivodeship Inspectorate for Environmental Protection was equally unfavourable due to the following factors: 1) pollution of surface waters (chiefly of the Warta), 2) noise (in 57 percent of the city's area allowable noise levels are exceeded), and to a lesser extent, 3) groundwater pollution. The level of air pollution has steadily declined owing to many investments made since the early 1990s and the restructuring of industry. Some state firms passed into the hands of international industrial consortia like Volkswagen, Skoda, GlaxoSmithKline, Exide, Beiersdorf, Unilever, Nestle Pernod-Rocard, Bridgestone, Kimbal Electronics, Wrigley's, and other. Over the years 1990–2003 the total stock of foreign investment in Poznań amounted to $3.5 billion, or 4.8 percent of total foreign investment in Poland. To improve the quality of surface waters, especially those of the Warta, which are significantly below purity standards, the sewage system was expanded and a new biological Central Treatment Plant was opened. However, despite all those measures, the Warta water is not likely to improve until similar investments are made in all the upstream towns. In the recent years, per capita water consumption declined significantly while that of electric power has increased. There has also been substantial investment at the Municipal Refuse Tip at Suchy Las, where a biogas-fuelled power plant and a leachate treatment plant were built. Recycling containers were placed on multi-family housing developments that permit the separation of waste and recycling. The city section of a motorway opened in 2003 relieved some of the heavy traffic on the intra-urban routes and alleviated some of the city's transport problems. There has yet to be any major investment designed to reduce the noise level in the city. Despite some omissions, there is no doubt that many steps have been taken and costly investments have been made to contain the city's detrimental external impact and improve the residents' living conditions, although the process of "ecological modernisation" has by no means been completed.

The economy

Currently, private economic entities predominate (at almost 98 percent) over the state-run ones in Poznań's economy. They are mostly small businesses employing up to five people. There has also been a shift in their lines of activity. The industrial production predominant under socialism has given way to services, chiefly trade and repair, construction, real estate, and business services. Big changes have also occurred in those industrial plants that have withstood adverse tendencies and maintained their position on the market. The changes include a severe reduction in output and employment, and the implementation, largely with the help of foreign capital (privatization), of new technologies. Many of these enterprises take part now in the Cleaner Production Movement, which is intended to work out and implement preventative strategies of environmental protection to reduce the negative impact of many technological processes on nature. However, the transformation of the city's economic structure has also meant mass redundancies and unemployment. A favourable development, in turn, has been the steady increase in average monthly wages. What should boost the city's economic growth, especially its modernisation and diversification, is the construction of the Poznań Scientific-Technological Park, the establishment of a Technology Transfer Centre, and an increase in the number of business-serving economic entities. From the perspective of sustainable development, the economic initiatives launched by the city's authorities and residents can be appraised as good.

The social

The economic changes in Poland since 1990 have been accompanied by social changes. For many people, the restructuring or collapse of their places of work has often meant loss of employment. The Poznań labor market initially resisted these unfavourable tendencies: in 1989 the unemployment rate was a mere 1.2 percent. However, it has been rising steadily ever since reaching 7.1 percent in 2002. Even so, it is one of the lowest figures among the Polish towns. The largest group among the jobless is that of people age 24 and under. There has also been an increase in the percentage of unemployed people with higher education. These undesirable developments cause many graduates, unsure about their future, to look for employment abroad or to take to crime as a way of making a fast and easy profit. Job seekers not entitled to unemployment compensation apply for all kinds of social benefits, making this portion of the city's budget grow from year to year. Furthermore, while average monthly wages keep growing, there has been an ever widening polarization between the incomes of individual households, which is also contrary to the assumptions of sustainable development.

What has improved since the 1990s is the accessibility of health care, pharmacies, medications, and higher education in the city as a result of the establishment of new private schools of higher education offering a variety of specializations. However, there has been a rapid drop in the number of nurseries and kindergartens, which is connected with Poznań's decreasing birth rate over the last years, an increase in older residents, and a steady decline in population.

The residents also enjoy better housing conditions now, because newly-built flats are better equipped with facilities and have more floor space than those in the socialist apartment blocks. The model of a development with blocks of flats has almost been abandoned, giving way to a new building pattern of small, cosy housing developments.

While the average monthly wages keep growing, which is a positive development; there has been an ever widening polarisation between the incomes of individual households, which is contrary to the assumptions of sustainable development, too.

The spatial

On the basis of demographic forecasts which suggest a slight increase in the city population by the year 2010, and taking into consideration the crisis in multi-family building construction and lack of new, developed lots fit for housing, the authorities have decided to look for suitable lots within the city. The policy adopted includes renovation and modernisation of the existing resources and providing them with the missing technical equipment. Thus, emphasis is put on the restructuring of already urbanised areas and elimination of the kind of development threatening the environment, which is consistent with the conception of the compact city. Rehabilitation measures have also been adopted, especially in post-industrial areas.

The overriding aims of Poznań's spatial policy are to counteract the degradation of already developed areas and to curb spatial expansion, which will help to keep large areas biologically active and thus create conditions for a "healthy city" model. This policy is compatible with the idea of sustainable development, as long as the population density in the central part of the city does not grow rapidly.

The institutional

What is needed in institutional terms is the adoption of such structures by local government administration that can identify, plan and coordinate measures taken to implement the sustainable development model. The situation in Poland is favourable in that the spatial development plan, which is a model of spatial order or a special case of balanced development, is an act of the local law (Mierzejewska 2003). It is worse in Poznań, however, because the Local General Spatial Development Plan passed in 1994 has now lost its validity. To improve matters, a plan for the years 2005–2010 was adopted in 2005 and together with other planning documents it now provides a basis for the city's sustainable development.

Conclusions

Under socialism, the Polish economy developed according to the rationalist attitude of man's dominion over nature. The consequence was extensive degradation of the environment threatening the population's health and life and producing barriers to further economic growth. Since 1989, there has been a radical turnabout in the attitude and policy of the Polish authorities toward first, eco-development and then sustainable development, which has become an obligatory model of growth in Poland. No such model has so far been devised in practice; and while it should accommodate the specific Polish conditions, use can also be made of the models worked out for towns in the other European countries. The environmental degradation and problems involved in the socio-economic transformation after 1989 has put Polish towns in a situation especially unfavourable to the idea of sustainable development. Lack of an explicit definition of such development in Poland is a barrier as well. Sustainable development models devised for Polish towns should put special emphasis on ecological and social aspects as explained earlier.

Analysis of Poznań's sustainable development shows a favorable assessment of progress in the protection of ecological systems and the restriction of the city's detrimental external impact. Equally favourable are the changes that have taken place in the city's economy and in the conception and implementation of its spatial development. The picture is much less reassuring in terms of social development, with the standards of living of many Poznań residents having fallen in the recent years. This leads to growing disparities between particular social groups, which do not correspond with the principles of sustainable development.

It is hard to say unequivocally if these assessments are generalizable to all Polish towns. Poznań is an example of a city that is now at a stage of "ecological modernisation". Also, since Poland has joined the European Union, it is hard to predict the future of the sustainable development idea, given the fact that EU directives focus on economic aspects while ignoring social questions.

Thus, what is needed to call Polish cities well-balanced is a change in people's attitude towards the natural environment and in the urban development model. Nature cannot be perceived solely as a resource to be used, but also as a living environment of the present and future generations. One of the means to achieve this is investment in the social sphere, including ecological education raising city-dwellers' awareness. The urban development model has to change too. There have been some spontaneous advantageous changes in Polish cities after the collapse of socialism (in the economy, construction, environmental protection, etc.), but sustainable development can only be achieved through a deliberate implementation of the selected model. In the case of large Polish cities, the most favourable seems to be the fair-share model, while small and medium-sized towns should strive towards maximum self-reliance possible.

References

Achterberg, W. (1986), 'Gronden van Moreel Respect Voor de Natuur', in *Milieufilosofie Tussen Theorie en Praktijk: Van Ekologisch Perspectief Naar Maatschappelijke Toepassing*, J. van Arkel (eds).

Bauman, R. (1991), *Domy w Zieleni* [Houses in Greenery] (Warszawa: Arkady).

Beatley, T. (1991), 'A Set of Ethical Principles to Guide Land Use Policy', *Land Use Policy*, Jan, 3–8

Bookchin, M. (1974), *The Limits of the City* (New York: Harper Colophon).

Breheny, M. (1997), 'Urban Compaction: Feasible and Acceptable', *Cities*, 14:4 (Warszawa: Instytut na Rzecz Ekorozwoju).

Carley, M. and Spapens P. (2000), *Dzielenie się światem* [Dividing World] (Warsaw: Instytut na rzecz ekorozwoju)

Chojnicki, Z. (1988), 'Koncepcja Terytorialnego Systemu Społecznego' [Conception of a Territorial Social System], *Przegląd Geograficzny*, 60:4, 491–507.

Chojnicki, Z. (1999), *Model Wzajemnych Zależności Między Systemem Społeczno-Ekonomicznym a Środowiskiem Geograficznym* [Model of Interdependences Between a Socio-economic System and a Geographical Environment] (Poznań: Bogucki Wydawnictwo Naukowe).

Girardet, H. (1992), *Cities: New Directions for Sustainable Urban Living* (London: Gaia Books).

Girardet, H. (1993), 'Sustainability: The Metabolism of London', *Regenerating Cities*, 6, 37–40.

Hall, T. (2001), *Urban Geography* (London/New York: Routledge).

Haughton, G. (1997), 'Developing Sustainable Urban Development Models', *Cities*, 14:1.

Kassenberg, A. and Rolewicz, Cz. (1985), *Przestrzenne Diagnoza Ochrony Środowiska w Polsce* [Spatial Diagnosis of Environmental Protection in Poland] (Warszawa: PWN).

Kozłowski, S. (2002), *Ekorozwój. Wyzwanie XXI Wieku* [Eco-development. A Challenge of the 21st Century] (Warszawa: PWN).

Leitman, J. (1994), 'Urban Enviromental Profile Series', *Cities*, 12:1.

Leitman, J. (1995), 'Urban Environmental Profile: A Global Synthesis of Seven Urban Environmental Profiles', *Cities*, 12:1.

Mierzejewska, L. (2001), *Tereny Zielone w Strukturze Przestrzennej Poznania* [Green Areas in the Spatial Structure of Poznań] (Poznań: PTPN).

Mierzejewska, L. (2003), 'Rozwój zrównoważonyJako Kategoria Ładu Przestrzennego' [Sustainable Development as a Category of Spatial Order] in Slezak and Ziolo (eds).

Mierzejewska, L. (2004), *Przyrodnicze Aspekty Rozwoju Zrównoważonego Miast* [Natural Aspects of the Sustainable Development of Towns] (Poznań: Bogucki Wydawnictwo Naukowe).

Mierzejewska, L. and Parysek, J. (2001), 'Environment and Planning, or Possible Approaches to the Environment in Physical Planning', *Geographia Polonica*, 74:1.

Morris, D. (1990), *The Ecological City as a Self-reliant City* (Montreal: Black Rose).

Morris, D. (1982), *Self-Reliant Cities: Energy and the Transformation of Urban America* (San Francisco: Sierra Club Books).

Odum, E. (1971), *Fundamentals of Ecology* (Philadelphia: W.B. Saunders Company).

Pacione, M. (2001), *Urban Geography* (London: Routledge).

Parysek, J. (1997), *Podstawy Gospodarki Lokalnej* [Foundations of the Local Economy] (Poznań: Wyd. Naukowe UAM).

Parysek, J. (2005), *Miasta Polskie na Przełomie XX i XXI Wieku. Rozwój i Przekształcenia Strukturalne* [Polish Towns at the Turn of the 21st Century: Development and Structural Changes] (Poznań: Bogucki Wydawnictwo Naukowe).

Pęski, W. (1999), *Zarządzanie Rozwojem Zrównoważonym Miasta* [Management of a City's Balanced Development] (Warszawa: Arkady).

Piontek, B. (2002), *Koncepcja Rozwoju Zrównoważonego i Trwałego Polsk* [Conception of Poland's Balanced and Sustainable Development] (Warszawa: Wyd. Naukowe PWN).

Pióro, Z. (1962), *Ekologia Społeczna w Urbanistyce na Przykładzie Badań Lubelskich i toruńskich* [Social Ecology in Town Planning: The Case of Lublin and Toruń Studies] (Warszawa: Arkady)

Ravetz, J. (1994), 'Manchester 2020 – A Sustainable City Region Project', *Town and Country Planning*, 63.

Rees, W.E. and Roseland M. (1991*)*, 'Sustainable Communities: Planning for 21st Century', *Plan Canada*, 31.

Słodczyk, J. (2002), *Przestrzenny Rozwój Miast a Rozwój Zrównoważony* [Spatial Growth of Towns and Balanced Development] in I. Jażdżewska (eds).

Slezak, T. and Ziolog, Z. (2003), *Społeczno-gospodarcze i Przyrodnicze Aspekty Ładu Przestrzennego* [Socio-economic and Natural Aspects of Spatial Order] (Warszawa: Biuletyn KPZK PAN).

Stren, R., et al. (1992), *Sustainable Cities: Urbanization and the Environment in International Perspective* (Boulder, CO: Westview).

Syrkus H. and Syrkus, Sz. (1946), 'Budownictwo Doświadczalne' [Experimental Construction] *Dom, Osiedle, Mieszkanie*, 6–8.

Wackernagel, M. and Rees, W. (1996), *Our Ecological Footprint: Reducing Human Impact on the Earth* (Gabriola Island, BC: New Society Publishers).

White, R. and Whitney J. (1992), 'Cities and Environment: An Overview', in Stren et al. (eds).

Chapter 7

The Efficiency of Land Use Conversion

Hai-Feng Hu and Tzu-Chia Chang

Introduction

In science and engineering the operational definition of "efficiency" is generally based upon some variation of a ratio of output over input. By contrast, in social science, the definition of efficiency is rather controversial. Most researchers enter into endless arguments whenever they talk about the issues regarding institutional efficiency (Parkin 2000). In this chapter, we seek to clarify the meaning of efficiency through two aspects. The first aspect concerns the connection between economic "efficiency" and individual utility.[1] Generally speaking, when we discuss "efficiency" in social science the criterion of judgment is based upon the utility changes of the individual. For example, in the case of the popularly used Pareto Efficiency we say an allocation of resources is Pareto efficient when there is no other possible allocation where some individuals can be made better off without making others worse off. In this example, for an individual, a state is said to improve or decline by measuring changes in the individual's utility. From the viewpoint of society, another definition of efficiency is the Marshall Efficiency. In Marshall's definition, an allocation is said to be efficient when it maximizes net social benefits – the sum of producers' surplus and consumers' surplus[2] (Mankiw 2001). In the same way, the measurement of surplus here derives from the utility changes of individual. In a sense, these definitions connect the economic efficiency and individual's utility; as a result, it means that efficiency is quite a subjective concept.

The second aspect concerns the relative concept of efficiency. At the beginning of the paper titled "Property Market Efficiency: An Institutional Economics Perspective", Keogh and D'Arcy (1999) stated:

> The concept of property market efficiency remains poorly developed and inadequately theorized despite a growing body of empirical research on the issue[3] ... the institutional dimension fundamentally alters the concept of efficiency and leads to a partial and

---

1 In economics, "utility" is a measure of individual's satisfaction or happiness.

2 Producers' surplus is the difference between the price sellers receive for the good and the minimum or lowest price they would be willing to sell the good for. Consumers' surplus is the difference between the maximum or highest amount buyers would be willing to pay and the price they actually pay (Arnold 2004: 86).

3 Keogh and D'Arcy (1999): Most work focuses on the issue of information-processing efficiency in the property investment market, adapting the work of Fama (1970) and his successors on other financial asset markets. The result is a limited interpretation of what

contingent judgment on achieved efficiency. Instead of seeking a judgment on whether the 'property market' as an entity is efficient, the institutional approach allows the possibility that the 'property market process' may be efficient for some market participants but not for others.

In fact, the relative concept is not a new idea, and has been emphasized in many subjects. In physics, for instance, when we describe an event or phenomenon, it is necessary to indicate the specified observer. For different observers the descriptions may vary.

This chapter applies the idea that the economic efficiency is a subjective concept which comes from the viewpoint of a particular observer to study the efficiency of institutions. More specifically, we focus attention on exploring the efficiency of institutions of land use conversion by comparing the current zoning system with the tender offer system as proposed by Colwell (1997).

The remainder of this chapter is organized as follows: Section two discusses the various conceptualizations of efficiency. Section three compares different institutions of land use conversion, while Section four looks at the role of government. Finally, Section Five concludes.

About "Efficiency"

In general, we use the Pareto criterion to judge the efficiency of resource allocation. As a globally recognized criterion for judging efficiency it takes into account all agents involved in the implementation of an institution. However, for a particular agent the information obtained from the Pareto Efficiency criterion is too loose; that is, even though the institution may satisfy the Pareto criterion, the agent still cannot know how much he is better off after an institutional policy is implemented. In other words, supposing that two institutions satisfy the requirements of Pareto Efficiency, an observer may still not be able to decide which institution is the better one. Therefore, we first seek to define the concept of *local efficiency*.

Since the utility concept is the key to judging the agent's situation, we can define the concept of local efficiency by observing changes in the agent's utility after an institution's policy has been implemented. For a specific agent, if the change is positive, then we can say that the institution is efficient in relation to that specific agent. The definition of local efficiency is only concerned with some specified agent. However, it is neither meant to reject Pareto Efficiency and Marshall Efficiency which in turn are concerned with all agents involved in an institution simultaneously, nor to simplify the analysis of efficiency. On the contrary, the purpose of local efficiency is to understand more of the information related to an institution. In other words, understanding the concept of local efficiency can deepen the analysis of an institution.

For these reasons, we need to use more words to describe the efficiency of an institution. For example, if there are two agents, A and B, in a society, then

---

constitutes efficiency and the application of empirical tests which might be ill-suited to assessments of the property market.

there will be three viewpoints regarding how efficiency should be described; the efficiency for agent A, the efficiency for agent B, and the efficiency for both A and B simultaneously. In general, if we do not identify the viewpoint we adopt, this means that the third scenario applies. Note that even when we apply the third viewpoint to consider all agents involved in an institution simultaneously, the comparison of economic efficiency of institutions is still a difficult task.

In economic analysis, we usually apply the Pareto criterion, but it is not operational in the real world due to the strict limitation that no agent should be made worse off. Consequently, the concept of Marshall Efficiency would be an alternative in this situation. In Marshall Efficiency, the change in the utility of all agents is summed. If the net change in value is positive, we can say that the institution is efficient.[4]

In order to clarify the meaning of efficiency one step further, it is useful to point out the difference between a "state" and a "path". As shown in Figure 7.1, for one agent or one kind of agent who is in state U_1, his psychic satisfaction level at a specific time point will be U_1, regardless of whether the value of utility U_1 can be numbered or not,[5] for it is still a "stock" concept. In other words, it is a quantity measured at a specific point in time. As time goes by the agent may change his utility value by means of some exchange or action, as in the case of the path R_1 in Figure 7.1, and then the agent will reach the new state U_2. In addition, it should be noted that the structure of Figure 7.1 has two other implications. First, there may be many kinds of exchanges or actions along the path R_1 and second, the role of R_1 may be explained as that of an institution in society.

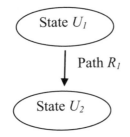

Figure 7.1 The relationship between state and path 1

---

4   In the same way, when we say: *the institution is efficient*; this is a viewpoint that takes all agents into consideration simultaneously. The efficiency of the institution is not for a specific agent.

5   There are two kinds of utility function in economics, namely, cardinal utility and ordinal utility. If utility level can be indicated in an exact number, then the utility function is said to be cardinal. On the other hand, if we can not use a number to indicate utility level, but only can rank different utility levels, then we say the utility function is ordinal. Which kind of utility function is the proper one to describe individual's behavior is still controversial.

In general, if agents volunteer to go to state U_2, this means that the utility value of agents in state U_2 is larger than that in U_1; this is a basic axiom of behaviorism.[6] The question then becomes how to measure the utility value of the state, and the answer depends upon the content of the state. If there is only one agent in the state, the answer is clear, for the total utility value of the state is equal to the utility value of the agent. If there are two agents in the state the answer is a little more complex. First, if we know the "common utility function"[7] of the two agents then we will know the utility value of the state by substituting the utility values of the two agents into the function. If we do not know the common utility function, we can still obtain some useful information from the axiom of behaviorism.

The situation can be categorized according to whether or not there is interaction between the two agents. In the case where there is interaction, there is a business transaction or exchange taking place between the two agents, the seller may give something to the buyer and receive some money from the buyer, or else the buyer may pay some money to obtain something. If they exchange on a voluntary basis they may both obtain higher utility values separately, in which case there will be a Pareto improvement. The gap in terms of the utility value between the two states is the so-called "psychic profit" of Mises (1963), which is similar to the concepts of consumer and producer surplus in economics. Then, even without the explicit form of a "common utility function", we can still be sure that the utility value in the final state will be higher than the corresponding value in the initial state, regardless of whether the utility of the agent is cardinal or ordinal.

If no interaction takes place between the two agents, then we cannot calculate the utility value of the state so easily and clearly. Let us consider the following hypothetical situation. One agent's utility value is ten, while another agent's utility value is five.[8] When both agents go through a specific path and reach a new state, then one agent's utility value will be eight, and that of another will be seven. According to the Pareto criterion, we cannot compare the efficiency of the two states because the situation cannot satisfy the strict limitations of Pareto Efficiency. In other words, we know that the Pareto criterion is very clear and elegant, but if there is any agent in the state who is worse off than before, then we cannot judge the gains or losses in efficiency merely by using that criterion. Regarding this non-operational property of the Pareto criterion, Friedman (2000: 24) has remarked:

> Modern economists often try to avoid some of the problems implicit in Marshall's approach[9] by using a different definition of economic improvement, due to Vilfredo

---

6 Regarding the axiom of behaviorism, please see Mises (1962, 1963) for more detailed information.

7 The meaning of "common utility function" is the same as the "public interest" of all people in the state.

8 We suppose the utility value of the agent is cardinal here.

9 In Marshall Efficiency, when the utility changes of all agents are summed up, if the net value is positive, we can say that the institution is efficient, and the concept is similar to the definition of efficiency in Mankiw (2001: 153): *the property of a resource allocation of maximizing the total surplus received by all members of society.*

Pareto, an Italian economist. Pareto avoided the problem of trading off gains to some losses to others by defining an improvement as a change that benefits some and injures nobody.

Unfortunately, this approach eliminates the solution as well as the problem ... In a complicated society it is very unlikely indeed that a change in legal rules will produce only benefits and no costs ... If we want to make an overall evaluation of the effects of such changes, we are stuck with the problem that Marshall solves, even if imperfectly, and Pareto only evades.

To broaden the scope of the Pareto criterion in judging the efficiency of an institution, we should use Marshall's concept to estimate the impact of institutional changes overall, i.e. we should calculate the net deviation in utility value for the whole state. For this purpose, we should use the cardinal form to measure the agent's utility level, and be familiar with the common utility function.[10] There is another point that we would like to mention here. If all agents increase or decrease their utility values simultaneously, we can come to a definite conclusion that the final state will be better off or worse off than the initial state, regardless of whether we use the Pareto criterion or Marshall's approach.

If there are three or more agents in a state, the inference is similar to the case of two agents. It is a generalization of two agents, but the calculations are more complex.

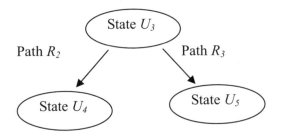

Figure 7.2 The relationship between state and path 2

In Figure 7.2, if the utility value of state U_4 is greater than that of U_5 we can say that state U_4 is more efficient than state U_5. The result then becomes irrelevant in terms

---

10 This way of summing up the utility changes of all members within a state is meaningful in a real society. For example, if there are two people A and B in a state, and after the implementation of a specific institution, A's utility value decreases by 1, and B's utility value increases by 5, then the net change in the utility value of the state will be +4. If we add a compensation mechanism and let B transfer utility value of 2 to A, then the joint institution will be efficient for A, will be efficient for B, and will also be efficient for (A+B) simultaneously. Pindyck and Rubinfeld (1989: 567) have illustrated the idea by using the example of imposing quotas on imports of cars in America.

of comparing the transaction costs of path R_2 and R_3, because the efficiency of a state depends upon the utility value directly and it is not necessary to measure the transaction costs indirectly.

On the other hand, even if we know that the utility value of state U_4 is bigger than that of U_5, we do not know that the society will follow the path R_2 definitely for, due to some special social structure, the process of history does not bring people to a higher utility value. In any case, there is no contradiction between this point and the axiom of behaviorism mentioned before, because some people do not volunteer to accept the process of history.[11]

In Figure 7.3, because of different initial states, we cannot compare the efficiency of State U_7 and State U_9. Even though the utility value of State U_7 is bigger than that of State U_9, we cannot say that State U_7 is better than State U_9 in terms of economic efficiency; otherwise we will make a logical mistake.

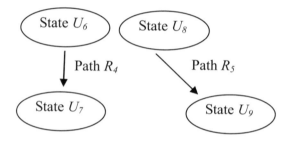

Figure 7.3 The relationship between state and path 3

The Efficiency of Land Use Conversion: A Utility Perspective

There are many kinds of regulations regarding land property rights within a society. For example, a zoning system is an institution that is expected to serve many purposes – including eliminating or reducing the uncompensated external cost of non-conforming land use, improving the environmental amenities, increasing the value of real estate, guiding urban growth, maintaining the level of public service, improving the landscape of a city, and economizing on fiscal expenditure.

To achieve these goals, the government[12] uses administrative discretion to make decisions regarding the type and the intensity of land use, these decisions being subject to adjustment according to the social and economic situation. As to the effectiveness of the zoning system, opinions are widely divided. In any case, with regard to the zoning system, the government has the absolute right to decide how the land should be used. This is a very important point when we study the issue

---

11 North (1982, 1990) has illustrated this thought in a study on the institution of property rights.

12 For the sake of accuracy, the "government" mentioned here is similar to the "proximate policy-makers" defined by Lindblom (1993). They are elected and appointed officials who mostly directly enact and administer laws.

of land use conversion. In many regions or countries,[13] regardless of whether the proposals to convert the use of land are made by the public sector or the private sector, there must be a process of investigation that is guided by local government. In other words, the government is an intermediary in addition to being a well-disposed agency in the zoning system.

With regard to land use conversion, Colwell (1997) has proposed a tender offer system, in which the risk that is caused by the government can be eliminated. The way in which the tender offer system operates is briefly described as follows:

1. A "partial property right" of land is created so that a landowner can prohibit the conversion or development of adjoining land within a specific range.[14]
2. If a landowner wishes to develop his own land and a surrounding landowner has a "partial property right" to prohibit the development, the developer needs to buy the approval from the surrounding landowner.
3. In a way similar to an auction, the developer will acquire rights from the surrounding landowners by offering to pay a specified price for the partial rights needed. The surrounding landowners can decide whether to sell their rights or not. The conversion of land is allowed only after a specific proportion[15] of the partial property rights are bought. Thus, if the developer cannot buy enough partial property rights at his first attempt, he should offer a higher price so that the proportion can be achieved; otherwise he will abandon his plan.
4. The second tier of rights is acquired involuntarily under a specific discount,[16] and then the problem of holdout is resolved.[17]

According to the ways in which the zoning system and the tender offer system are structured, plus the definition of efficiency mentioned in the previous section, this section of the chapter analyzes the economic efficiency of institutions in relation to land use conversion.

First, the framework of analysis is similar to that depicted by Figure 7.2, in which state U_3 represents the initial state of land use, and paths R_2 and R_3 represent the zoning system and the tender offer system, respectively. The zoning system will create a new state U_4, and the tender offer system will create U_5. If we wish to compare the efficiency of the two institutions, this means that we will compare the utility values of states U_4 and U_5.

---

13 For example, in Taiwan the zoning system is the main body of rules concerning land use.

14 Colwell (1997) suggested 150 feet, and of course this is arbitrary. This distance may depend on the kind of development, and may need some scientific or empirical study. The tender offer system that we refer to here focuses on the contractual structure, and the decision regarding the exact or best number in relation to the distance is not the issue.

15 Colwell (1997) suggested 80 percent, and of course it is arbitrary, too.

16 Colwell (1997) suggested 10 percent. He thought the discount was arbitrary, but reasonable.

17 The two-tiered, front-end-loaded tender offer device proposed by Comment and Jarrel (1987) is supposed to handle the holdout problem.

There are three kinds of agents in this analysis, the government, the landowner of the land to be converted, and the landowner of the surrounding land.[18] In Figure 7.4, if the landowner of region A wishes to change the land's use or develop it, any such development will have an impact on the surrounding land, which will be deemed an "externality" if there is no transfer of money between landowners A and B.

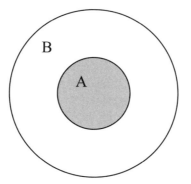

Figure 7.4 Sketch map of conversion land and surrounding land

For the sake of simplicity, we assume that the externality is negative and note that in the zoning system landowner B does not have any legal right to stop the development of region A. Also note that, if landowner B is unable to obtain any compensation, the development of region A will reduce landowner B's utility level. On the other hand, for landowner A, if he still volunteers to develop his land after paying some money to the government, this implies that he will increase his utility level after the development is completed.

Usually, when we talk about the development of land it means that we are increasing the intensity of land use which almost always raises the value or market price of the land. That is to say, landowner A can increase his nominal wealth through the development and, if he does not need to pay any money to landowner B whose utility value is reduced by a negative externality, this implies that A can earn more.[19]

In accordance with the regulations governing land use in the current zoning system, the government can obtain money or land from the developer by the approval of land use conversion. The amount of such money is a specific proportion of the total profit which the developer can earn from developing his land, but regardless of how much the proportion is it cannot change the way in which the government

18 There is no limit to the number of each kind of agent. In other words, the numbers of each kind of agent do not affect the conclusion.

19 For the sake of simplicity, we assume that the conversion involves a negative externality. This means that the utility value of the surrounding landowner will decrease after the conversion. If the developer cannot benefit from the conversion, there will be no need to develop the land.

is able to take the profit that accompanies the development of the land. Therefore, the nature of land use conversion gives the impression that the government and developer share the implicit wealth hidden in the regulations of land use.

In the tender offer system, the role of the government is neutral. It is not involved in the development, and the conversion of land use is a simple contractual relationship between landowner A and landowner B. Based upon the discussion in the previous section, we know that A and B can increase their utility values simultaneously by means of a voluntary exchange.

To summarize the above analysis, we present Tables 7.1 and 7.2 regarding the issue of land use conversion. Table 7.1 depicts the conversion of land use where there is a negative externality, and Table 7.2 illustrates where there is a positive externality. The main difference between these two tables is the change in utility of the surrounding landowner B. Landowner B will either suffer from a negative externality or benefit from a positive externality based on the current zoning system, but will always benefit under the tender offer system. This distinction may be illustrated as follows:

Table 7.1 The impact of land use conversion on the agents' utility (*negative* externality)

Agent/Institution	Zoning system	Tender offer system
Government	↑	→
Landowner A	↑	↑
Surrounding Landowner B	↓	↑

Note: ↑ utility increases; → utility remains constant; ↓ utility decreases.

Table 7.2 The impact of land use conversion on the agents' utility (*positive* externality)

Agent/Institution	Zoning system	Tender offer system
Government	↑	→
Landowner A	↑	↑
Surrounding Landowner B	↑	↑

Note: ↑ utility increases; → utility remains constant; ↓ utility decreases.

In the case of the land use conversion with a positive externality, the utility levels of all agents will increase simultaneously under both the zoning system and the tender offer system. Although the distributions of the benefits will be different, there will be very little dispute in this case. That is, if the externality is positive the two institutions will be efficient for all agents from all perspectives. Which one will be more efficient for a specific agent? This, however, is not the point of this chapter.[20] What we like to emphasize is that the benefit accruing to the government from the zoning system actually comes from both landowner A and landowner B, for the way in which the burden is shared will depend upon the bargaining power of both sides in a way similar to the concept of elasticity in economics. That is, the burden for those who show a larger price elasticity is smaller. However, regardless of how much the proportion is, no one will be worse off than before, and therefore there will be no or very little dispute in this situation.

In the case of land use conversion with a negative externality, the surrounding landowner is the only one who suffers, for both landowner A and the government will benefit from the conversion. However, Mises (1963: 734) has said:

> There are hardly any acts of government interference with the market process that, seen from the point of view of the citizens concerned, would not have to be qualified either as confiscations or as gifts. As a rule, one individual or a group of individuals is enriched at the expense of other individuals or groups of individuals. But in many cases, the harm done to some people does not correspond to any advantage for other people.

Under the tender offer system, the surrounding landowner B can obtain some compensation from landowner A, provided that B agrees to the development of region A by accepting a specific amount of money. This means that B can reach a higher utility level from the conversion of land use and, in the same way, if landowner A still wishes to develop his land after paying some money to B, it means that A can still benefit. In short, both landowners A and B can increase their utility values by means of a voluntary exchange under the tender offer system. Therefore we can say that the tender offer system is efficient for A, for B, and most importantly for (A+B).

On the other hand, if the surrounding landowner B cannot obtain any compensation under the zoning system, the conversion of land use will enable landowner A and the government to benefit, but B will suffer. In other words, we can say that the zoning system is efficient for A and is efficient for the government, but it is not efficient for B. As for all agents simultaneously, we are not sure. From the viewpoint of Marshall Efficiency, if we want to know whether the institution is efficient or not, we need to calculate the utility level of the whole state. Therefore we need to know in advance the utility level of each individual and the form of common utility function. However, the existence of a common utility function is still controversial.

Since the calculation of the utility level of the whole state needs to consider all agents involved in the state simultaneously, it implies that different agent

---

20 If the conversion of land use has positive effects on surrounding land, then the conversion will increase each individual's utility level simultaneously. Hence, the focus of discussion is the distribution of profits caused by the conversion. This issue, anyway, is not as much controversial as the land use conversion with a negative externality.

combinations will have different common utility functions. Thus if the agent composition in the state is different, there will be different results when we compare the efficiency of institutions. For example, if we only consider landowner A and surrounding landowner B in a case regarding land use conversion, the result of comparing efficiency between the current zoning system and the tender offer system will be different from the result that considers landowner A, B, and the government simultaneously. Furthermore, since the utility level of whole state is an increasing function with respect to each agent's utility level, although we do not know the exact form of the common utility function, there is still one thing of which we are sure. Namely, if we exclude the government in the situation and only consider landowners A and B, the new state resulting from the zoning system path will be worse than the state that includes the three agents. The reason for this is that we have neglected the benefit accruing to the government in the zoning system. In other words, when we evaluate the efficiency of an institution, the agents chosen to be included in the state is very crucial. However, even if we only consider landowner A and landowner B for the sake of simplicity, we note that A benefits and B suffers under the current zoning system, and that both A and B will benefit under the tender offer system. Since we do not have enough information regarding the common utility function, we still cannot compare directly the efficiencies of states caused by these two institutions.

Nevertheless, if A's benefit under the zoning system is no bigger than that under the tender offer system, and B's utility increases in the tender offer system but decreases in the zoning system, we can come to the conclusion that the tender offer system is more efficient than the zoning system in relation to the land use conversion where there is a negative externality.

In brief, although we try to compare the efficiency of institutions by measuring the utility values of agents in a state directly, we cannot come to a clear and simple conclusion due to the lack of an explicit form of common utility function. However, we are still able to draw a rough conclusion here. In the case of land use conversion involving a negative externality, if we only consider two kinds of agent, namely, landowner A and surrounding landowner B, unless A can get much more profit under the zoning system than under the tender offer system, we can almost say that "the tender offer system is more efficient than the zoning system".[21] Due to the lack of an explicit form of the common utility function and a partial lack of empirical evidence we cannot be absolutely certain. Even though the word "almost" implies some weakness in our conclusion, the chance of being wrong is very small. Only if the common utility function takes on a very strange form, for example, will the weight of landowner A's utility in the common utility function be very high.

Under the current zoning system, if the government transfers a payment to surrounding landowner B after receiving money from landowner A, the content of the compound institution will be similar to that under the tender offer system, only the government will serve as the intermediary between landowner A and landowner B, regardless of whether the compound institution is better than the tender offer system. This is an area that needs more study.

---

21 If surrounding landowner B suffers very significant damage and even landowner A benefits greatly, this conclusion is still tenable over a reasonable range.

In the real world, although the institutions of land use are very complex, we are of the opinion that the spirit of voluntary exchange under the tender offer system is generally quite suitable. Furthermore, the details regarding its implementation, for example, the relative proportions or numbers should depend upon the kind of land use conversion. Conversely, because there are many people involved in the negotiation process, the current zoning system apparently has more scale economies than the tender offer system. We think this is part of the reason why only a small part of land use conversion adopts the spirit of voluntary exchange. We find that there is no logical contradiction between the technical viewpoint and the efficiency viewpoint that we have mentioned above.

The Role of Government

According to the mechanism of implementation, the main difference between the current zoning system and the tender offer system lies in the allocation of land property rights, especially in the "partial right" as proposed under the tender offer system in which the working of the right can be seen as some sort of power of approving land use conversion or land development. In a sense, under the zoning system, this power belongs to the government, whereas under the tender offer system, the power is given to the surrounding landowners. The difference not only reflects different levels of economic efficiency, but also different roles as played by the government.

In general, there are two theories describing the bureaucratic behavior of government. One is contract theory and the other is exploitation theory. In contract theory the goal of government is to maximize the total social welfare; by contrast, in exploitation theory the goal of government is to maximize its own profit. Our observations from the real world indicate that much bureaucratic behavior conforms to the description of exploitation theory. Additionally, in public choice theory, a well-known premise is that the government is not always well intentioned, and that the government's information is not perfect. The motive of self-interest is prevalent not only among the individuals in the private sector, but also among those in the public sector (Buchanan and Tullock 1962; Buchanan 1987). Therefore, there will be much political risk in the current zoning system in which the right of approving land use conversion belongs to the government, and, expectedly, the land developers will have to pay for the approval. Many scandals regarding land use conversion in Taiwan could support this inference.

Some articles in related literature put forward the view that when the government receives an amount of money from the land developer when the land use conversion takes place; this is equivalent to giving money back to the whole society. However, we do not agree with this point. From observations of the way in which the real world operates, we find that the money which comes from the developers is a very important source of income for the government, which means that the land use conversion has the potential to become a financial or political instrument in the hands of the government. On the other hand, in the case of land use conversion that involves a negative externality, there is no doubt that the surrounding landowners are the only ones who suffer, and not the whole of society. The government should, therefore, not take the money from the developer to compensate the general public, but rather the money should belong to the surrounding landowners who suffered as a result of the negative externality. In other words, the statement that the economic profits or windfalls from land use conversion should be held over for the government deserves more discussion.

Additionally, under the current zoning system, the government takes away the rights of people who suffer from bad externalities in advance, and distributes them later in the form of government purchases. Such an approach does not satisfy the need for fairness and justice, and instead is detrimental to the efficiency of land use. Furthermore, under the current zoning system the government and the developer share the intrinsic value of the right of approving land use conversion. Regardless of how much compensation there is, the nature of the misallocation of land property rights is not changed.[22]

Even if the government is well intentioned, and always makes every effort to maximize social welfare, she will still levy a Pigouvian tax[23] on developers to compensate the surrounding landowners who are suffering from the negative externality. But to impose a fair Pigouvian tax, the government will have to know the exact form of utility function of individuals in advance; and the latter is an impossible mission according to Coase's judgment. On the contrary, in regards to the surrounding landowners under the tender offer system, the price that he will accept for agreeing to the conversion of land use will depend upon his own subjective judgment of the change in utility. Making self-judgments in this way avoids the difficulties associated with collecting information regarding the agent's utility, which is the foundation for imposing the Pigouvian tax. This approach also conforms to the so-called "Austrian" approach to economics.

In short, in a general case of land use conversion, it is very clear that the surrounding landowners will shoulder some of the impacts of the conversion. Hence, based on the premise that everyone is ruled by self-interest, it is natural in such circumstances for the landowners who are seeking to convert the use of land to draw up a contractual agreement with the surrounding landowners directly. In this the government does not need to make a decision instead of the surrounding landowners. Furthermore, the motive of self-interest that prevails in the private sector serves to further increase the level of welfare (Buchanan and Tullock 1962; Buchanan 1987).

Although the tender offer system fits in with the spirit of voluntary exchange, it still needs the government's help. It needs the government to maintain the order of exchange, to determine the relative numbers and proportions within the system,

---

22 In accordance with the ideas put forward by Castells (1983: 249), we combine some empirical research with some lawsuit cases, for example, *Hsiao and Liu* (1997), *Nollan v. California Coastal Commission* (1987), *Guinnane v. San Francisco City Planning Commission* (1989), *Mitri Saad v. City of Berkeley* (1994), and *Dolan v. City of Tigard* (1994), etc. We can find a misallocation of land property rights under the current zoning system.

23 Pigouvian tax is supposed to solve the externality problem, but Coase (1960) did not agree, his main reason having to do with the difficulties associated with collecting enough information regarding the agent's utility.

to protect the private property rights, and to eliminate the indistinct public areas that arise from the allocation of property rights. These are the basic tasks of the government.

Conclusion

Based upon the differences between a "state" and a "path" discussed in this chapter, we point out that the economic efficiency, which must be both relative and subjective, is evaluated by measuring the subjective changes in the utilities of agents. In general, we lack sufficient information regarding the common utility function of a state, but we can still come to a conclusion based on the premise of catallactis. That is, if agents exchange voluntarily, each of them can reach a higher level of utility. And we note that the common utility function is an increasing function of each individual's utility level. Therefore, if the agents within the state make voluntary exchanges with each other, we can conclude that the utility level of the state will increase no matter what the form of common utility function is. On the contrary, if they do not exchange voluntarily, the outcome is ambiguous.

Roughly speaking, in the conversion of land use involving a negative externality, if we exclude the singular form of the common utility function, and only consider two kinds of agents, the conversion landowner and the surrounding landowner, there is only one situation in which the conversion landowner will obtain much more profit under the zoning system than under the tender offer system. Otherwise, we can come to a definite conclusion that the tender offer system proposed by Colwell (1997) will result in better economic efficiency than the zoning system in terms of the land use conversion policy.

By extension, the above viewpoint implies that the intervention of government in public issues does not guarantee an increase in economic efficiency, especially in those instances where the institutions are implemented by the government's force. In other words, we cannot confuse the meanings of "efficiency" and "easy exchange". Efficiency is not equivalent to easy exchange, and we cannot ignore the premise of catallactis, for exchanges are processes of voluntary agreement among persons. Otherwise, we might come to a wrong conclusion that is caused by a flaw in our logic.

References

Arnold, R. (1987), *Economics*, 6th edition (Ohio: South-Western).
Buchanan, J. (1987), 'The Constitution of Economic Policy', *American Economic Review*, 77, 243–250.
Buchanan, J. and Tullock, G. (1962), *The Calculus of Consent: Logical Foundation of Constitutional Democracy* (Ann Arbor: University of Michigan Press).
Castells, M. (1983), *The City and Grassroots: A Cross-Cultural Theory of Urban Social Movements* (London: E. Arnold).
Coase, R. (1960), 'The Problem of Social Cost', *Journal of Law and Economics*, 3, 1–44.

Colwell, P. (1997), 'Tender Mercies: Efficient and Equitable Land Use Change', *Real Estate Economics*, 25:4, 525–537.

Comment, R. and Jarrel, G. (1987), 'Two-tier and Negotiation Tender Offers: The Imprisonment of the Free-riding Shareholders', *Journal of Financial Economics*, 19:4, 283–310.

Dolan v. City of Tigard (1994), 512 US 374, 114 S. Ct. 2309.

Fama, E. (1970), 'Efficient Capital Markets: A Review of Theory and Empirical Work', *Journal of Finance*, 25, 383–417.

Friedman, D. (2000), *Law's Order: An Economic Account* (New Jersey: Princeton University Press).

Guinnane v. San Francisco City Planning Commission (1989), 209 Cal.App.3d 732, 257 Cal.Rptr. 742.

Hsiao, H. and Liu, H. (1997), 'Collective Action Toward a Sustainable City: Citizens Movements and Environmental Politics in Taipei', presented at the International Symposium on Sustainability, Livelihood and Degradation in the Third World Cities, December 5–7.

Keogh, G. and D'Arcy, E. (1999), 'Property Market Efficiency: An Institutional Economics Perspective', *Urban Studies*, 36:13, 2401–2414.

Lindblom, C. (1993), *The Policy-Making Process*, 3rd edition (Englewood Cliffs, NJ: Prentice-Hall).

Mankiw, N.G. (2001), *Essentials of Economics*, 2nd edition (Orlando, FL: Harcourt College).

Mises, L. (1963), *Human Action: A Treatise on Economics* (US: Yale University Press).

Mises, L. (1981), *The Ultimate Foundation of Economic Science*, 2nd edition (New York University Press).

Mitri Saad v. City of Berkeley (1994), 24 Cal.App.4th 206, 30 Cal.Rptr.2d 95.

North, D. (1982), *Structure and Change in Economic History* (New York: W.W. Norton).

North, D. (1990), *Institutions, Institutional Change and Economic Performance* (Cambridge: Cambridge University Press).

Parkin, M. (2000), *Economics*, 5th edition (US: Pearson Education).

Pindyck, R. and Rubinfeld, D. (1989), *Microeconomics* (New York: Macmillan).

Chapter 8

Moving Toward Urban Sustainability: A Comparison of the Development of Sustainability Indicators in Seattle and Minneapolis

Katrina M. Harmon

The Case for Sustainable Development in Cities

Sustainability may well prove to be the buzz word of the twenty-first century. Some 6.5 billion people now live on our planet, with the global population expected to surpass 9 billion by 2042 (US Census Bureau 2006). This projected increase of 50 percent in just over four decades must be considered in its historical, spatial, and socioeconomic context. In the four previous decades, from 1959 to 1999, the world experienced a doubling of its population from 3 billion to 6 billion. The twentieth century also saw the rapid urbanization of the global population. In 1900, an estimated 14 percent of the world's people resided in cities. Today, over half of the global population is believed to be living in urban areas. Cities are also getting bigger. In 1950, there were 83 cities with populations exceeding one million; by 2000, there were 411, including 20 "mega-cities" with more than 10 million inhabitants each (Whitehouse 2005).

Accompanying the demographic trends of the last century has been a rise in consumption fueled by a still globalizing capitalist economy. Economic development is driving a seemingly endless expansion of the definition of basic human *needs*. The evolution of populous Third-World economies, such as India and China, has particularly severe implications for global consumption rates. As noted in a recent PBS documentary on global climate change, more than one billion Chinese are soon likely to want the same sized cars and appliances that are now considered to be essential components of the American middle-class standard of living (*Global Warming: The Signs and the Science* 2005).

When taken together population growth, urbanization and economic development can have serious consequences for the environment. Simply meeting basic human needs for food, shelter and clothing for 9 billion people implies unprecedented and daunting levels of natural resource consumption. Coupled with rising lifestyle aspirations and the spatial concentration of ever larger numbers of people in cities, the conditions likely to characterize the next century could threaten the very social and political stability of society. Going forward, the viability and efficacy of local policy making institutions and processes will depend upon their ability to accommodate the demands of their constituents in the face of growing resource constraints.

In this context, "sustainability" and "sustainable development" have emerged as popular terms for the shift in mindset that will be required to deal with so-called "third-generation" environmental issues. As environmental challenges are increasingly trans-boundary and interdisciplinary in nature, cities have become crucial testing grounds for putting the broad concepts of sustainability and sustainable development into practice. Because meaningful change must ultimately occur at the local level, urban experiments with sustainability can be illustrative of the usefulness of sustainability as a framework for engendering participation and for translating sustainability concepts into terms that are locally relevant and actionable.

In order to explore the movement toward sustainability in cities, this chapter will briefly review the international sustainability framework emergent from United Nations' conferences and activities within the last three decades. This framework is important since it strives to establish a working definition and broad principles of sustainability for calibrating efforts to address environmental issues at the global, national and sub-national levels. Sustainability indicators will then be considered as an important tool for implementing sustainability-based goals and programs. The development of sustainability indicators in two cities – Seattle and Minneapolis – will be reviewed and evaluated in order to consider the realities of putting sustainability into practice. Although these cities are both generally affluent and progressive communities located in the United States, they nonetheless represent two separate attempts to pursue urban sustainability through deliberately participatory means. A comparison of their experiences can help to identify factors that influence differential implementation of sustainability and assess the prospects for sustainable development in other cities – both in the United States and abroad.

The International Sustainability Framework

Environmental issues began appearing on the global agenda in the early 1970s. The proliferation of conferences and commissions sponsored by the United Nations since then is indicative of the increasing salience of the environment. The Stockholm Conference on the Human Environment, held in 1972, marked the earliest acknowledgement of conflicts between environment and development (Kates et al. 2005). In 1983, as a follow-up to Stockholm, the UN established the Commission on Environment and Development (UNCED), also known as the Brundtland Commission. In 1987, the Brundtland Commission published *Our Common Future*, widely considered a major milestone in the global environmental movement because it "push(ed) sustainable development into the mainstream of worldwide policy debates" (Wheeler and Beatley 2004).

Based on its work in twenty-one countries over five years, the Brundtland Commission provided the first common formulation of sustainability, defining it as: "development that meets the needs of the present without compromising the ability of future generations to meet their own needs" (World Commission on Environment and Development 1987). The success of the report in calling global attention to the need for sustainability was evidenced by the numerous national and NGO activities and reports that followed it. The Brundtland Commission's definition of sustainability continues to be the one most frequently cited; yet, it has come under attack for being vague and anthropocentric and for positioning economic development as the key to an improvement in human well-being (Wheeler and Beatley 2004). Others have touted its "creative ambiguity" (Kates et al., 2005), recognizing the essence of sustainable development as "a political and social construct" that must be broad enough to allow for flexibility in interpretation to meet local needs (Vig and Kraft 2005). In any case, the Brundtland Commission's report marked the beginning of a global framework for sustainable development that incorporated the dual concepts of needs and limitations. Thus, it underscored the importance of reconciling concerns for the environment with development.

The next major milestone for the creation of an international sustainability framework came with the 1992 UN Conference on Environment and Development in Rio de Janeiro (Earth Summit). Attended by leaders of 178 countries, the event had an extremely high profile that signified the growing international attention given to sustainable development. The Earth Summit produced two important documents: a declaration of principles and an "Agenda 21" of desired actions for the twenty-first century. It also resulted in the creation of the UN Commission on Sustainable Development to review international implementation efforts and the UN Division for Sustainable Development to coordinate the agency's work on sustainable development in the field).

Agenda 21 emphasized the importance of local and public participation in sustainability efforts. Principle 10 of Agenda 21 stated that: "Environmental issues are best handled with the participation of all concerned citizens, at the relevant level". Principle 21 emphasized the vital role of local communities and local knowledge, particularly of indigenous communities, in guiding sustainable development. Chapter 7 established directions for sustainable urban development, while chapter 28 explicitly recognized the importance of local government in realizing sustainability objectives: "By 1996, most local authorities in each country should have undertaken a consultative process with their population and achieved consensus on a local Agenda 21 for their communities". In response to this call to action, Local Agenda 21 (LA21) emerged from the Summit as an international sustainability planning process to encourage and facilitate the cooperation of local governments and their citizens in creating a sustainable future.

The use of indicators was also incorporated into Agenda 21. Chapter 40 called on countries, as well as international, governmental and non-governmental organizations, to develop and identify indicators of sustainable development to provide a basis for decision-making at all levels. Agenda 21 noted the importance of the harmonization of efforts at multiple levels, including the incorporation of a set of sustainability indicators in common, regularly updated, and widely accessible reports and databases.

The momentum generated by the Rio Summit and Agenda 21 resulted in additional UN-sponsored conferences on sustainability-related topics, including the 1996 Habitat II City Summit in Istanbul. These conferences consistently reiterated a commitment to the principles of public participation and partnership with local authorities as key components of sustainable development. In 2002, the World Summit on Sustainable Development in Johannesburg was held as a ten-year follow-up to the Rio Summit. Although the Johannesburg Summit reviewed progress in sustainability implementation and produced some additional financial commitments, it was widely considered a disappointment for its failure to generate significant international commitments to address environmental concerns.

Despite the lack of coordinated, global movement toward sustainable development since Rio, a number of localities have begun to taken action consistent with Local Agenda 21. According to a survey by the International Council for Local Environmental Initiatives (ICLEI), "6,416 local authorities in 113 countries have either made a formal commitment to Local Agenda 21 or are actively undertaking the process" (ICLEI 2001). As Wheeler and Beatley point out: "There is no single, universally acknowledged manifesto that by itself sets out a sustainable *urban* development agenda", (2005). Yet, most local sustainability initiatives have some common elements. These typically include: the creation of a local sustainability forum; articulation of a shared vision of the community's future; the development of sustainability indicators; the production of local state-of-the-community reports; and preparation of local sustainability action plans. In the absence of a standard, detailed template to guide local sustainability efforts, indicators take on an especially important role in defining sustainability in locally relevant terms, establishing goals and tracking implementation progress.

Sustainability Indicators: "Measure What You Treasure"

According to the International Institute for Sustainable Development (IISD), an indicator "… quantifies and simplifies phenomena and helps us understand complex realities. Indicators are aggregates of raw and processed data but they can be further aggregated to form complex indices" (IISD 2006). In the context of sustainability, indicators offer a way for translating a vague and complex phenomenon into a more clearly articulated and interrelated set of factors and processes. Despite frequent reference to the Brundtland Commission's definition of sustainability, there is no widely accepted standard definition of the concept (Farrell and Hart 1998). As a result, the development of a set of indicators often becomes a means for defining sustainability in locally meaningful terms (Kates et al., 2005). Once defined, indicators are helpful for tracking progress in achieving goals and for considering the intended and unintended effects of sustainability-oriented policies on other variables. Indicators can also serve as a useful tool for educating the public about the direction of current trends and the complexity and interrelationship of variables at work in the community. Politically, indicators can serve to justify past expenditures on sustainability initiatives and build support for new initiatives. In this way, they serve a critical function in informing decision making and promoting government accountability and transparency.

Given the potential usefulness of indicators, much effort has been channeled into developing them. As the concepts of "sustainability" and "sustainable development" have been popularized, governmental and non-governmental organizations have been joined by private consulting firms in devising sets of sustainability indicators for use at the international, national, and sub-national levels. According to the IISD, there are at least 100 systems for assessing progress in sustainable development at the community level (IISD 2006). More realistically, there are likely as many sets of indicators as there are groups defining them. Since sustainability tends to be a value-laden and context-sensitive concept (Levett 1998), the indicators that are defined and operationalized in any given urban context are likely to reflect the values, experiences, needs and interests of those who create them (Farrell and Hart 1998). Furthermore, because indicators are often developed using a participatory, consensus-based approach, the set of indicators in place in any given community tends to be relatively lengthy and wide-ranging.

Despite the absence of a single, *best* definition of urban sustainability, a set of criteria for considering some desirable characteristics of sustainability indicators can still be helpful. Virginia Maclaren, a professor at the University of Toronto's Centre for the Environment, has identified certain "fundamental properties" of sustainability indicators that all communities "may wish to consider" (Maclaren 1996). Although many sets of alternative criteria exist, Maclaren's approach is appealing for its simplicity and straightforwardness. Furthermore, it reflects the common threads found in similar proposals for criteria for sustainability indicators: that they must reflect the mindset shift that sustainability requires, and that the process of defining, tracking, and improving upon indicators is as important as the end product.

According to Maclaren, sustainability indicators should have four essential characteristics (1996). Indicators should be "integrating" in that they portray linkages among the economic, environmental, and social dimensions of sustainability. Indicators should also be "forward looking" in that they assess impact on intergenerational equity. As noted by Kates et al. (2005), few efforts at defining sustainability indicators are explicit about the time period in which they are intended to operate. This often results in a short-term focus for sustainability efforts, in spite of a commitment to both current and future generations in principle. Sustainability indicators should be "distributional" in that they measure the degree of equity in social, economic and environmental conditions within a population or across geographic regions. Importantly, this implies that data should be considered in both aggregate and disaggregated forms in order to distinguish between local and non-local sources and effects of environmental degradation. Finally, indicators should be developed with input from multiple stakeholders. Citing the history of the social indicator movement, Maclaren points out that indicators created with input from a broad range of participants in the policy process tend to be the most influential, valid and reliable.

Although not all indicators must satisfy each criterion, every indicator must be the product of a participatory process and, together, the set of indicators should display all four of these basic characteristics. In addition to these fundamental properties, Maclaren also proposes a sustainability reporting process. While not discussed in detail here, her emphasis on the need for a structured reporting method suggests the importance of placing sustainability indicators in the larger policy making context. Therefore, an additional criterion of "usability", or usefulness in decision making, could be added to Maclaren's list.

Hart (2006) expands on the concept of "effective indicators" by suggesting that they should be relevant, easy to understand, reliable, and based on accessible data. Essentially, to be of value, indicators need to provide information in a form that is understandable to relevant audiences and useful as an input to decision making processes. Maclaren's emphasis on the importance of process also suggests the need to assess the quality of indicators on an ongoing basis and to refine them over time. Viewed as a product as well as a process, sustainability indicators can serve as a catalyst for improving a community's ability to work together and learn from one another over the long term.

A Comparison of Sustainability Indicators in Two Cities

The sustainable Seattle Initiative and the Indicators Commons Project

The City of Seattle is widely cited for its leadership in urban sustainability. With a population of 563,374 in the year 2000, the city of Seattle serves as the core of the Seattle-Tacoma-Washington Combined Statistical Area. The larger metropolitan area population of 3.8 million qualifies it as the thirteenth largest in the United States (US Census Bureau 2006). Seattle's location in the American Pacific Northwest has endowed it with physical and socio-cultural features that have supported the development of a progressive community concerned about its natural environment. Seattle's organized sustainability efforts date back to 1990. Although not explicitly linked to the UN's Local Agenda 21 program, the Sustainable Seattle Initiative was recognized by the United Nations Centre for Human Settlements in 1996 with an "Excellence in Indicators Best Performance" by the Community Sector. Seattle's sustainability indicators have also served as a model for other urban sustainability initiatives in the United States.

Sustainable Seattle was established in 1991 as a non-profit organization "dedicated to enhancing the long term quality of life in the Seattle/King County area" (Sustainable Seattle 2006). It grew out of a conference sponsored by the Global Tomorrow Coalition, when a small amount of grant money was assembled to undertake a two-year series of public meetings for the promotion of community sustainability. With a grass-roots foundation, Sustainable Seattle continues to be positioned as a multi-stakeholder group, volunteer network, and civic forum intrinsically based on community participation. Groups with a broad range of interests – including educators, religious organizations, social activists, environmental groups, government officials, and business leaders – have consistently been represented in the process. The Sustainable Seattle initiative is overseen by an independent board of trustees, with the maintenance of sustainability indicators and other administrative activities performed by a volunteer center at the Seattle Metrocenter YMCA. Notably, it is not affiliated with any governmental organization. Although it has no formal policy making role, its active role in education and outreach activities and its visible presence in the community provides it with some ability to influence public priorities and initiatives. As an example, the sustainability indicators identified by Sustainable

Seattle have been integrated into the City of Seattle's twenty-year comprehensive plan, which is entitled "Toward a Sustainable Seattle" (Portney 2003).

From the outset, Sustainable Seattle has identified members of the community and the media as its primary audiences, considering businesses and local government only secondarily. It has pursued the development of a "community-based indicator set" through an iterative process involving public meetings with a wide range of citizen groups, a technical advisory group and a taskforce of community decision makers. In this model, citizen values and needs drive the process, but technical experts provide advice, scientific data, and methods to ensure the integrity of the measures. Explicitly, the Indicators of Sustainable Seattle are "intended to be used by citizens and policymakers to guide behavior changes that will steer our community on a more sustainable course ... [They] are a call to action – to spur critical thinking, to inspire us to reconsider our priorities, and to leverage actions that will ensure our community's long-term health" (Sustainable Seattle 1998).

Sustainable Seattle has published three indicator reports for Seattle/King County since its inception. Its first report, issued in 1993, included 20 indicators that met five criteria based on a definition of sustainability as "long-term health and vitality – cultural, economic, environmental, and social". Specifically, any indicator should be: 1) a bellwether of sustainability; 2) accepted by the community; 3) attractive to local media; 4) statistically measurable; and 5) logically or scientifically defensible. In 1995, the indicator set was expanded by an additional 20 indicators for a total of 40 that were grouped into five main areas: 1) Environment; 2) Population and Resources; 3) Economy; 4) Youth and Education; and 5) Health and Community. In 1998, Sustainable Seattle released its third report on "Indicators of Sustainable Community". The 1998 report was based on the 40 indicators used in the 1995 report, although some modifications were made to improve their usefulness (see Table 8.1). For example, the Wetlands and Biodiversity indicators for 1995 were combined into one Ecological Health indicator, and an Energy Use per Dollar of Income indicator was added. Overall, almost half of the indicator data sources or trend analyses were in some manner improved upon from 1995 to 1998 (Sustainable Seattle 1998). The 1998 report also included "Success Stories" of projects and programs working to advance the goal of community sustainability.

While Sustainable Seattle planned to publish its fourth indicators report in 2002, its Board decided after the release of the 1998 report to reassess the indicator program. As noted in the 1998 report itself, "while our methods for measuring progress are better, our application of the indicators as a tool for social change still needs to improve" (Sustainable Seattle 1998). Specifically, the Sustainable Seattle Board noted the need for expansion of the indicators to the neighborhood and regional levels, as well as the development of specific strategies and actions in response to indicator trends: "After the release of its 1998 indicators ... the Board was concerned that merely publishing the indicators ... was not sufficient and that a successful program should include programs which support actions by citizens, businesses and policy makers to affect the trends documented by the indicators" (Sustainable Seattle 2006).

Table 8.1 1998 Sustainability indicators for Seattle, Washington

Category	Indicator	Trend (1995–1998)
Environment	Wild Salmon	↔
	Ecological Health	?
	Soil Erosion	↔
	Air Quality	↑
	Pedestrian – and Bicycle-Friendly Streets	?
	Open Space near Urban Villages	?
	Impervious Surfaces	?
Population and Resources	Population	↔
	Water Consumption	↑
	Solid Waste Generated and Recycled	↓
	Pollution Prevention	↑
	Local Farm Production	↓
	Vehicle Miles Traveled and Fuel Consumption	↓
	Renewable and Nonrenewable Energy Use	↓
Economy	Energy Use Per Dollar of Income	↑
	Employment Concentration	↑
	Unemployment	↑
	Distribution of Personal Income	↓
	Health Care Expenditures	↓
	Work Required for Basic Needs	↓
	Housing Affordability	↔
	Children Living in Poverty	↓
	Emergency Room Use for Non-ER Purposes	↔
	Community Reinvestment	?
Youth and Education	High School Graduation	?
	Ethnic Diversity of Teachers	↔
	Arts Instruction	?
	Volunteer Involvement in Schools	↑
	Juvenile Crime	↔
	Youth Involvement in Community Service	?
	Equity in Justice	↑
	Adult Literacy	?
Health and Community	Low Birthweight Infants	↔
	Asthma Hospitalizations for Children	↔
	Voter Participation	↑
	Library and Community Center Usage	↔
	Public Participation in the Arts	↑
	Gardening Activity	↑
	Neighborliness	?
	Perceived Quality of Life	↔

Source: Indicators of Sustainable Community (1998) (Seattle, WA: Sustainable Seattle).

Note: ↑ improving trend; ↓ declining trend; ↔ neutral trend; ? insufficient or inconclusive data.

The 2002 report was thus suspended, and a series of actions to revamp the indicator program were initiated. In 2003, Sustainable Seattle started collecting data and publishing indicators at the neighborhood level via the Sustainable Urban Neighborhoods Initiative. In 2004, a 24-member Indicators Steering Committee was assembled to develop a new mission statement, along with new goals, principles, and criteria for sustainability indicators (see Tables 8.2 and 8.3 for recently approved sustainability principles and criteria). In April 2005, a Civic Panel of over 100 community leaders met to identify "assets and concerns" and to prioritize an initial set of indicators accordingly. The Technical Advisory Committee worked throughout the first half of 2006 to refine the indicators and develop a common framework for facilitating an integrated approach to sustainable development. On September 21, 2006, the Steering Committee approved the "Indicators Commons" work plan based on a group of 24 sustainability goals. When completed, the Indicators Commons project will have revised and refined the Indicators of Sustainable Community, identified strategies and actions for using indicators and sustainability principles and put into place five-year plans for implementing and tracking sustainability actions (Sustainable Seattle 2006).

The city of Minneapolis sustainability program and sustainability indicators

Minneapolis shares many similarities with Seattle. With a metropolitan area population of 2,968,806, Minneapolis – St Paul ranks fifteenth in the country, two places behind 13th ranked Metro Seattle. The City of Minneapolis itself had a population of 382,618 in 2000. Located in the Upper Midwest, Minneapolis is known as "The City of Lakes". It has a reputation as a culturally and politically progressive community with a demonstrated commitment to quality of life. The sustainability movement in Minneapolis is more recent than that in Seattle; yet, in just a few years, Minneapolis has made a significant commitment to sustainability and has developed and implemented a set of sustainability indicators for its community.

In contrast to the community-based Sustainable Seattle Initiative and its Indicators Commons Project, the Minneapolis Sustainability Program has been visibly government-led. In 2003, the Minneapolis City Council passed Resolution 2003R-133 to initiate the development of the Minneapolis Sustainability Plan and a set of Sustainability Indicators. According to the Council's resolution, the Sustainability Plan was to be integrated into the Minneapolis Plan, the city's comprehensive planning document. In fact, one of the eight goals of the current Minneapolis Plan now reads: "To preserve and enhance our environmental, economic and social realms to promote a sustainable Minneapolis". Resolution 2003R-133 also made an explicit commitment to incorporating the "three E's" of sustainability, Environment, Economy and Equity, into City operations and decision making processes. The City has defined sustainability as: "meeting current needs without sacrificing the ability of future generations to meet their own needs by balancing environmental, economic, and social (equity) concerns" (City of Minneapolis 2006). Although public documents do not make official reference to UN sustainability principles or the Local Agenda 21 program, Minneapolis' definition of sustainability clearly shows a strong resemblance to the Brundtland Commission's definition. In this way, the influence of the global sustainability framework is evident.

Table 8.2 Sustainable Seattle indicator criteria (adopted March 2005)

The Steering Committee adopted criteria for the development of indicators at its March 2005 meeting. Criteria will be used to evaluate and select indicators fitting within the principles and framework of sustainability indicators for this project.

1. **Links Essential Conditions**: Individual indicators must show some aspect of human wellbeing, healthy ecosystems, or symbiotic relationships within and between each.
2. **Reflect community values**: Community assets and concerns are reflected in the data and analyses of each indicator.
3. **Linkages**: Indicators are linked by activities of individuals, governments, businesses, institutions, and together as a linked set frame a holistic perspective of King County.
4. **Actionable**: Measures conditions or activities that can be changed in a positive direction by local actions.
5. **Future Vision Oriented**: Measure trends that relate to the vision of a sustainable future.
6. **Long term strategies and medium term action**: The set of indicators must reflect a balance between long term vision for which strategies can be developed, and short term needs for which immediate action can be taken.
7. **Attractive to local media**: The press publicizes them and uses them to monitor and analyze.
8. **Policy relevant**: Most of the indicators must relate to opportunities for policy change, in governments, businesses, non-profit organizations, institutions, and individuals.
9. **Measurable**: The indicator uses data that can be collected and analyzed through established methods.
10. **Valid**: The indicator data accurately represents and measures what it is designed to measure.
11. **Reliable**: The data for the indicator are measured in a consistent manner that can be repeated from one time interval to another.
12. **Demographic detail**: Data for the indicator are available on age, race/ethnicity, income/socioeconomic status, and education levels as appropriate.
13. **Geographic detail**: Data for the indicator are available and/or can be gathered at a sub-regional level.
14. **Data availability**: Data are available and there is established ongoing data collection. If a selected indicator requires primary data collection, it should be cost effective and have potential for funding.
15. **Leading**: Indicators must give information while there is still time to act.

Accessed from: <www.sustainableseattle.org/Programs/RegionalIndicators/IndCriteria>.

Table 8.3 Sustainable Seattle indicator principles (adopted March 2005)

The following are a set of principles adopted by the Steering Committee that together form the guidelines that will lead to successful development of a set of sustainability indicators.

1. **Link human and ecological wellbeing**: Seek to measure the status or effect of interdependence between the wellbeing of humans and the health of natural ecosystems.
2. **Diverse groups**: Include people from a variety of experiences including across age and income, ethnic and race, geographic location, expertise.
3. **Engaging**: Draw peoples attention and engage them in understanding sustainability concepts and how they apply to indicator selection.
4. **Understandable**: Indicator data and analyses can be easily understood by citizens
5. **Collaborative and consensus based**: Process of developing indicators is accomplished through collaboration of many people and based on consensus-style decisions.
6. **Continuity of participation**: Participants attend all meetings and most commit to on-going participation in projects developed by this project.
7. **Considering cross-boundary effects**: Address flows and effects crossing the King County border as well as conditions and process inside those borders.
8. **Capacity building/catalyze action**: Activities developing indicators will build skills, networks, and knowledge about using sustainability indicators and principles to solve problems. The experience will inspire people to further action.
9. **Clear end point**: Indicators will have a clear point identified, that when reached represents reaching a sustainable condition for that indicator and associated components.
10. **Broad involvement**: Participants must be from all sectors and cover the variety of expertise implied by the indicator framework.
11. **Stakeholder driven**: Stakeholders initiate selection of indicators, with experts supporting developing of those indicators.
12. **Iterative learning dynamic**: The sequence of events and activities and the specific participant tasks will constitute a stepped learning process, each successive step building on the previous one.

Accessed from: <http://www.sustainableseattle.org/Programs/RegionalIndicators/IndPrinciples>.

In pursuit of its vision for a sustainable community, the City of Minneapolis sponsored two roundtable meetings in 2004, involving over 100 business leaders and residents in articulating a fifty-year vision for the city. The roundtables were funded by a grant from the Minnesota Office of Environmental Assistance and facilitated by the non-profit Crossroads Resource Center. Thirty sustainability indicators were initially identified for the community; in 2005, the Minneapolis City Council adopted 24 of these. The City's Environmental Coordinating Team and a Citizen Advisory Panel worked together to develop quantifiable targets for the indicators and collect baseline data where possible. In March 2006, the Minneapolis City Council approved a revised listing of indicators and related targets (see Table 8.4 for the list of adopted indicators). In June 2006, the City published its first Annual Report (for 2005) on indicator goals, targets, and strategies "for both City government and the community to conserve local resources, protect human health, maintain a healthy economy and improve our quality of life" (City of Minneapolis, 2006). The report also notes its intent "to serve as a foundation for civic activism and future policy decisions". Publication of the annual report is scheduled for June each year, and it is expected to increasingly focus on trend analysis and evaluation of progress toward meeting goals as its tracking efforts mature.

Table 8.4 2005 Sustainability indicators for Minneapolis, Minnesota

Indicator
Affordable Housing Units
AIDS and Gonorrhea Rate
Air Quality
Airport Noise and Impacts
Asthma Morbidity
Bicycle Lanes and Paths (miles)
Block Clubs
Brownfield Sites
Carbon Dioxide Emissions
Combined Sewer Overflow
Downtown Transportation Mode Split
Graduation Rate at Minneapolis Public Schools
Healthy Weight
Homeless in Minneapolis/Number of People Using Housing Shelters
Homicides
Infant Mortality Rate
Lead Testing of Children 9 to 36 Months
Permeable Surface
Renewable Energy Use
Students in the Arts
Teen Pregnancy Rate
Urban Tree Canopy
Water Quality of Lakes, Streams and the Mississippi River
Workers Earning a Living Wage / Unemployment Rate of City Residents Compared to Metro Average

Accessed from: <http://www.ci.minneapolis.mn.us/environment/indicators.asp>.

In addition to the publication of an annual report on sustainability indicators, the City Council has also called for their incorporation into the business planning processes of all City government departments. Every department is thus expected to calibrate its priorities and plans to the city's sustainability goals, and at the end of 2006, departments are expected to outline their progress in meeting sustainability-related objectives (City of Minneapolis 2006).

Evaluation of indicators

A consideration of the experiences of Seattle and Minneapolis with sustainability indicators yields several initial observations. Most apparently, a comparison of the list of indicators in use in each city reveals significant variation. The brief case histories outlined above demonstrate similar variation in the *process* by which the indicators have been developed, tracked, and modified. This underscores the malleable and highly subjective nature of sustainability as a concept as well as the importance of process in articulating the community values and goals that sustainability indicators should ultimately reflect.

Revisiting Maclaren's criteria for desirable "fundamental properties" of sustainability indicators supports a more in-depth analysis of the Seattle and Minneapolis cases. Maclaren's first criterion suggests that an indictor should be "integrating". From their inception, the sustainability projects of Seattle and Minneapolis were explicitly oriented around the integration of the economy, environment, and social equity. A look at the indicators for both cities reveals the inclusion of traditional measures of economic and environmental well-being (e.g. air quality and unemployment metrics) as well as broader social and cultural factors (e.g. measures of civic engagement like volunteer rates and block club participation). The interdependence of indicators is less straightforward, though metrics such as brownfield sites and library and community center usage certainly capture cumulative influences of environmental, economic, and equity dynamics. In practice, the "integrating" challenge is not only to accurately assess the interrelatedness of factors but also to link measurement into an action planning process that will move indicators in the desired direction. The decision by Sustainable Seattle to suspend its 2002 indicators report and overhaul its indicators program after nearly a decade of experience indicates the extent of this challenge.

Maclaren's second criterion for sustainability indicators is that they should be "forward looking". In both the Seattle and Minneapolis cases, indicators are based on a long-term vision of the future and a stated commitment to both current and future generations. Targets have been set for indicators in each city, guided by concern that the indicators should demonstrate progress in moving toward sustainability over time. However, the timeline specified by each indicator varies and is focused on the near term. The ability of the complete indicator set to assess impact on intergenerational equity is thus questionable. For example, Minneapolis' target for the air quality indicator is based on a percentage reduction of CO_2 emissions by 2012 (12 percent) and 2020 (20 percent) from a 1988 baseline. Goals for airport noise and related environmental impacts establish targets for 2015 using a 2004 baseline, while affordable housing objectives establish targets for 2009. As observed by Kates et al. (2005), lack of an explicit and consistent timeframe in which indicators operate can lead to a shorter term focus for sustainability efforts than may be desirable.

Sustainability indicators, according to Maclaren, should also be "distributional" in that they should assess intra-generational equity in social, economic, and environmental conditions within a population or across geographic regions. Both Seattle and Minneapolis have incorporated measures of well-being in their indicator sets. Metrics based on incidence of disease, homelessness, affordable housing, infant mortality, and public school graduation rates certainly do assess dimensions of equity. Yet, both cases lack a disciplined approach to consideration of spatial patterns across indicators or of differential effects on people based on race, ethnicity, education or socioeconomic levels. Consideration of the geographic distribution of any particular indicator, in addition to how it overlaps with the spatial incidence of other indicators, could be extremely insightful in uncovering the cumulative impact of sustainability trends. Building in some type of formal risk assessment by spatial and demographic characteristics could assist both cities in better understanding the nuances of intra-generational equity and advancing their indicators initiatives to the next level of sophistication. This underscores the need for a level of technical capability that takes time to develop but is essential for maximizing the value of indicator initiatives.

Furthermore, Maclaren suggests that data should be considered in both aggregate and disaggregated forms in order to distinguish between local and non-local sources and effects of environmental degradation. Her emphasis of this point underscores the need to assess distributional equity not just within the locality using the indicators but outside of it as well. In other words, the sustainability of a single community can only be completely evaluated by considering its relationship with and impact on the broader world in which it exists. In this light, the integration of urban sustainability initiatives with other regional, national, and international programs and benchmarks is critical. While the indicators in use by Minneapolis and Seattle may be influenced by factors outside of their boundaries, they do not explicitly provide a framework by which to systematically consider non-local influences.

As a fourth criterion, Maclaren suggests that indicators be developed with input from multiple stakeholders. The use of participatory processes is one of the hallmarks of the Seattle and Minneapolis cases. Indeed, they both seem to reflect a primary concern for the involvement of a wide range of stakeholders. Comparison of the two cases nonetheless highlights how public participation can look very different. Seattle's community-led sustainability initiative has involved a larger number of individuals, forums, and iterations in developing its indicators in comparison to Minneapolis' government-led initiative. While some of this difference may be due to maturity (Minneapolis' effort is more recent than Seattle's by a decade), variations in local culture may also play a role. Although beyond the scope of this chapter, investigation of local culture and socially constructed definitions of "public participation" could yield useful insights. In any case, defining public participation – in terms of whose involvement, to what degree and with what result – is likely to be the first meaningful task for any sustainability initiative.

Finally, Maclaren's concern for a systematic sustainability reporting process points to a need for sustainability indicators to be usable in a policy making context. Both the Seattle and the Minneapolis efforts have acknowledged the need to translate the information yielded by indicators into meaningful action. Both efforts have admitted that precisely how to do that is their greatest challenge. Minneapolis is explicitly integrating its indicators into the City Government's planning processes, documents, and metrics. This may be an advantage in calibrating local government policies and priorities to sustainability indicators, but it does not address the bigger question of translating indicators into action among private and other community-based actors. As Seattle's current revamping of its indicators project demonstrates, mobilizing strategic, broad-based action to move a community toward urban sustainability is much different that simply measuring indicators and forming small-scale, issue-specific projects around them.

Additional observations

Maclaren's criteria are useful in highlighting some of the challenges of developing and deriving maximum value out of sustainability indicators. Two additional observations warrant mention. First, the Seattle and Minneapolis cases demonstrate the importance and value of process in good environmental decision making. Participatory processes undoubtedly help create shared values and understanding (Dietz 2003). Because sustainability requires behavior change at the most local levels, public participation is critical. As reflected by the experiences of both cities, the use of sustainability indicators may be as much a journey as a destination. Seattle, one of the earliest experimenters with sustainability indicators, is overhauling its program more than a decade after it issued its first sustainability report. This highlights the need to evolve sustainability programs over time in response to community learning. It also highlights that the transition to a truly sustainable community simply takes time. Yet, Seattle and Minneapolis should both be commended for their commitment to undertaking the journey. Given that both cities have incorporated a commitment to sustainability and have integrated specific sustainability principles into their long-term strategic plans, it is a fair observation that sustainability has made it onto the public agenda in these communities. By this measure, these cities can be said to be "taking sustainability seriously" (Portney 2003).

A final, yet crucial, observation from the cases of Minneapolis and Seattle is the absence of explicit linkage to the United Nations-sponsored international sustainability framework. Sustainability principles as outlined in Agenda 21, for example, can be detected in both indicator programs, but the absence of clear integration of these urban-level initiatives into a national and international framework is striking. In a global context, the cities of Minneapolis and Seattle are more similar than they are different. The variations in their sustainability indicator projects point to the challenges of connecting local relevance to global significance. Agenda 21 aspired to the development of international indicator sets for two purposes: 1) the coordination of national and sub-national efforts; and 2) the evaluation of global scale processes and effects (Farrell and Hart 1998). In light of the two cases considered here, fragmentation of local efforts is likely to pose a significant challenge for the coordination and comparison of efforts over time and space. Although urban-based initiatives are crucial to the achievability of sustainability, their integration into the larger global system and the establishment of a truly global-to-local link will be vital. This raises the potentially important role that a national and/or regional framework can play in providing a nexus between global and local sustainability efforts. In the absence of commitment to and leadership in developing sustainability indicators at the national level in this country, US cities have been left to pioneer sustainability on their own. An interesting area for future investigation would be to compare indicators in countries that have established a national sustainability framework to the cases discussed here. Europe, for example, has made a significant commitment to sustainability at both the EU and national levels. Therefore, additional research comparing European and American experiences with urban sustainability could yield important insights about how to most effectively construct regional and national interfaces for connecting urban initiatives and priorities to the global sustainability framework.

Conclusion

This chapter has considered cities as crucial testing grounds for the pursuit of sustainable development. The definition, measurement and ongoing revision of indicators can serve as an important tool in the journey toward sustainability. As demonstrated by the experiences of Minneapolis and Seattle, the use of a participatory process to develop and deploy sustainability indicators can facilitate the formulation of a shared understanding of what sustainability means to a community. By engaging a wide range of perspectives, the process can yield a shared vision of the future, articulate community priorities and clarify required tradeoffs. With meaningful public dialogue about which indicators to use and what findings from their measurement imply, the use of indicators can help expand the range of policy options considered in addressing issues of sustainability, and the accountability of political institutions can ultimately be improved.

With due respect to the importance of community-based processes and the need to establish local relevance of broad sustainability concepts, the Seattle and Minneapolis cases reveal at least two areas of opportunity that should be considered by other localities considering sustainability indicator initiatives. As community familiarity and experience with indicators evolves over time, the need for a well-defined, integrated action planning process becomes apparent. Specifying an initial course of action for how indicator measurements will be acted upon – from the very outset of the indicator initiative – could help ensure timely follow-up. Establishing an extra-local connection for sustainability efforts also deserves more consideration. As third generation environmental issues become more salient, the need for effective multi-level governance is striking. Local initiative and innovation must ultimately be accompanied by regional and national action in order for visions of a truly sustainable society to be realized. Cities committed to sustainability can increase the political pressure on extra-local institutions by reaching out to regional and national policy makers and calibrating local initiatives to regional, state and national processes and priorities wherever possible.

References

Beatley, T. (2000), *Green Urbanism: Learning from European Cities* (Washington, DC: Island Press).

Bulkeley, H. (2006), 'Urban Sustainability: Learning from Best Practice?' *Environment and Planning*, 38:6, 1029–1044.

City of Minneapolis (2006), *Sustainability Initiatives*, accessed from: <http://www.ci.minneapolis.mn.us/environment/Sustainability-Initiatives.asp>.

City of Minneapolis (2005), *Sustainability Initiative: 2005 Annual Report*, accessed from: <http://www.ci.minneapolis.mn.us/environment/annualreport.asp>.

Dietz, T. (2003), 'What is a Good Decision? Criteria for Environmental Decision Making', *Human Ecology Review*, 10:1, 33–39.

Farrell, A. and Hart, M. (1998), 'What Does Sustainability Really Mean? The Search for Useful Indicators', *Environment*, 40, 4–9, 26–31.

Hallsmith, G. (2003), *The Key to Sustainable Cities: Meeting Human Needs, Transforming Community Systems* (Philadelphia: New Society Publishers).

Hart, M. (2006), *Sustainable Measures*, accessed from: <http://www.sustainable measures.com>.

The International Council for Local Environmental Initiatives (2001), *Second Local Agenda 21 Survey: Background paper No. 15*, accessed from: <http://www.iclei. org>.

International Institute for Sustainable Development (2006), *Community Sustainability*, accessed from: <http://www.iisd.org/communities/>.

James, S. and Lahti, T. (2005), *The Natural Step for Communities: How Cities and Towns Can Change to Sustainable Practices* (Philadelphia: New Society Publishers).

Kahn, M.E. (2006), *Green Cities: Urban Growth and the Environment* (Washington, DC: Brookings Institution Press).

Kates, R.W., et al. (2005), 'What is Sustainable Development? Goals, Indicators, Values and Practice', *Environment*, 47:3, 8–21.

Levett, R. (1998), 'Sustainability Indicators: Integrating Quality of Life and Environmental Protection', *Journal of the Royal Statistical Society: Series A, Statistics in Society*, 161:3, 291–302.

Ling, O.G. (2005), *Sustainability and Cities: Concept and Assessment* (World Scientific Publishing Company).

Maclaren, V. (1996), 'Urban Sustainability Reporting', *Journal of the American Planning Association*, 62:2, 184–202.

Mazmanian, D. and Kraft, M. (eds) (1999), *Toward Sustainable Communities: Transitions and Transformations in Environmental Policy* (Cambridge, MA: MIT Press).

Newman, P. and Kenworthy, J. (1999), *Sustainability and Cities: Overcoming Automobile Dependence* (Washington, DC: Island Press).

O'Riordan, T. (1998), 'Sustainability Indicators and the New Democracy', *Environment*, 40:9, 1.

Organization for Economic Cooperation and Development (1998), *Towards Sustainable Development: Environmental Indicators*.

Portney, K.E. (2003), *Taking Sustainable Communities Seriously: Economic Development, the Environment and Quality of Life in American Cities* (Cambridge, MA: MIT Press).

South Carolina Educational Television and Stonehaven Productions (Co-producers) (2005) *Global Warming: The Signs and the Science* [Motion picture] (available from PBS at: <http://www.shoppbs.org/home/index.jsp>).

Strachan, J., et al. (2005), *The Plain Language Guide to the World Summit on Sustainable Development* (London: Earthscan).

Sustainable Seattle (2006), *Sustainability Indicators*, accessed from: <http://www.sustainableseattle.org/Programs/RegionalIndicators/>.

United Nations (1992), *Rio Declaration on Environment and Development* (Report of the UN Conference on Environment and Development) (New York: The United Nations).

United Nations (1993), *Agenda 21: Earth Summit – The United Nations Programme of Action from Rio* (New York: The United Nations Press).

US Census Bureau (2006), *World Population Information*, accessed from: <http://www.census.gov/ipc/www/world.html>.

Vig, N. and Kraft, M. (eds) (2005), *Environmental Policy: New Directions for the 21st Century* (Washington, DC: CQ Press).

Wheeler, S. and Beatley, T. (eds) (2004), *The Sustainable Urban Development Reader* (London: Routledge).

Whitehouse, D. (2005), 'Half of humanity set to go urban', *BBC News*, May 19, accessed from: <http://news.bbc.co.uk/1/hi/sci/tech/4561183.stm>.

World Commission on Environment and Development (1987) *Our Common Future* (New York: Oxford University Press).

Chapter 9

Assessing Sustainability in Urban Planning: The Potential and Limitations of Indicators as a Means to Measure and Monitor Outcomes of Policy Implementation

Robin Ganser

The Quest for Sustainability and the Necessity to Monitor the Outcomes of Policy Implementation

It is international consensus that spatial planning has an important role in delivering sustainable urban development. A requirement for Local Authorities (LAs) to make every effort to achieve sustainable urban development has therefore been incorporated in many national strategies and in planning law. The complex relationship between – sometimes conflicting – sustainability targets makes monitoring of policy implementation a necessity at all levels of the planning system.

This chapter explores how some of the challenges to achieving sustainable development goals can be overcome through the use of sustainability indicators. This analysis draws upon experiences from the English system of national indicators which has been operational for several years and from the German research-field "Cities of the Future" – which includes pilot-projects that implement indicator systems at the local level. An in-depth analysis of quantified targets and indicators linked to sustainability objectives to reduce greenfield development and to further urban regeneration through re-use of previously developed land – including brownfields – exemplifies both the potential and the limitations of indicator based monitoring.

With regard to monitoring practice, the following two questions need to be addressed in due course:

- Are the existing monitoring requirements and mechanisms geared for the tasks at hand?
- Which improvements and further developments are necessary?

Before these questions can be answered, the rationale behind monitoring and the consequent demands on planning practice must be analyzed. There are several reasons for monitoring:

First, the potentially conflicting targets in national strategies for sustainable development (DETR 1992; Bundesregierung 2002) require early detection, and resolution of such conflicts, in order to allow effective policy implementation in planning and development control procedures. In this context it is equally important to measure the effectiveness of planning instruments and to maximize synergy.

Second, past lessons point to the need for monitoring – particularly given that the previous implementation of local land-use plans has not been satisfactory. Lengthy and resource intensive procedures, postponed plan reviews and outdated plans, frequent departures from the plan, and parallel plan alterations dominated by day to day political reflections led to a loss of the intended strategic function of the local land use plans (Cullingworth and Nadin 2003; Steinebach 2003). In the light of ongoing economic, social, and environmental changes, the need for a strategic local plan was rediscovered and thus requires monitoring to ensure efficient implementation.

Third, the implementation of any land-use plan is always dependent upon the acceptance by relevant stakeholders and subsequent activities to accomplish the plan objectives. Acceptance can be increased by monitoring arrangements which work to highlight links between policy implementation and the achievement of targets, thereby demonstrating the progress and the need for change (BBR 2003). Additionally, the traditionally tight budgets of Local Authorities require monitoring arrangements which ensure the best use is made of resources and that planning furthers economic development and stability (BBR 2003). Increasingly, programs require monitoring as part of determining eligibility for subsidies, particularly in Europe. These are evaluated by means of indicators which ensure that the program objectives are met. For example, the European Environmental Agency uses a set of indicators for environmental reporting (EEA 2004). In this context the main intention is to guarantee the efficient deployment of resources.

In the US, the 1990 amendments to the National Environmental Policy Act (NEPA) (US House of Representatives 1990) suggested monitoring requirements for all federal agencies (Glasson et al., 1999). This bill was not passed, thus, monitoring of projects and plans is not compulsory for the US in its entirety. However, the Environmental Protection Agency (EPA) stresses the importance of monitoring progress towards goals of federal or state environmental policy (EPA 2004). Furthermore, strategies like "Smart Growth" that have been adopted by the US EPA indicate that in the medium to long term, monitoring will likely play an increasingly important role.

In England, national Planning Policy calls for a full sustainability appraisal of local land-use plans (DETR 1999e; ODPM 2004b). The responsible Local Authorities are required to define targets which provide the relevant benchmark for monitoring by use of adequate indicators (DETR 1999e). This informs the decision on the need for and the scope of a plan review (DETR 1999e).

In Germany, the Federal Planning Act (Baugesetzbuch) places a statutory monitoring duty on Local Authorities. This involves environmental monitoring of the implementation of preliminary local land-use plans (Flaechennutzungsplan) and binding local land-use plans (Bebauungsplan) in the scope of the obligatory Strategic Environmental Assessment (European Parliament 2001).

The Role of Monitoring in the Planning System – Basic Principles and Requirements

Strategic and operative role of monitoring

The above requirements provide a first indication as to the specific tasks monitoring should fulfill in planning systems. In this context, the following three core monitoring functions can be identified.

Monitoring general trends and conditions which are of environmental and spatial relevance should be part of survey and review processes of statutory plans and programs as well as an integrated part of strategic environmental assessments and sustainability appraisals. Monitoring quantifiable targets and overall objectives in terms of progress towards these goals can provide the basis for an evaluation of target achievement, the effectiveness of measures, and the need to adapt targets. Monitoring effects – including potential conflicts and synergies – goes hand-in-hand with the achievement of the aforementioned targets and should inform decision makers.

The three monitoring tasks above thereby form a "strategic level" of monitoring which is primarily concerned with the evaluation of achievements. Additionally, an "operative level" can be identified which focuses on the implementation of quantifiable targets and linked indicators in planning documents or strategies and in the scope of development control. This includes making sure that all necessary targets and indicators are in place and controlling formal planning processes – e.g. dynamic determination of plan reviews according to monitoring results. Additionally the decision making process should be supported through monitoring – e.g. providing a frame for discretionary decision making in the scope of planning and application procedures.

The monitoring system is therefore not confined to informing policy makers and the public of the real world effects of policy implementation. Its role in the planning system is far more comprehensive, as it can provide an active means of controlling and managing planning processes and urban development if used correctly.

Sustainability indicators – principal requirements

The United Nations Commission on Sustainable Development (CSD) developed a core set of 58 indicators (CSD 1995) and methodology sheets (United Nations 2004). The development of national monitoring systems for planning practice has been widely influenced by this international proposal for indicator-based monitoring. These documents and indicators continue to provide the primary reference for national indicator systems to date. The CSD model – in line with Agenda 21 – distinguishes four broad monitoring fields (social, economic, environmental, and institutional aspects) and three indicator categories: "driving force indicators"[1] which show effects due to human activities; "state indicators" which describe the current state of the environment, economic and social aspects and "response indicators" which highlight reactions of a community to the above effects (Libbe 1999). Due to the inherent simplification of reality and the close link to political objectives, the CSD model lacks scientific consistency, a problem which needs to be resolved. A big plus of the model is its simplicity, while at the same time allowing transparent monitoring. This model is the basis for both the English and the German indicator systems.

Regardless of the planning level indicators are devised for, some common principles can be defined. Box 9.1 highlights principal requirements based on English research and good practice (DETR 1999d; UK Roundtable 1997).

Box 9.1 Principal requirements based on English research and good practice

a. be sensitive to social, ecologic and economic changes,
b. allow simple, sound and economic data collection (by empirical means or by measurements of status quo or progress),
c. be readily understandable – yet allow adequate measuring, and
d. include specific thresholds (targets or limits) which highlight important changes.

These requirements are very broad and consequent variation, particularly of local indicator systems, can lead to problems of compatibility. The following suggestion of additional requirements (Box 9.2) may be helpful to overcome these inherent uncertainties (BBR 2003; Birkmann et al., 1999; Libbe 1999; Ganser 1999; UK Roundtable 1997).

Box 9.2 Additional requirements for indicators

a. Clear cut targets and clearly defined links to indicators – are essential for transparency and implementation. Further to this compatibility of targets and indicators on different levels of scale has to be ensured (universally valid or transferable).
b. The absolute number of indicators should be limited – to ensure a good overview and avoid distractions from important changes. A limited set of "key-indicators" or "headline indicators" is essential for highlighting progress towards objectives of particular importance.
c. The set of indicators should equally comprise quantitative as well as qualitative indicators to avoid an unbalanced emphasis on fields which allow easy (quantitative) measuring.

---

1   Other models include: FEST (Forschungsstaette evangelische Studiengemeinschaft, FRG), LEF (Lahti Environment Forum, Finland), Sustainable Seattle, Jacksonville – Quality of Life Indicators (USA).

In the material demands highlighted above, several procedural requirements can be identified. The definition of the indicators should involve participation and consultation in order to facilitate data collection and to further the acceptance of targets and monitoring. A transparent process of defining indicators is equally important. It is also essential to define clear responsibilities for data collection and monitoring at the appropriate level – to minimize the workload and duplication of actions. The above requirements not only provide a frame for the future development of indicators, but can also be used as a benchmark for the following evaluation of existing national indicators in England.

Practical Experiences with Systems of Sustainability Indicators – England

Monitoring in England – national level

Since experience with the recently reformed English planning and monitoring system is very limited, the following analysis focuses on the system that was operational up to the recent planning reforms and the 2005 monitoring regime (DEFRA 2005). It is important to point out that the new system does not introduce big structural changes, rather, it comprises fewer indicators than its predecessor established in 1999 (DETR 1999c). The latter consists of 15 "Headline Indicators" which cover the pillars of sustainable development as defined by the national strategy. Progress is outlined in the scope of the overall assessment of 147 national indicators on the basis of "Change since Strategy" (baseline assessment 1999) (DETR 1999c).

The characteristic strengths and weaknesses of indicator-based monitoring at national and subordinate levels are exemplified through a focused analysis of the monitoring arrangements for the sustainability target "to deliver 60 percent of new housing on Previously Developed Land (PDL) and through conversions of existing buildings by 2008" (hereafter: 60 percent target) (DETR 1999b; ODPM 2005a) – linked with the national headline indicator: "Percentage of new dwellings built on PDL" per year (Sustainable Development 2004). Both are based on the overarching objectives of reducing greenfield development and encouraging urban regeneration through the reuse of PDL.

The 60 percent target is binding for land-use allocations in the statutory Local Development Plan and for the determination of planning applications (DETR 2000b). The national target is adapted for the regional level in the scope of so-called Regional Planning Guidance (RPG) which is currently being replaced by new Regional Spatial Strategies (RSS) – issued by the national Secretary of State. These set the frame for Structure Plans (sub-regional) and Local Plans in each region. Under the new regime, Structure plans will be integrated in RSS and Local Development Frameworks at sub-regional and local levels.

The following analysis first evaluates the national indicator against the requirements a) to g) defined above. Subsequently, the subordinate levels of planning are scrutinized for consistency with the national frame and internal logic.

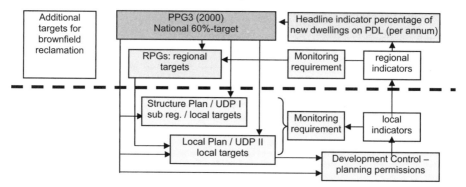

Figure 9.1 Overview of targets, indicators, and monitoring

Fulfillment of principal requirements

The headline indicator "percentage of new dwellings on PDL (per year)", integrated in the national system, fulfils most of the defined requirements a) to g) as the overview in Box 9.3 demonstrates.

Box 9.3 Overview of procedural requirements and remaining deficits

a.   it is sensitive to land use changes and clearly focused on the national target – but only limited conclusions can be drawn on social, ecologic and economic changes,

b.   it allows simple and economic data collection drawing on so called ordnance survey data (mapping of entire country),

c.   it is readily understandable but it is not free of transparency problems (see e, below),

d.   the indicator does not include specific thresholds or alert zones which highlight the necessity of policy changes,

e.   clear links between national objective, 60 percent target and national headline indicator seem to be established at first sight. However target and indicator are too narrowly focused to cover the overarching objectives in their entirety.

f.   the number of indicators is high but the limited set of headline indicators secures an overview of key monitoring aspects and priorities – and

g.   the system includes quantitative as well as qualitative indicators. Although number and therefore emphasis leans towards the former.

Procedural requirements like consultation and public participation in the scope of defining national indicators were fulfilled.

The English indicator system relates to national political objectives. Therefore, similar to the CSD proposal, the chosen indicators show some gaps and do not provide scientific consistency. There are several fundamental deficiencies which are the underlying reason for implementation problems. These are elaborated upon subsequently.

Deficits of national target and resulting monitoring problems

The 60 percent target has the following three main characteristics:

a. It is set in relative terms – i.e. it is focused on a proportion of all new buildings rather than absolute numbers.
b. It focuses on (dwelling) units rather than the land area upon which these are built, and
c. It focuses on residential use and thereby excludes other land uses such as industry; transport infrastructure and leisure facilities.

These characteristics account for the following potential problems. a) The desired 60 percent proportion may be achieved, yet in a situation with a high rate of building completions, 40 percent of those completions would be on greenfields. This in turn is counterproductive for the overarching objective of reduced greenfield development. b) Built densities at present are higher on brownfields than on greenfields. This means that for each unit on greenfields relatively more land area is developed. As a consequence, although currently approximately 70 percent of all new housing units are built on PDL, only 58 percent of all land types developed for housing actually is brownfield land (ODPM 2003; ODPM 2005b). c) The housing focus on PDL can lead to the displacement of more suitable land-uses on these sites, such as more employment uses on greenfields which again is counterproductive. In conclusion, this means that the headline indicator only adequately measures progress towards the 60 percent target but not towards the overarching sustainability objectives. As a consequence, transparency issues concerning the information of the broad public arise.

To permit an adequate assessment of progress towards furthering regeneration and reducing the absolute amount of greenfield development – the following additional indicators should be monitored:

a. – Absolute amount of PDL re-use,
   – Proportion of PDL stock that is re-used (particularly on/off-flows),
   – Percentage of PDL of entire newly-developed area (with distinction between housing and other uses).
b. – Absolute amount of greenfield development (with distinction between housing and other uses),
   – Percentage of greenfields of entire newly developed area (with distinction between housing and other uses).

Database-related problems of monitoring

The data source for the headline indicator, National Land-use Change Statistics (LUCS), is based on Ordnance Survey (OS) information which includes a time-lag between completion of development and incorporation into OS maps. Therefore, precise information on the achievement of the 60 percent target can only by supplied with considerable delay. Depending upon location there can be a time lag of several years[2] (ODPM 2003; ODPM 2005b). Additionally, the character of OS data implies that only the status quo of development is captured without information on plan allocations and outstanding planning permissions. Therefore, information on the future achievability of the 60 percent target is limited. In addition, Development Control Statistics (DCLG 2004) lack the distinction between permissions (for all uses) issued on greenfields and on PDL. Comprehensive information on the renewal and on outstanding planning permissions is also missing (ODPM 2004a). Most of these deficits could be remedied in the scope of LA annual reports.

Monitoring of potentially conflicting targets

Potential conflicts such as a lack of affordable housing due to reduced greenfield development (Barker 2003) or displacement of uses other than housing from brownfields onto greenfields require monitoring through additional indicators. As far as the potential conflict with the housing target is concerned, the following indicators have to be monitored: a) allocation of housing land in plans compared to future housing requirements; b) permission rates and c) completion rates. The analysis of these can indicate whether enough sites for development are coming forward to meet housing requirements or whether a time lag between permission and completion is due to economic considerations.

Monitoring of PDL on-/off-flows

A central presupposition for the achievement of the 60 percent target is an adequate supply of PDL. First compiled in 1998, the National Land-use Database (NLUD) contains comprehensive information on available PDL in England (DTLR 2000). This includes facts on location, land type, type of dereliction, physical constraints and planning status. A big plus of NLUD is the categorization of PDL which includes "latent" PDL thereby reducing uncertainty over future availability for redevelopment (English Partnerships 2003). Unfortunately, NLUD currently does not offer estimates on the commercial viability of PDL nor does it allow the comparison of timelines or does it include qualitative data such as the ecological value of the sites.

---

2   In 1992, proportion of PDL of all newly developed sites: 49 percent (Greenfields 51 percent). In 1999, PDL 53 percent (Greenfields 47 percent) – 1999 data is subject to some uncertainty due to incomplete data.

Combined measuring of sustainability indicators and local authority performance

A key characteristic of the English system is the combination of sustainability indicators and so-called Best Value Performance Indicators (BVPIs). The latter are used to assess the performance of local authorities (LAs) (DCLG 2004). While some of the BVPI targets and indicators are focused on procedural performance only – such as the Development Control which attempts to determine 60 percent of major applications in 13 weeks[3] – others link LA performance with the implementation of the Local Plan. A central example is the indicator: "BV 106 – Percentage of new homes built on PDL". This direct link between LA performance, consequential resource implications for each LA, and the achievement of sustainability targets can have a positive effect, providing an additional incentive. On the downside, some of the BVPIs can have negative effects such as when LAs have to consider applications under the pressure of tight deadlines thereby reducing the quality of planning decisions.

Monitoring at regional, sub-regional and local level in English planning practice

The strengths and potential weaknesses of monitoring at the regional, sub-regional, and local levels are exemplified by case studies in the South East of England. In this region, which is experiencing high development pressure, monitoring in the context of the 60 percent target is of particular importance for sustainable urban development. This is characterized by reduced greenfield development and increased brownfield reuse, thereby making the most efficient use of scarce spatial resources.

   In the scope of this analysis, the first question above that addresses the adequacy of monitoring, is examined using the following criteria related to the quality of monitoring practice:

   a. Adequate monitoring of the contribution to the national 60 percent target and compatibility of the local and national indicators
   b. Overcoming national monitoring gaps and deficits
   c. Internal logic of indicator systems and operative issues

Subsequently, the monitoring practice at the different tiers of planning can be tested against these criteria.

Monitoring at the regional level

Monitoring at the regional level is the core responsibility of Regional Assemblies (RAs) currently consisting of LA representatives. Looking at the South East Region for example, the RA's Planning Committee agreed to a set of 40 indicators for monitoring policies in Regional Planning Guidance 9 (RPG9), which is to be superseded by a new South East Plan (SEERA 2002). Data is collected

---

   3   BV 109 Indicator: Percentage of planning applications determined in line with the Government's new development.

through surveys (completed by LAs) analyzed by the RA and fed into a Regional Monitoring Report.

The test against criterion a) reveals that the central target of RPG9: "At least 60 percent of development to take place on PDL" (SEERA 2002) is more comprehensive than the national 60 percent target as it is set for all land uses. The issue of potential displacement problems, whereby the housing priority on brownfields can result in displacement of more suitable (e.g. industrial) uses, is therefore avoided.

The regional indicator "proportion of dwellings completed on PDL" is compatible with the national indicator. The average target across all English regions defined by respective regional planning documents – is to provide 66 percent of new dwellings on PDL, therefore the national target is met.

The analysis with regard to criterion b) shows the following result: the national monitoring deficit of "planned land-uses" and of "future availability of PDL" as a presupposition for the achievement of the 60 percent target is partially remedied (SEERA 2003). However, central deficits of regional monitoring still include the lack of indicators for the absolute amount of greenfield development and for the proportion of greenfields of the entire newly developed land area. Only the "Number and area of designated sites affected by development" (SEERA 2003) are monitored. The latter only include sites designated for environmental reasons and therefore do not provide a complete picture of greenfield loss to development.

Moving on to the assessment against criterion c) a central deficit of the Regional Monitoring Report becomes evident: The target which requires that at least 60 percent of all development should take place on PDL is not adequately monitored as the regional indicators fail to include several types of development, such as infrastructure and leisure uses. As a consequence, the monitoring system provides an incomplete picture of the types of development and the location and site type to which the former relates. It is therefore not possible to evaluate the achievement of the overarching targets to reduce greenfield development and to further regeneration through increased PDL reuse.

A particular strength of the regional monitoring system is the fact that a comparison of housing requirements (future demand) and issued permissions is incorporated. This indicates whether additional measures are necessary to achieve this potentially conflicting target while at the same time reducing residential development on greenfields.

Additionally, monitoring of the indicator "Net density of additional dwellings completed" (SEERA 2003) supports the effective use of land resources. In this context, however, a further distinction of net densities according to land type (PDL/greenfields) is necessary.

Summarizing the above, it can be said that, although monitoring in the South East region closes some of the national monitoring gaps, some deficits remain. A key unanswered question is whether sub-regional and local monitoring can close these remaining gaps in order to improve the overall quality of the monitoring system.

Monitoring at the sub-regional level

Applying the criterion a) of adequate monitoring and indicator compatibility as regards the 60 percent target at the subordinate tiers of the planning system leads to the following results: At the sub-regional level, Structure Plans should include a compatible indicator and specific targets for new housing provisions on PDL in each district within the county's respective sub-region. In Kent, for example, a county in the South East of England, the cumulative average as a whole is 70 percent of housing to be provided on PDL which clearly exceeds the national 60 percent target (Kent County Council 2003). However, there is no quantified target to complement the regional 60 percent target for all new development to be provided on PDL. Therefore, an implementation and monitoring gap exists within the South East region. This means that the more comprehensive target may not be met because it is not incorporated in all of the subordinate planning documents.

As far as the test against criterion b) is concerned, it has to be noted, that the proposed monitoring arrangements close one of the gaps identified at the national level: the indicator "Extent of greenfield land newly committed to development" for example, indicates progress towards the overarching national objective of reduced greenfield development (Kent County Council 2003). Monitoring of the absolute PDL re-use in Kent shows deficits similar to the national level.

Additionally, monitoring includes indicators which to some extent cover potentially conflicting targets such as the adequate supply of housing and reduced greenfield development (Kent County Council 2003). Yet information derived from these indicators does not provide insight into the reasons for a potential housing shortfall. Additional information is necessary to interpret the monitoring results correctly and to devise adequate improvement measures.

As far as the issues of potential displacement problems are concerned, an additional indicator covering the "proportion of housing and business development permitted" (Kent County Council 2003) can be used as a proxy measure of current and future land use plans. This, in turn, is the basis for corrective action in form of revised targets and location priorities for specific land-uses.

The test against criterion c) internal logic of the indicator system reveals that the sub-regional targets are complemented by policies for the sequence of development which prioritize the reuse of PDL. These require (Kent County Council 2003):

- That PDL is considered first, followed by greenfield land
- Then the sequential consideration of major urban areas, rural service centers and smaller rural settlements as locations for development (Kent County Council 2003).

These complementary policies facilitate the implementation of the 60 percent target.

Additionally, monitoring density on PDL and greenfields (Kent County Council 2003) highlights progress towards the more efficient use of land resources. This indicator helps to interpret the 60 percent target monitoring results in a wider context: in a situation where there are equally high densities on PDL and on greenfields and the 60 percent target is met, it can be assumed that progress towards reduced greenfield development and increased PDL re-use is made.

In addition to monitoring of urban development, sub-regional monitoring includes targets and indicators which complement national BVPI monitoring. These include the preparation of statutory planning documents through subordinate LAs. This is valuable in the scope of operative monitoring as it indicates where sub-regional targets are actually incorporated and implemented in planning practice. This provides the necessary basis to highlight shortfalls in the planning system and to use control as well as default powers to influence LAs to adhere to the framework set by the super ordinate planning documents. These issues are closely linked to the interesting field of monitoring practice at the local level which is explored subsequently.

Monitoring at the local level

Local monitoring problems are most visible and also most noticable in terms of real world effects. There are two main reasons for this: in contrast to highly aggregated data at the superordinate levels, monitoring refers to a relatively small area which means that there is little scope to balance results between different locations. On the other hand, monitoring informs decision making which is directly linked to project related planning decisions and actual development. Therefore correct and comprehensive monitoring results are crucial in the scope of the determination of plan reviews and of applications.

A joint initiative between local and central government developed sustainability indicators which were tested in 30 LAs (DETR 200a). These are based on local versions of national indicators and act as a point of reference. Some Local Plans include a central matrix with local objectives, targets, policies, and indicators which form the core of the monitoring arrangements (Dartford 2001). Evidence from the following exemplary analysis of Dartford Borough's Local Plan suggests that the above joint initiative can result in a successful implementation at the local level.

When tested against criterion a) – compatibility and adequate monitoring of the contribution to the national 60 percent target – it is evident that the Local Plan incorporates the more comprehensive regional target to locate 60 percent of all new development on PDL. The national and Structure Plan targets are therefore covered. Unfortunately the Local Plan target for all new development is not adequately monitored as information is only collected for housing completions on PDL. To end this part of the assessment on a positive note it has to be stated that the indicator is compatible with the national monitoring system.

However, there is also still room for further improvements with regard to criterion b) as the local monitoring arrangements do not remedy the national deficits concerning the absolute amount of greenfield development. As a consequence, the monitoring results do not indicate progress towards the overarching objective of reduced greenfield development.

By contrast, the national monitoring gap regarding PDL availability and re-use is closed. In this context, status quo information from the National Land Use Data Base (NLUD) and a sub-regional study on future housing land supply is combined and provides a good overview of progress towards the overarching objective of furthering regeneration through increased PDL reuse (Dartford 2004).

Now moving on to test the local monitoring arrangements against criterion c), the internal logic of the local system, the following observations are crucial. The Local Plan strives to focus new development at central locations, including monitoring the success of greenbelt policies through a specific indicator which measures the amount of exceptional development in the greenbelt (Dartford 2001). This should be complemented by a requirement for a sequential test to be carried out in the scope of Development Control, in line with the sub-regional policies mentioned above. Additionally, as mentioned above, the total amount of greenfield development should be monitored at the local level.

The relevant density targets of super ordinate planning tiers are sustained by targets requiring residential densities of at least 30 or 60 dwellings per hectare in central locations. This density target is linked to a local indicator which can show whether progress towards the overarching objectives is made. As discussed above, if residential densities on PDL and greenfields are similar and the 60 percent target is achieved, one can deduce that progress towards reduced greenfield development and increased PDL reuse is made in absolute terms, as far as housing is concerned. However, to improve monitoring and provide a complete picture of spatial development, all land-uses should be covered in the future.

Another important monitoring issue at the local level is that of potentially conflicting targets, for example reduced greenfield development on the one hand and increased completions of housing units on the other hand. It is important that, in addition to monitoring of the 60 percent target, appropriate indicators are incorporated in the annual monitoring reports which cover housing completions compared to the requirements set by super ordinate planning tiers (Dartford 2001, 2004). If the monitoring results indicate that either one of the targets is not met, corrective action, such as furthering of brownfield reuse through planning briefs for specific sites, needs to be taken. However, not all Local Plans define a specific indicator for housing completions (Dartford 2001, 2004).

After analyzing the core material monitoring considerations it is now time to explore the monitoring mechanisms for the operative level. Monitoring of the completion of specific planning documents which provide a framework for future development is of great importance. In England, the goal is to have in place an up-to-date area-wide local land-use plan as well as supplementary site-specific planning documents for all major development sites which incorporate the 60 percent target and the linked density targets. If these documents are not in place, chances are that decisions on project applications will not consider all relevant targets or that the decision making process will not reflect the weight these targets have when they are incorporated in local planning documents. The timely completion of the latter should therefore be monitored. The exemplary analysis shows that not all of these monitoring requirements are met. Merely periodic reviews of site-specific supplementary planning guidance are carried out (Dartford 2001).

It is equally important to monitor the implementation of the above planning documents once they are in place. The case study example demonstrates how this can be achieved: the implementation of the Local Plan is monitored in terms of policies given effect through Development Control. This can be measured through the number of planning permissions that adhere to the policies and do not require any waivers or alterations of the plan to legalize the project. This can be complemented by analyzing the proportion of conditional planning permissions which are upheld by the appeal authority in case of objections against the conditions imposed on a planning permission. Such conditional permissions are normally issued when a specific planning application does not conform to the local development plan in its entirety but is accepted providing that certain conditions are complied with which in turn usually comprise certain amendments to the application. The number and the reasons for variances or departures from the plan are monitored (Dartford 2001). Both of the above provide a solid basic understanding of the effectiveness of planning documents and the specific policies within them which in turn ensures that the 60 percent target and the linked objectives can be met.

Detailed local indicators should provide a clear picture of local progress towards sustainability objectives. However there are limitations that can arise due to a complete or partial lack of data, missing baseline information, necessary to set a benchmark for progress reporting, or time lags in measuring. A minimum requirement therefore is an indicator that provides an overview of the monitoring quality of the entire indicator set – for example in terms of the "number of targets which are monitored and where meaningful monitoring results could be obtained" (Dartford 2001). This element of quality control can highlight problems and help to optimize monitoring in future (Dartford 2001). In addition, it shows where a higher level of interpretation of the monitoring results is necessary, especially when these results are fed into the decision making process.

As an interim conclusion regarding the monitoring of the 60 percent target for sustainable spatial development, the English monitoring practice suffers from various deficits at different levels of the planning system. This requires the careful interpretation of monitoring results when they are used as evidence in the scope of the decision-making process. Some of these problems are rooted at the national level and subsequently feed through all tiers of planning.

Emerging national framework and research findings from pilot projects in Germany

Looking at the German situation can be helpful since Germany is the only other country in Europe that has introduced a fairly similar national target for sustainable spatial development. Germany's sustainability strategy includes the objectives of reduced greenfield development and furthering regeneration through re-use of PDL. These are concretized by a target to limit greenfield development to 30 hectares per day for the whole of Germany by 2020 (hereafter: 30ha target). As the German target is more comprehensive, covering all land-uses and referring to an absolute amount of permissible greenfield development, the achievement of this target is more likely to go hand in hand with the overall objectives. Also, displacement effects of development types other than housing, potentially induced by the 60 percent target, are not to be expected. Monitoring is nonetheless vital in order to evaluate the achievement of the target and if necessary to adjust the policy context.

The German national indicator system is not fully operational and several regional systems are in a test phase (BBR 2003). Therefore, the pilot research project: "Cities of the future", which focuses on local indicators is at the heart of the following analysis.

Results from research linked to pilot projects

Although research on "Cities of the future" started before the adoption of the national strategy, the overarching objectives have a central role. They were concretized by a quantified target that provides future development at a ratio of 3:1 inside and outside of urban areas (BBR 2003). All four model cities that took part in the research project achieved this target.[4] Additionally, a field test with 50 participating LAs was conducted to assess practicality and robustness of the devised indicators. As a result, 12 standard and 12 additional indicators were developed (BBR 2003). The former allow economic data collection, mostly integrated in existing statistics. The latter provide more distinctive information but require additional data collection. Several indicators are introduced to assess progress towards the objectives and the quantified target. For example, the "proportion of new development inside: outside urban areas" and "square meters of developed area" highlights progress towards the national target. The indicator "proportion of developed land compared to total area of the LA" provides complementary information on the local context which is of particular relevance to assess future development options. The intended focus on urban areas and on PDL re-use is supported by the target and the linked indicators: "intensity of land-use" (BBR 2003) and "floor space required for workplaces" (BBR 2003) aiming at more efficient land-use.

An indication of future PDL availability is provided by the indicators "PDL available for development: proportion of entire developed area" (BBR 2003) and "Mobilizing PDL and existing buildings: square-meters of sites which can be developed immediately or in the short term in comparison to entire developed area" (BBR 2003). However, the absolute amount of PDL re-use and the ratio of PDL on- and off-flows are not monitored. The indicator: "Sum of area designated as: Natura 2000 sites, nature reserves and national parks" (BBR 2003) complements measures to reduce greenfield development as development is prohibited on these sites.

Only a crude indication of progress towards the potentially conflicting housing target is provided by the indicators: "Population moving to suburban areas ..." (BBR 2003) and "... sum of entire housing allowance paid per year" (BBR 2003). The local English indicators which allow a comparison between housing requirements, permissions and completions permit a more accurate assessment of the reasons for housing shortages. There seems to be scope to learn from both systems.

The emerging national indicator framework

The above research results and experiences gained in the pilot projects have informed the discussion on the monitoring of the 30ha target and the 3:1 target as well as the linked objectives to reduce greenfield development and further urban regeneration at national level. This includes, amongst others, the following central indicators (German Federal Government 2004):

- The absolute amount of greenfield development (all land-uses) which is already measured (ha/a) as part of the so-called "German Environmental Index" which comprises six highly aggregated indicators that cover important environmental objectives (Umweltbundesamt 2004).
- The absolute amount of PDL reuse.
- The proportion of development inside and outside urban areas.
- The absolute amount of developable PDL.

The central deficits of the proposed German indicators are similar to their English counterparts. First of all, the national set does not indicate potential conflicts, particularly between reduced greenfield development and resulting restrictions for the realization of land-uses. The elimination of this deficit should not pose a major hurdle as issued planning permissions, building completions and outstanding planning permissions are already monitored and therefore allow a comparison with projected demand and respective targets. A missing piece of information to date, however, is the distinction between completions on PDL and on greenfields. Monitoring cannot readily highlight hindrances in the planning system as the implementation of policies and allocations in land-use plans supporting the national target are not covered.

In order to attain a balanced set of indicators, not only quantitative but also qualitative aspects of PDL redevelopment have to be covered. The latter, however, also poses a weak spot in the German system. Monitoring thus far does not provide a complete nationwide picture of PDL potential. In this respect it will be necessary to install an equivalent to NLUD in Germany, exclusive of the deficits mentioned before. Finally, looking at the planning statistics, the same flaws discovered when analyzing the English statistics become apparent with the exception that the German system does provide information on planned land-use allocations and thereby gives an indication of future possibilities to achieve the national targets and meet market demand.

Conclusions and relevance for the US

The undisputed necessity of monitoring policy implementation in the scope of land-use planning leads to the vision of interlinked indicator systems from the international to the local level. This is broadened by plans to combine monitoring of sustainability targets and monitoring of LA planning performance. In addition, it would be helpful to make monitoring a compulsory presupposition for subsidies. Specific requirements set the frame for the definition and development of indicator systems. The core deficits which were detected in the exemplary analysis of the English system lead to the following generalized conclusions on potential deficits of sustainability indicators (Box 9.4):

Box 9.4 Generalized conclusions on deficits

- Too narrowly defined targets and indicators (e.g. 60 percent target) – cannot adequately monitor overarching sustainability objectives. A set of corresponding additional indicators is necessary.
- Varying comprehensiveness of targets and linked indicators (e.g. 60 percent housing/all uses on PDL) leads to monitoring gaps.
- At some levels not merely national objectives but also specific targets were only partially monitored (indicators too narrowly defined).
- Organisational deficits (e.g. unclear feedback) lead to problems of data availability (opportunities to gather information are lost).
- Data base problems (missing information, time lags) feed into the indicator system thereby reducing the potential to inform policy.
- Not all LAs currently fulfil their monitoring duties. Some show monitoring arrangements of differing quality. Therefore aggregation at different levels of scale is obstructed.
- There is acute need for harmonizing different systems and catalogues of indicators at EU, member-state and regional levels.

Using this analysis, one can draw the following conclusions about chances and limitations of monitoring by means of indicators (Box 9.5):

Box 9.5 Risks and limitations of monitoring through indicators

- Some aspects of life and of urban development simply can not be assessed due to a lack of specific values attached to them.
- Methods of measuring depend on the target and the definition of "success". The measurement of quantitative and qualitative aspects requires a different method of data collection and analysis.
- Indicator sets which fulfill the above requirements give a good outline of strengths, weaknesses and conflicts. Yet regularly the complexity of reality is reduced – as a consequence a degree of interpretation and additional analysis is required.
- Headline indicators therefore regularly need complementary indicators to provide a complete picture of policy implementation.
- Ranking of local authorities according to performance is difficult as local context makes interpretation of monitoring results necessary (e.g. due to differing PDL availability). Therefore the broad vision: performance measuring has to be implemented with great care.

The introduction of the 60 percent target and consequent monitoring in England remarkably reduced the amount of greenfield development. This and the above organizational and methodical conclusions are of particular interest for the US in the context of smart growth efforts: There are similar objectives of refocusing regional growth within central cities and inner suburbs, away from rural and undeveloped areas in order to enhance the overall quality of life. The central concept is to avoid piecemeal planning and to combine regional and local planning levels as well as public and private subsidies (Cullingworth and Caves 2003). In the US where 50 state governments are operational that each convey varying powers to local and regional planning authorities by either constitution or enabling act, the coordination of compatible targets, indicator sets, and data collection in the scope of monitoring at different levels of the planning system is of particular importance. The same holds true for Europe. Although data collection takes place at member-state level, there is no requirement for national indicator sets to comply with the European system which can lead to inconsistencies.

References

Barker, K. (2003), 'Review of Housing Supply, Securing our Future Housing Needs, Interim Report – Analysis', available at: <http://news.bbc.co.uk/1/shared/spl/hi/uk/03/budget/documents/pdf/barker_review_foretoch3_396.pdf>.

Birkmann et al. (1999), Indikatoren fuer eine nachh. Raumentwicklund, Methoden u. Konzepte d. Indikatorenforschung [Indicators for Sustainable Spatial Development, Methods, Concepts, Indicators] (Dortmund: Blaue Reihe).

Bundesamt fuer Bauwesen und Raumordnung (BBR) [Federal Office for Building and Regional Planning] (2003), *Zukunft Findet Stadt* [Future Discovers City] (Bonn).

Bundesregierung [Federal Government] (2002), Perspektiven fuer Deutschland: Unsere Strategie fuer eine Nachhaltige Entwicklund [Perspectives for German: Our strategy for Sustainable Development] (Berlin: Bundesregierung).

Commission on Sustainable Development (CSD) (1995), 'Third Session' (United Nations).

Cullingworth, B. and Caves, R. (2003), *Planning in the USA* (New York: Routledge).

Cullingworth, B. and Nadin, V. (2003), *Town and Country Planning in the UK* (London: Routledge).

Dartford Borough Council (2001), 'Local Plan' (second deposit, draft) (Dartford).

Dartford Borough Council (2004), 'Local Plan Review: First Monitoring Report' (Dartford).

Department for Communities and Local Government (DCLG) (2004), 'Local Government Performance', available at: < http://www.bvpi.gov.uk/pages/index.asp>.

Department of the Environment, Food, and Rural Affairs (DEFRA) (2005), 'Securing the Future: Delivering UK Sustainable Development Strategy' (London: The Stationery Office).

Department of the Environment, Transport, and the Regions (DETR) (1999a), 'A Better Quality of Life – A Strategy for Sustainable Development in the UK' (London).

DETR (1999b), 'Draft Planning Policy Guidance Note 3 – Housing' (London).

DETR (1999c), '1999 Indicator Report: A Baseline Assessment – Quality of Life Counts' (London).

DETR (1999d), 'Planning for Sustainable Development – Towards Better Practice' (London).

DETR (1999e), 'PPG12 Development Plans' (London).

DETR (2000a), 'Handbook: Local Quality of Life Counts' (London).

DETR (2000b), 'Planning Policy Guidance Note 3 – Housing' (London).

Deutsches Institut für Urbanistik (DIFU) (German Institute for Urban Studies) (1999), *Indikatorensysteme fuer eine nachhaltige Entwicklung in Kommunen* (Indicator Systems for Sustainable Development in Local Authorities) (Berlin, DIFU).

Department of Tranport, Local Government and the Regions (DTLR) (2000), 'National Land Use Database: Data Specification' (London: DTLR).

English Partnerships (2003), *Towards a National Brownfield Strategy: Research findings for the Deputy Prime Minister* (London: EP).

Environmental Protection Agency (EPA) (2004), 'EPA Report on the Environment', available at: <www.epa.gov/indicators>.

European Environment Agency (2004), 'Overview of EEA Products', available at: <http://www.eea.eu.int/products>.

European Parliament (2001), 'Directive 2001/42/EC' (Council on the Assessment of the Effects of Certain Plans and Programs on the Environment).

Ganser, R. (1999), 'Sustainable Urban Development as "Leitmotiv" for Town Planning in Great Britain and Germany'. Thesis, Dipl. (University of Kaiserslautern).

German Federal Government (2004), 'Status Report 2004' (Berlin).

Glasson, J., et al. (1999), *Introduction to Environmental Impact Assessment*, 2nd edition (London: Routledge).

Kent County Council/Medway Council (2003), 'Structure Plan: Policy HP 3'.

Libbe, J. (1999), 'Indikatorensysteme fuer eine Nachhaltige Entwicklung in Kommunen, Dokumentation Forum Stadtoekologie 11' [Indicator systems for sustainable development in local authories, Documentation of the Forum Urban Ecology] (Berlin: DIFU).

Office of the Deputy Prime Minister (ODPM) (2003), 'Land Use Change Statistical Release 18' (London: ODPM Publications).

ODPM (2004a), 'Outstanding Planning Permissions for Housing Development in Northern England' (London: ODPM Publications).

ODPM (2004b), 'Planning Policy Statement 12: Local Development Frameworks' (London: ODPM Publications).

ODPM (2005a), 'Draft Planning Policy Statement 3: Housing' (London: ODPM Publications).

ODPM (2005b), 'Land Use Change in England: Residential Development to 2004' (London: ODPM Publications).

South East England Regional Assembly (SEERA) (2002), 'RPG9 Regional Monitoring Report' (Guildford).

SEERA (2003), 'RPG9 Regional Monitoring Report: Annex 1' (Guildford).

Steinebach, G. (2003) *Ergebnisse der Kommunalbefragung in Rheinland – Pfalz zum Stand der Flaechennutzungsplanung und Einsatz von IuK-Systemen in der oeffentlichen Verwaltung und raeumlichen Planung* [Results of the Communal Survey in Rheinland-Pfalz on the Situation of Area Wide Local Planning and the

Implementation of ICT Systems in Public Administration and Spatial Planning] Kaiserslautern, Integrated Communication Systems).

UK Government (2004), 'Sustainable Development: The Government's Approach', available at: <http://www.sustainable-development.gov.uk/index.asp>.

UK Round Table on Sustainable Indicators (1997), 'Getting the Best out of Indicators' (London).

Umweltbundesamt [Federal Office for Environmental Protection] (2004), 'Boden' [Soil], available at: < http://www.umweltbundesamt.de/dux/bo-inf.htm>.

United Nations Department of Economic and Social Affairs (2004), 'Indicators of Sustainable Development', available at: <http://www.un.org/esa/sustdev/natinfo/ indicators/isd.htm>.

US House of Representatives (1990), HR 1113.

European Parliament (2001), Directive 2001/42/EC, section 4c BauGB (German Federal Planning Act).

Chapter 10

Measuring Sustainability: The Role of Ecological Footprinting in Assessing the Impact of Development

Andrea Collins and Andrew Flynn

Introduction

As sustainable development has moved from the realms of rhetoric and into practice, policy makers operating at different levels of government have become increasingly concerned about measuring whether their activities are having the desired impact. In addition to policy makers; researchers, non-governmental organizations, environmental protection bodies, businesses, and communities have also been interested in analyzing the extent to which government commitments to sustainability have substance. The measurement of sustainability (or unsustainability) has, however, proven to be problematic with ongoing debates over what and how things should be measured. Since its development in the early 1990s in Canada by Mathis Wackernagel and William Rees (see Wackernagel and Rees 1996), the Ecological Footprint has rapidly grown in popularity. In a remarkably short space of time Footprint studies have been undertaken in North America, Europe, and Scandinavia. Additionally, several specialist Footprint consultancies have been formed to take advantage of what appears to be a booming market for their expertise. It is now timely to critically analyze what Footprint studies have delivered and what difference they have made to the way in which environmental protection or sustainability decisions are made.

One of our main interests has been to analyze how corporate commitments to sustainable development in Cardiff Council play themselves out when a major urban development – International Sports Village – is at the planning and implementation stage. The Footprint has provided a new window by which to gain insights into the development process and to begin to assess the likely environmental impacts of the International Sports Village (ISV). As we argue later, the Environmental Statement arising from the Environmental Impact Assessment (the conventional decision-making tool to determine the environmental effects of a new development) is so much a part of the development process that it may seriously underplay the environmental impact findings. An Ecological Footprint, by contrast, provides an alternative measure and different insights on economic and political imperatives on decision-making for land use development. Key sources of data from which we have drawn evidence in preparing this chapter are existing Footprint reports from the UK and elsewhere, the developing literature on Ecological Footprinting, and key person interviews that we undertook with UK Footprint practitioners, non-governmental organizations, and officials in government. Given that the Footprint community in the UK is small, for reasons of confidentiality, we have not been able to identify interviewees.

This chapter is divided into six sections. In the following section we briefly outline the purpose of an Ecological Footprint. The third section notes the adoption of the Ecological Footprint as a sustainability indicator by the National Assembly for Wales and the promotion of the Footprint within Cardiff, the capital city of Wales. The next section outlines the nature of development in Cardiff's International Sports Village (ISV) – the key development within the city. This is followed by a review of the Cardiff Ecological Footprint and the estimated Footprint of visitors to ISV. Finally, the chapter points out that despite the evidence that the Footprint produces of environmental impact, developmental pressures are likely to remain at the fore.

What is an Ecological Footprint?

A Footprint provides a "snapshot" estimate or measure of the area of land and water ecosystems required to provide the resources and to assimilate the wastes of a given population. More simply stated, an Ecological Footprint indicates the demand on the environment for resources. Typically the population studied is that of a nation-state, however the Footprint can also be applied to a region, city (or other administrative area), business, person, or product. Politico-administrative areas are favored units for analysis because they have a defined geographical boundary that can then be compared to the Footprint area. By showing the impact of a population in terms of area, the Footprint provides a clear illustration of the ways in which "… biologically productive land area produces or absorbs flows of many of the materials utilized by our society. Uses are often mutually exclusive and are therefore in competition for the finite area of productive land in the world" (ECOTEC 2001). The Ecological Footprint has the potential to visualize human demands upon the environment in terms of the use of the earth's available land making it an intuitive and attractive means of measurement.

The Ecological Footprint is measured using a standardized area unit equivalent to a world average productive hectare or "global hectare" (gha) and is usually expressed in global hectares per person (gha/capita). It is derived for each study area by estimating the area of land required to support the demand for resources consumed. This demand on nature can be compared with the available Earth's biocapacity, which translates into an average of 1.8 gha/cap in 2001 (WWF 2004). However, humanity is currently using 2.2 gha/cap which indicates a situation of "overshoot" with nature's capital being spent faster then it is being regenerated (WWF 2004). Overshoot may permanently reduce the Earth's ecological capacity.

Being able to clearly identify different levels of resource use is, for the advocates of Ecological Footprinting, one of its major strengths. The metaphor of an *Ecological Footprint* has an intuitive appeal since it communicates critical dimensions of human ecology. It personalizes sustainability by focusing upon consumption and it quantifies the impact of consumption using a single land area that is both easily understood and a useful approach to visualizing the current ecological crises. The Ecological Footprint aggregates the impacts of consumption into a single measure and offers policy makers the potential to clearly identify and compare the environmental impact of different human activities and to monitor change. From the point of view of one of its UK promoters, the Ecological Footprint is one of the best tools currently available to help decision makers become aware of the environmental impacts of different policy options (Barrett et al., 2004).

Ecological Footprinting in Wales

As part of a process of devolution in the UK in the late 1990s, Wales – one of the constituent countries of the UK with a population of about 3 million – was given limited powers across a range of policy areas (e.g. health, education). There was, though, one exception in relation to sustainability. The National Assembly for Wales (the name of the devolved body) was given a unique duty among legislatures in the European Union. It was directed to promote sustainable development in all of its activities. Adoption of the Footprint as an indicator is a considerable source of pride to the Assembly and distinguishes it as a leader on sustainability. As the Assembly's first report on its sustainability performance commented: "We believe that this makes Wales the first country in the world to adopt the Ecological Footprint as an official indicator" (National Assembly for Wales 2000–2001). The rise to prominence of the Footprint indicator is something of a surprise as work on environmental indicators in Wales had generally "run into the sand" (interview with local government official).

There is, however, likely to be a gap between the adoption of an indicator and any impact it may have on an organization's performance. From a review of Footprint studies and key person interviews with staff in local government, Footprint researchers and non-governmental organizations a general feeling emerged that Footprint studies had been "done" as an academic exercise to the organization rather than developing as a collaborative project, where the Footprint results could be trusted and used by the client organization to inform policy. The evidence indicates that these Footprint studies have actually made little difference to policy. The paucity of tangible examples of the Footprint informing policy debate within local government brings into question the validity of the Footprint "study" itself as a policy tool.

Within Cardiff Council there has been a strong determination from the outset that the Footprint results should have validity and resonance for policy makers. For the Footprint study to be used to its best effect and to make a difference, Ecological Footprinting must focus as much on process as it does on methodology. The partners engaged in the Cardiff study – the Council, Stockholm Environment Institute – York, and Cardiff University – have sought from the beginning to concentrate on process as well as the "nuts and bolts" of material flow analysis and the Ecological Footprint calculation. Uniquely, for a UK study, Cardiff University is working with the Council not only to collect locally relevant data for the Ecological Footprint calculation (undertaken by SEI-York), but also with policy officers from the Council to develop sustainable policy scenarios. This new model of Footprinting is developing new processes and ways of working together for the organizations involved.

Partly as a result of the raised level of expectations among Council staff as to how Footprint results might inform their own work and partly because of the significance of the ISV for the City, attempts have been made to assess the environmental impacts of the proposed development. This is a novel application for the Footprint tool. Moreover, because of the relationships that have developed over time with key Council staff, there is the opportunity to analyze how environmental issues inform the development process from early discussions with developers to the actual buildings.

International Sports Village

The International Sports Village (ISV) is to be "a key development in the context of Cardiff as a European Capital celebrating its centenary as a city in 2005" (Ove Arup 2001). In addition to creating a landmark sports tourism destination for national and international events, the ISV complex is to be an important component of economic regeneration by creating jobs in the area.

Promoters of the ISV envision that the development will attract further development and inward investment which will be important in capitalizing on the investment potential from future events in South Wales, including the Ryder Cup in 2010 (Ove Arup 2001). In addition to use by local residents in Cardiff and the surrounding area, it is also anticipated that the ISV development will promote itself as

> an urban 'Centre Parcs' role as it will provide long stay accommodation so that visitors will have full use of the site's extensive sports, leisure and entertainment facilities as well as providing a convenient base for exploring the rest of Cardiff and the surrounding area (Ove Arup 2001).

There are some exceedingly high expectations for the site and according to one consultancy: "the International Sports Village will unquestionably become part of and play a key role in one of the most exciting visitor destinations in Europe" (B3 Burgess Partnership 2002). Or from another consultancy: "The development [the ISV] will create a landmark sports tourism destination for national and international events" (Ove Arup 2001). Within the ISV there is to be a flagship project that will be the focus of development activity. The plan is to build a new fifty meter swimming pool to replace the Wales Empire Pool (initially built for the 1958 Commonwealth Games) which was demolished to make way for the development of the Millennium Stadium in the center of Cardiff in the late 1990s. The pool had symbolic, sporting, and recreational value and because of this significance, promises were given that it would be replaced.

Land use allocations at the ISV are grouped into four principal categories: sports, leisure and entertainment; visitor accommodation; residential units; and commercial retail. Proposed developments include an Aquatic center (including water slides, flumes and waves and a separate fifty meter pool facility, to replace the Welsh Empire Pool). Activities will include swimming, diving, surfboarding, and wind surfing. The proposal also includes an indoor Arena with a seating capacity of between 6,000 and 10,000 which will host a range of events including ice-based performances, other indoor sporting activities, concerts, exhibitions, and TV spectaculars. Other sporting facilities will include a snow dome, ice pad, ice climbing wall, rock climbing, indoor caving, and health and fitness facilities. Alongside these developments will be sports retail, bars, restaurants, and food courts.

The key mechanism by which the likely environmental impacts of the development have been assessed to date has been through a small number of Environmental Statements (ES). These Environmental Statements have been prepared for Cardiff Council by an independent team of specialists drawn from Ove Arup (a large consultancy). For our purposes, the most important ES accompanied the outline planning application submitted to Cardiff Council, which was to establish the principle that development would be approved. The ES is one of a number of documents produced to support the planning application; a Traffic Impact Assessment, a Planning Statement, and a Retail Impact Assessment have also been produced. The ES is highly competent in the way in which it tackles suggestions for the remediation of contaminated land on the site. It is also particularly strong in identifying the impacts that will arise during and following the development. Issues that are noted as of particular importance are transport, landscaping, and car parking provisions. The ES also includes a lengthy consideration of how these impacts might be mitigated to reduce their environmental impact. One of the most interesting features of the ES is the way in which it tackles tourism and its impacts. The ES notes the types of attractions intended for the ISV and the accommodation and other services to support them. Indeed, it likens the development to,

> an urban holiday village. The intention of the mix is to complement and integrate with other key attractions in the City (Millennium Stadium, Cardiff Castle etc) to consolidate Cardiff's overall appeal as a tourism destination and reinforce sport/leisure related economic activity and employment (Ove Arup 2001).

The tenor of the assessment is to consider the economic benefits of tourism and to ignore any environmental impacts that might arise. The assumption appears to be that urban tourism does not have environmental impacts and therefore they are not worthy of consideration (see Ove Arup 2001). And yet at two levels at least, it is possible to suggest that visitors to the ISV will have environmental impacts and that these may be significant. One is that ISV attractions are intended to complement those in the City (e.g. Millennium Stadium, Cardiff Castle) and those just outside (e.g. Museum of Welsh Life) and will inevitably involve travel to and from these destinations. The ISV will thus accentuate an emerging multi-site visitor experience in Cardiff. Despite the aspirations for the use of public transport between locations, it is likely that there will be a heavy reliance on the private car. Second, visitors to Cardiff will consume resources and generate waste and these will be additional to those of Cardiff residents but will need to be "absorbed" by the local Cardiff environment, its surrounding areas, and beyond.

To assess the additional impact that ISV will have on the Ecological Footprint of Cardiff we must first briefly report on the Cardiff Footprint.

The Cardiff Footprint

Cardiff's Ecological Footprint was 1.7 million global hectares (gha) in 2001 – the year for which the most recent household expenditure data was available at a sub-national level (see Collins et al. 2005 and 2006). This is equivalent to 82 percent of the total land area of Wales (2.1 million hectares). On a per capita basis, the Ecological Footprint of an average Cardiff resident is 5.59 gha per capita, and is greater than the Footprint of an average UK and Welsh resident (5.35 gha/cap and 5.25 gha/cap respectively) (see Table 10.1). The magnitudes of these figures show that the level of consumption by Cardiff residents is currently inequitable as they are using resources more than three times the average "earthshare" of 1.8 gha/cap. In terms of equity, Cardiff residents would need to reduce their ecological demand by 68 percent before they could say they were living sustainably. Table 10.1 below highlights the individual components of the Cardiff Footprint and its similarities and differences to Wales and the UK. (For a fuller account of the Cardiff Ecological Footprint see Collins et al., 2005 and 2006.)

Table 10.1 Ecological footprints of Cardiff, Wales and the UK (2001)

	Cardiff [gha/cap]	Wales [gha/cap]	UK [gha/cap]
Food and drink [a]	1.33	1.29	1.34
Energy	0.99	0.92	0.90
Travel [b]	0.99	0.78	0.72
Capital investment [c]	0.74	0.74	0.74
Consumables	0.67	0.67	0.75
Government [d]	0.41	0.41	0.41
Housing	0.16	0.17	0.18
Services	0.26	0.24	0.32
Holiday activities	0.10	0.10	0.12
Other [e]	-0.03	-0.03	-0.03
Total	**5.59**	**5.25**	**5.34**
Waste	0.81	0.67	0.67

Note: gha = global hectares.

[a] includes catering services.

[b] includes transport services and air travel.

[c] Capital Investment or Gross Fixed Capital Formation (GFCF): Relates principally to investment in tangible fixed assets such as plant and machinery, transport equipment, dwellings and other buildings and structures. However, it also includes investment in intangible fixed assets, improvements to land and also the costs associated with the transfer of assets. The investment relates to assets which are used repeatedly in the production process for more than

one year and as such covers such purchases as: software, mineral exploration and purchases of dairy cattle. The Footprint calculations assume shared responsibility, i.e. equal values for UK and Wales.

d) Includes central and local government. The Footprint calculations assume shared responsibility, i.e. equal values for UK and Wales.

e) includes non-profit institutions serving households, valuables, changes in inventories and overseas tourists in the UK; the latter one leading to an overall negative Footprint.

We can now look at how we might assess the environmental impact of the ISV. The brief review above of the Ecological Footprint data for Cardiff residents provides important clues as to where we might expect tourists to be making significant ecological impacts. So, for example, food and drink, transport, and waste are likely to loom large in a tourist Ecological Footprint as they do for residents. Of course, what this implies is that Cardiff's development strategy will be heightening the pressure on areas where the City's residents are already making significant ecological impacts.

Calculating the Ecological Footprint for ISV Visitors

Since discussions with developers on the physical structure of the ISV site are still at an early stage, we have concentrated on calculating the potential impact of ISV visitors' consumption. As the broad outlines for the development of the ISV are known, we have used this to estimate the ecological pressure (i.e. Footprint) of visitors to the ISV. It is important that the environmental impact of visitors be recognized because so far, in the model of development for the Bay promoted by Cardiff Bay Development Corporation (CBDC) and shared by the Wales Tourist Board (see CBDC 1995) and replicated in the Environmental Statement for the site, visitors are assumed to be economically positive and environmentally benign. However, it is important that we begin to recognize the environmental impacts of tourism and ensure that these impacts become part of the decision-making process. An indication of the scale of the likely environmental impact of the ISV is contained in Table 10.2. Based on information contained in reports supporting the development of the ISV, it is estimated that the development will attract over two million visitors each year. This figure is almost equivalent to one fifth of Cardiff's total visitor figures for 2001.

We have sought to identify the likely ecological impacts of ISV visitors by comparing them with the traditional Cardiff visitor in the following consumption areas: passenger transport, food and drink, energy use, and infrastructure (accommodation establishments), and waste. Table 10.3 provides a summary of the data sources that were used for each of the component areas. Details on how visitor's consumption and their corresponding Ecological Footprints were calculated for each of the areas listed above are fully explained in Collins and Flynn (2005) and here we simply report the results.

Table 10.2 Visitor numbers and days for ISV and Cardiff

	Cardiff [a]	ISV [b]
Visitor numbers per year	10,643,000	2,062,068
Visitor days per year	12,076,000	2,297,055
Average duration of stay per visitor [days]	1.13	1.11

[a] 2001 STEAM Report (Cardiff County Council, 2002. STEAM, the Scarborough Tourism Economic Activity Monitor is a mathematical model used for estimating volume, value, expenditure and basic tourism characteristics. It measures all aspects of tourism, including visitors who stay with friends or relatives and day visitors. STEAM figures are produced annually.

[b] Based on estimates contained in Visitor and Tourist Traffic Estimates Report Final Report (Stevens & Associates, 2001).

Calculating the Ecological Footprint of Cardiff visitors

The consumption patterns and corresponding Ecological Footprint of Cardiff visitors was calculated using a similar methodology and set of assumptions as for ISV visitors. The same data sources were used to provide an estimate for food and drink consumption, energy use, and waste. Visitor travel to Cardiff was estimated using data from the 2001 Cardiff Visitors survey (e.g. visitors' home location and mode of transport used). Travel in Cardiff was estimated using data on visitor numbers at key attractions, mode of transport, and distance from the city center. The Footprint for visitor accommodation was not calculated as there was insufficient detailed data available on categories of accommodation.

The ecological impacts of the traditional Cardiff visitor can now be compared with those who are likely to visit the ISV. Below, we express the Footprint results as all visitors per year and also on a per visitor per day basis. The latter involves calculating the Footprint of all visitors per day and dividing this by the estimated number of visitors at each destination for one year. As the average Cardiff visitor has a longer duration of stay compared to an ISV visitor, presenting the Footprint results per day will allow the Footprint of both visitors can be analyzed for the same period of time (i.e. one day).

Ecological Footprint Results for Cardiff and ISV Visitors

The Ecological Footprints results for both visitor types show that visitors at both destinations can produce a large ecological impact (see Table 10.4). The number of visitors, how they travel to and within their destination, the food and drink they consume, the energy they use, and the wastes that they produce will result in large global ecological impacts. Moreover, those areas of consumption where visitors are likely to have the greatest effect such as transport and food and drink are also those that impact most on the Cardiff resident's Footprint (see Table 10.1).

Table 10.3 Estimated consumption by ISV visitors

Area of consumption	Data source	Calculation notes
Passenger travel (to ISV)	*Visitor and Tourist Traffic Estimates* (Stevens & Associates, 2001) *Cardiff Visitors Survey* (2001)	Estimated using: Visitor demand for 15 facilities and number of journeys per transport mode. Distances travelled to ISV using home location or airport of departure (for overseas visitors).
Passenger travel (at ISV)	*Summary Transport Assessment* (TPK Consulting, 2001) *National Travel Survey* (2004)	Estimated using: Total journeys per mode of transport (weekday and Saturday) based on an event taking place in the arena. Average distances travelled by different modes of transport.
Food and drink	*Cardiff's Ecological Footprint* (Collins et al., 2005)	Estimated using: Quantity and type of food and drink consumed per Cardiff resident per day. Number of meals consumed by visitors at each ISV facility.
Energy use (accommodation establishments)	*"Ecological Footprint Analysis as a tool to assess tourism sustainability"* (Gossling et al., 2002)	Estimated using: Energy use per bed night in each category of accommodation. Total visitor bed nights per category.
Infrastructure (accommodation establishments)	*"Sustainability Rating for Homes – The Ecological Footprint Component"* (Wiedmann et al., 2003)	Estimated using: Average floor area per bed unit for each type of accommodation. Building materials needed for a 2002 Building regulations dwelling.
Waste	*Cardiff's Ecological Footprint* (Collins et al., 2005)	Estimated using: Amount and composition of waste landfilled and recycled per Cardiff resident per day.

Based upon those consumption activities that have been considered so far, the overall Footprint for a Cardiff visitor is considerably larger than that of an ISV visitor. Air travel was responsible for a significant proportion of a Cardiff visitor's travel Footprint. However, as air travel by an ISV visitor may be underestimated in our discussion of the results, we have largely excluded air travel from our discussion because the difference between both visitor types is unrealistic.

When the impacts of each type of visitor are considered, the results show that individual components contribute differently to a visitor's Footprint. For Cardiff and the ISV visitors, travel has the largest impact because both visitor types travel further distances, are more likely to use private transport, and are less inclined to use public transport. Cardiff visitors have a larger Footprint for food and drink because they have more opportunities to eat out in the city. This higher level of consumption is also reflected in Cardiff visitors' Footprint result for waste. Cardiff visitors also have a large Footprint result for energy use. The difference in energy use is because there is more visitor accommodation available in Cardiff.

So, it appears that ISV visitors are likely to have a lower impact than the traditional Cardiff visitor. However, this assumption could be thrown into doubt by changes to mix of developments at the ISV site and to the estimations of the behavior of ISV visitors. For example, if there should be more opportunity to stay at the ISV, then the ISV visitor Ecological Footprint will much more closely mirror that of the Cardiff visitor. From the marketing perspective, increasing the number of visitors who stay overnight is a positive action since it increases spending in the local economy. The philosophy at the ISV development, however, is to increase visitor days by encouraging repeat visits to the facilities. As ISV visitors are more likely to use private transport, especially travel by car and to travel further by car, this would have negative consequences for the Ecological Footprint.

Analysis of the Ecological Footprint of the traditional Cardiff visitor and the ISV visitor has shown that it is a sophisticated tool which can be used to measure the potential impact of a development and identify key environmental pressure points. The Footprint results also indicate how a proposed development, such as that at ISV, can exacerbate the visitor Footprint in Cardiff. However, the Footprint also has the potential to suggest ways in which those pressures might be reduced. For example, if 50 percent of distances travelled by car to the ISV were replaced by public transport, this could reduce the visitors travel Footprint by as much as 12 percent (5,190 global hectares).

Table 10.4 Summary of ecological footprint results for Cardiff and ISV visitor

Component activities	Cardiff visitor			ISV visitor			
	EF/visitor/ day [gha]	% (Incl air)	% (Excl air)	EF/visitor/ day [gha]	% (Incl air)	% (Excl air)
Travel	0.000502	92.3	–	0.000059	77.9	–
(excl air)	0.000043	–	51.1	0.000054	–	76.5
Food	0.000024	4.3	27.7	0.000015	19.7	20.9
Energy	0.000018	3.3	21.2	0.000002	2.4	2.6
Infrastructure	–			0.000001	–	–
Total [a] (incl air)	0.000544	100.0		0.000076	100.0	
Total [a] (excl air)	0.000085		100.0	0.000071		100.0
Total [a] (incl air) (all visitors/yr)	2,111,388			56,896		
Waste	0.000007			0.000007		

Note: EF = Ecological Footprint; gha = global hectare

[a] Infrastructure is excluded from the total footprint figure as the equivalent data for Cardiff was not available.

Conclusions

While the Ecological Footprint can highlight key environmental resource impacts arising from the development of ISV and also give a sense of their scale, on its own it will not change the trajectory of development. The challenge for Cardiff Council and its developers is to put in place strategies which reduce the potential environmental impact of ISV. So, will key actors be "persuaded" to act on the Footprint results?

At one extreme, and a highly unrealistic one, the Footprint results are uncritically accepted and quickly acted upon. At the other extreme, the Footprint data and its advocates are completely ignored. This too is rather unlikely because of the individual and collective commitments that have been made to the exercise in Cardiff. In between these two extremes there is the possibility that the Footprint results for Cardiff and ISV are regarded as credible and offering a baseline against which to measure, in a way that is different to an EIA, the environmental impact of ISV. On this line, environmental data is seen as shedding light on a problem that, to be reduced, will require input from across the Council and from the Council's partners. Another possibility is that the Footprint results for ISV are viewed as telling a bad news story about the environmental pressures arising from tourists and that such data runs counter to a favored development strategy and is therefore to be challenged or marginalized.

Thus, the use of the Footprint results and the tool itself as part of a case to persuade other actors to adopt a more sensitive environmental position must recognize that at least some of those actors will be wedded to more developmental positions, will deploy counter arguments, and will bring to bear their own favored tools. Here, we have to try and make sense of tools (including the Footprint) that will often be promoted as a more rational way of making a decision with the recognition that decisions are not made in a rational way. One of the most stimulating studies of rationality and decision making has been that by Flyvbjerg (1998). He contends that "rationality is context-dependent and that the context of rationality is power" (Flyvbjerg 1998). Power will vary across space and time and be contingent upon social-structural processes and organizational and actor context (Flyvbjerg 1998). These insights suggest the outputs of tools for sustainable decision-making (like the Footprint) may become rationalizations for decisions that are made by powerful actors. In other words, the Footprint results lend weight to existing developmental trajectories rather than challenging them. So while the Footprint should raise challenging questions about the level of resource consumption, the balance of interests at both an official and political level may mean that these are kept to the margins of an organization. At the end of the day, political considerations (no matter how formulated) are likely to be paramount. A key issue for Cardiff Council is whether a new administration elected in the Spring of 2004, and having stronger environmental credentials than its predecessor, will make the push to put the environment closer to the heart of decision making on ISV.

References

B3 Burgess Partnership Limited (2002), *Cardiff International Sports Village Heritage Strategy*, May: B3 Burgess Partnership Limited (Cardiff: Cardiff County Council).

Barrett, J., Cherrett, N., and Birch, R. (2004), 'Exploring the Application of the Ecological Footprint to Sustainable Consumption Policy', *Proceedings of the International Workshop on Driving Forces of and Barriers to Sustainable Consumption* (University of Leeds, UK), available at: <http://www.env.leeds. ac.uk/~hubacek/leeds04/call.htm>, accessed March 2004.

Cardiff Council (2004), *Cardiff Visitors Survey 2001* (Cardiff: Cardiff County Council).

Collins, A. and Flynn, A. (2006), 'A New Perspective on the Environmental Impacts of Planning: a case study of Cardiff's International Sports Village', *Journal of Environmental Policy and Planning*, 7, 277–302.

Collins, A., Flynn, A. and Netherwood, A. (2005), *Reducing Cardiff's' Ecological Footprint – Main Report*. BRASS (Cardiff University, Cardiff: WWF Cymru). Available at: <http://www.walesfootprint.org>, accessed March 2005.

Collins, A., Flynn, A., Wiedmann, T. and Barrett, J. (2006), 'The Environmental Impacts of Consumption at a Subnational Level: The Ecological Footprint of Cardiff', *Journal of Industrial Ecology*, 10:3, 1–16.

Department of Transport (2004), National Travel Survey: 2002. Transport Statistics Bulletin – SB (04) 22 (London: HMSO).

ECOTEC (2001) *Ecological Footprinting*. A Technical Report for the Scientific and Technological Options Assessment (STOA) Panel (EP/IV/STOA/2000/09/03) (March) (Brussels: European Parliament).

Flyvbjerg, B. (1998), *Rationality and Power* (Chicago: University of Chicago Press).

Gössling, S., et al. (2002), 'Ecological Footprint Analysis as a Tool to Assess Tourism Sustainability', *Ecological Economics*, 43, 199–211.

Ove Arup and Partners International Ltd. (2001), *International Sports Village Environment Statement* (December 2001).

Stevens and Associates (2001), *Cardiff International Sports Village Visitor and Tourist Traffic Estimates*. Prepared for Cardiff County Council (December 2001).

TPK Consulting (2001), *Cardiff International Sports Village Summary Transport Assessment*. Prepared for Cardiff County Council (December 2001).

Wackernagel, M., and Rees, W. (1996), *Our Ecological Footprint: Reducing Human Impact on the Earth* (Gabriola Island, BC: New Society Publishers).

Welsh Assembly Government (2000–2001) *The First Sustainable Development Report of the National Assembly for Wales under Section 121(6) of the Government of Wales Act 1998* (Cardiff: Welsh Assembly Government).

Wiedmann, T., Barrett, J. and Cherrett, N. (2003), *Sustainability Rating for Homes – the Ecological Footprint Component* (York: SEI), available at: <http:// regionalsustainability.org>, accessed June 2004.

WWF (2004), *Living Planet Report 2004*, World-Wide Fund for Nature International (WWF), Global Footprint Network, UNEP World Conservation Monitoring Centre. (Gland, Switzerland, WWF). Available at: <http://www.panda.org/livingplanet>.

Chapter 11

Regional Environmental Capacity for Sustainable Growth: A Historical Approach

Mamoru Taniguchi, Hirofumi Abe, and Yoshiro Ono

Introduction

The concept of sustainable development was introduced in 1980 by the publication *World Conservation Strategy* (IUCH 1980) and became widely disseminated after the UN's World Commission on Environment and Development published *Our Common Future* in 1987. The Commission defined the concept as follows: "…sustainable development is development that meets the needs of the present without compromising the ability of future generations to meet their needs" (WCED 1987). While this definition of sustainable development is somewhat anthropocentric, if it is assumed that the future generations are only those of *Homo sapiens*, other authors see sustainability as synonymous with carrying capacity (Healey and Shaw 1993) which applies to any species. *Carrying capacity* is the maximum population that the particular environment or ecosystem can support with the resources available. For example, Beatley (1995) states "… a given ecosystem or environment can sustain a certain animal population and that, beyond that level, overpopulation and species collapse will occur" (Beatley 1995).

While the concept of sustainability is popular and potentially useful, the word is frequently misapplied. One reason may be the lack of a quantitative definition of sustainability. From a regional point of view, the condition required to achieve sustainability is that areas need to be environmentally self-reliant. Therefore, to arrive at a quantitative definition of sustainability, it is necessary to measure the environmental capacity in each region. What numbers can the region support with the resources located within the specific ecosystem? Determining environmental capacity is critical in understanding the region's resources and demands upon these. An assessment of what it would mean for the region to be "self-reliant", or have internal resources sufficient for regional needs, allows the subsequent evaluation of potential growth factors which could impact the environmental load for that region.

This study presents a methodology for the measurement of environmental capacity. The method is applied using real data, and the environmental load for each study region is evaluated. Factors that influence environmental loads are estimated by the model analysis. This methodology is composed of the following three steps:

1. The notion of *sustainable population* is proposed on the basis of rice harvest data converted to a population scale. Rice is a staple in Japan, and its production is much more important than that of bread or meat in the West. During Japan's *Edo* Period (1603–1867) the rice production in each area was measured by the scale "*koku*". The word *koku* itself also referred to the income of feudal lords and warriors.

2. The *sustainable population* in each region is calculated. The *environmental load ratio* in each region is estimated by comparing the present population and the *sustainable population*. If the present population is larger than the *sustainable population*, it is assumed that environmental pressure, or the environmental load, in the region increases.

3. A multiple-regression model is used to investigate factors that affect the difference in the *environmental load ratio* among regions. A variety of factors including political control, infrastructure, natural disasters, and other regional characteristics, are considered.

Assumptions and Data

A simple search of the term "environmental capacity" yields more than 500 Web sites (www.jacses.org 2006). However, few sites refer to measuring regional capacity. Most quantitative research concerning environmental capacity focuses only on counting the numbers of a certain species within a limited narrow biotope space, rather than within a specific region. In order to investigate and measure regional environmental capacity, it is necessary to first develop a method to describe the regional environment.

This research assumes that the beginning of the *Edo* period (1603–1867) in Japan was an example of a sustainable and stable society. At that time, modern technologies such as chemical fertilizers and high-speed transportation systems were not available. People's lives had not been westernized, and there was little opportunity for import and export of goods beyond the local region. Residents of each region had to sustain themselves on the resources available locally. Therefore, the environmental capacity in each region could be estimated as the regional population during this era.

The *Edo* period was the age of feudalism. The social structure of this time was different from that of modern Japan. In each region or *han*, the feudal lord (*daimyo*) was solemnly entrusted to his territory by the reigning Tokugawa *shogun*. The *shogun* was "the hereditary commander of the Japanese army who until 1867 exercised absolute rule under the nominal leadership of the emperor" (http://dictionary.reference.com).

The Tokugawa government or *bakufu* established its headquarters in *Edo*, now known as Tokyo. The Tokugawa shoguns retained direct control over approximately a quarter of the territory and people of Japan. This area was known as the *tenryo* or "heavenly domain". The remaining three-quarters of the country and its people were parceled out among the *daimyo*, feudal lords, for them to rule as their own domains (*han*). The 260 domains or regions varied greatly in size. The official productive capacity of the largest *han* was over five million bushels of rice (1,000,000 *koku*)

(Mason and Caiger 1997). The relationship between the central government and the local authorities was known as the *Baku-Han* system.

Government procedures for tax assessment and collection made the village (*mura*) the basic unit, rather than the individual farmer, and taxes were levied annually in the form of an agreed percentage of the village rice crop. Outside of the villages, within the larger *han* or region, the tax rate may have been somewhere between 30 and 50 percent (Mason and Caiger 1997). Without a high-speed transportation system, the local population was limited to occupation of the *han* and its resources. Therefore, as mentioned previously, the population size of the largest *han* could be viewed as the maximum in terms of the sustainable capacity of the region. The environmental capacity of the *han* provides an appropriate unit for analysis.

As the *Edo* period lasted more than two hundred years, many social conditions shifted with the passing of time. For example, in the era of *Iemitsu Tokugawa*, the third shogun (1623–1651), the *bakufu*'s (government's) control system was at its height. Surveys by tax collectors of rice production for each village were completed until the *Iemitsu* era. Rice is regarded as a staple food in Japan, which means that the level of *koku* indicates the production power of each region. On the other hand, the level of *koku* or rice production in each region was not changed until the end of the *Edo* period. This led to the inconsistency in historical documentation that "in 1841, 48 percent of *bakufu* income came from sources other than agricultural taxes, and half of this was direct merchant levies" (Mason and Caiger 1997).

For the reasons discussed, *sustainable population* is defined on the basis of the data from the middle of the seventeenth century, as the *koku* level and the real production capacity in each region were possibly equal at that time. In this study, the data from 1664 were used for analysis, as the information concerning boundaries among *hans* was also obtained for this year (Kodama 1956).

Many researchers have investigated the Japanese *koku* system (Shirakawabe 2000), but most of these studies have a historical and sociological viewpoint, rather than a quantitative analysis to determine environmental capacity. From a statistical point of view few studies discuss the *koku* system or use data from the *koku* districts as the base for study (Hattori 1997). Additionally, this is the first time that *koku* data has been utilized in environmental investigation.

The Method to Calculate *Sustainable Population*

Sustainable population

Sustainable population is defined as the population maintained by the primitive agricultural processes within the region. Here, the word "primitive" means the cultivation style is not based on modern technology, chemical fertilizers, or a mechanized transportation system. Under these conditions, it is assumed the agricultural product level expresses the real fertility of the region. Resources and technology are not imported from beyond the region's boundaries. There are little or no external human factors influencing production. From this, the figures for rice production at the beginning of the Edo period are the best index to estimate the *sustainable population* in Japan. Based on this idea, the *sustainable population* in each region is defined by the following equation. No. 1:

$$P_i = \alpha \cdot K_i$$

P_i : *sustainable population* in region (*han*) i

α : population that could be maintained by one *koku*

K_i : *koku* level in region i in 1664

It is not easy to estimate an accurate α value, as it may fluctuate under various conditions. To estimate a more accurate α value, it is necessary to adopt different methods for calculation and collection of results. This study uses the following two methods: 1) a calculation based on the total population, and 2) a calculation based on the rice consumption per capita. Two possible α values are calculated by each method. One is the maximum value, and the other is the minimum value. The average α value between the possible maximum value and the possible minimum value is defined as the represented value in each method. The final α value is obtained from the average of the two represented α values calculated by each method.

Calculation of α: Total Population Method
The first calculation method is based on the total population in 1664. The total regional population divided by the total regional *koku* level determines the value α. No. 2:

$$\alpha = \{ Q - \Sigma P_j \} / \Sigma K_i$$

Q : total Japanese population in 1664

P_j : population of the urban area j that did not depend on rice products coming from the specified *han*

The procedure for calculation is composed of five parts:

1. Q is calculated from two original population estimations of 1573–1614 and 1721 (Statistical Bureau 1985, Takashi bonen suisan 2006, and Komiyayama youkaisetsu 2006). The result of the determination of Q is 22,473,790 persons.
2. The population of a highly urbanized area, *Edo (Tokyo)*, *Osaka*, and *Kyoto* (Chandler 1987), should be included as P_j. It is also assumed that people occupying territories run by the Imperial Household, as well as temples and shrines, are also included in this category. As a result, two million people should be excluded from the total population Q. P_j is difficult to estimate accurately as most of the population relied on the agricultural industry in that era. An exclusion of two million, less than 10 percent of the total population, is appropriate for a rough estimation.

3. The total rice production level is calculated as 17.98 million *koku*. This calculation is based on the accurate *koku* level of an individual *han* in 1664 (Editing Committee 2000).
4. Based on this data, the numerical value of α is derived from equation No. 2 as 1.138. On the other hand, not all the rice products in a region were always used by the residents. The highest tax rate for a rice harvest was around 50 percent (Shin-Jinbutu-Ohoraisha 1997). This means that the real numerical value of α should be larger than 1.138. Consequently, it is assumed that the possible maximum value of α could be 2.276, under a 50 percent tax rate, as a calculation from 1.138 × 2. Simultaneously, the possible minimum value of α could be assumed to be 1.138.
5. The average α value between the possible maximum value and the possible minimum value is calculated as (1.138+2.276)/2 = 1.707. From this calculation, 1.707 is considered as the estimated average α value based on the total population method.

Calculation of α: Rice Consumption Method
Though there might be some differences among individuals and eras, this research estimates the value of α from the amount of personal rice consumption. At the present time, rice consumption per capita in Japan is 66kg (Himass 1996). This number is converted into α value of 2.273, as one *koku* equals 150kg. Rice is still the main food source for the modern Japanese, but consumption has decreased considerably from that in the past. Based on these findings, the numerical value 2.273 is assumed to be the possible maximum value of α based on the rice consumption method.

Tracing back the decreasing trend of rice consumption, it is possible to estimate a possible minimum value of α. In the last 30 years, per capita rice consumption in Japan decreased by about 50kg (Himass 1996). Some references (Honnma and Komuro 1987) indicate that rice consumption at the beginning of the Showa era (about 75 years ago) was 164.25kg per capita annually. This number is converted into α value of 0.913, as the possible minimum value based on the rice consumption method.

The average α value between the possible maximum value and the possible minimum value is calculated as (0.913+2.273)/2 = 1.593. From this calculation, 1.593 is considered as the estimated average α value based on the rice consumption method.

Numerical Value of α
The numerical value of α is calculated as the average value of these two numbers derived from these two methods, namely (1.593+1.707)/2 = 1.65. The value 1.65 is adopted as α for the following analysis.

Zones for Our Case Study: *Hans* and Their Boundaries

Three types of *hans* are excluded from this analysis to guarantee more accurate calculation:

- very small *hans* that produced under 50 thousand *koku* in 1964,
- some exceptional *hans* whose *koku* production rates do not express the real production capacity. Tsushima and some northern territories (Nanbu, Tsugaru, and Matsumae) are included in this group, as these regions were not suitable to cultivate rice, and
- the territories of *tenryo*, the Imperial Household, temples and shrines, as accurate details of their *koku* levels were not available.

Consequently, the case study includes 87 Japanese local *hans* throughout a 330 year term. Table 11.1 lists these 87 *hans*, and Figure 11.1 shows their location and boundaries. As the following studies are not based on the point base analysis but on the extent of each *han*'s region, it is necessary to check these boundaries against their modern counterparts to get accurate present population data. When the *han*'s boundary does not match the modern boundary, the population data of the modern region is divided according to the amount or ratio of their area covered by the *han*. National census data from 1995 is used to calculate the present population in each *han*'s region.

Table 11.1 List of han: 87 zones for case study

1	Akita	23	Kawagoe	45	Wakayama	67	Tokushima
2	Senda Ichinoseki	24	Sakura	46	Hikone	68	Takamatsu
3	Yamagata	25	Odawara	47	Zeze	69	Marugame
4	Shiniou	26	Shibata	48	Kishiwada	70	Matsuyama
5	Shounai	27	Nagaoka	49	Izushi	71	Ohzu
6	Yonezawa	28	Takada	50	Akashi	72	Uwajima
7	Aizu	29	Takada	51	Akashi	73	Kohchi
8	Nakamura	30	Toyama	52	Sasayama	74	Kohchi
9	N Honmatu	31	Kanazawa	53	Himeji	75	Kurume
10	M haru	32	Ohno	54	Akou	76	Yanagawa
11	Taira	33	Fukui	55	Yodo	77	Saga
12	Tanakura	34	Obama	56	Kohriyama	78	Karatsu
13	Shirakawa	35	Koufu	57	Tottori	79	Fukuoka
14	Mito	36	Ueda	58	Matsue	80	Hirado
15	Kasama	37	Matsushiro	59	Hamada	81	Kumamoto
16	Kogo	38	Matsumoto	60	Okayama	82	Oka
17	Tatebayashi	39	Nagoya	61	Tsuyama	83	Nkatsu
18	Utsunomiya	40	Kanou	62	Fukuyama	84	Usuki
19	Maebashi	41	Ohgaki	63	Takahashi	85	Agata
20	Takasaki	42	Kuwana	64	Miyoshi	86	Obi
21	Shinobu	43	Kameyama	65	Hiroshima	87	Kagoshima
22	Iwatsuki	44	Anozu	66	Choufu		

Figure 11.1 Territory of each han (1664)

Sustainable population and environmental load

Distribution pattern of sustainable population
The distribution pattern of *sustainable population* is shown in Figure 11.2. As α values are consistent through Japan, the ratios of *sustainable population* among the *hans* are equal to the ratios of *koku*.

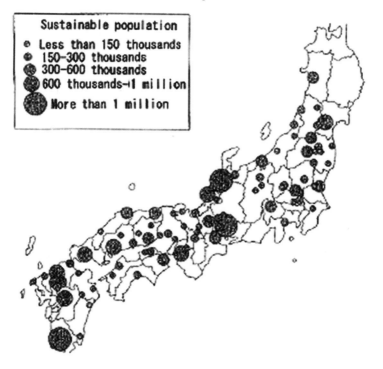

Figure 11.2 Sustainable population in each han

The method to calculate the environmental load ratio
The *environmental load ratio* is defined by the following equation. The term refers
to the comparison between present population and *sustainable population*.

$E_i = P P_i / P_i \times 100\%$

E_i : *Environmental load ratio* at region i

P_i : *Sustainable population* at region i

$P P_i$: Present population at region i

The *environmental load ratio* may be interpreted from two different points of view.
One possibility is that this ratio expresses the existing environmental load level due
to the population level, as the term itself indicates. The other interpretation is that it

indicates regional growth due to modernization and development, or use of resources beyond those obtainable within the region's boundaries.

The pattern of environmental load ratio
Figure 11.3 shows the calculation results of the *environmental load ratio* for each *han*. *Hans* located within the three largest metropolitan areas (*Tokyo, Osaka,* and *Nagoya*) or along the Pacific Ocean tend to show a larger load ratio than other regions. On the other hand, *hans* located along the Sea of Japan tend to show a low load ratio, and some of them are under 100 percent.

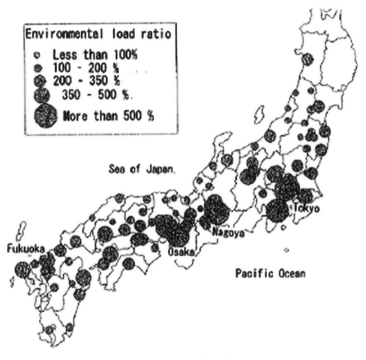

Figure 11.3 Pattern of environmental load ratio

The apparent diversity of *environmental load ratio* for *hans* is influenced by many factors. For more accurate analysis, a multiple-regression model is used to explain environmental load factors.

Factor Analysis of Environmental Load Ratios

The multiple-regression model uses the variables listed in Table 11.2. Figures 11.4–11.6 provide detailed information concerning the variables. The result of the model calibration is shown in Table 11.3. The estimated model is accurate enough to estimate the *environmental load ratio* for each region, as the correlation coefficient is 0.920, and the coefficient of determination adjusted for the degrees of freedom is 0.811. The plus parameter value shows factors causing the environmental load to increase, producing regional population growth. On the other hand, the minus parameter value means that factor contributes to a decreased environmental load, thus leading to regional population decline. This dual meaning of each parameter value embodies the antinomy or paradox of the relationship between "environment" and "growth".

Figure 11.4 Japanese shinkansen lines (high speed rail)

Table 11.2 Explanatory variables for environmental ratio

	Explanatory variables	Remarks
1	Hans that include satellite city in the met. region	Tokyo, Osaka and Nagoya metropolitan regions
2	Hans that include regional center city	Adjusted by number of prefectures of each region
3	Hans that include military city	The divisional headquarters and key navalport
4	Hans that belong to the Kanto region	Kanto region also includes Tokyo metropolitan area
5	Hans with domestic airport	Category II (1) airport that provides domestic service
6	Hans with prefectural capital	Hans such as Matsushiro, Kanou, Chousyuu and Usukiare also included
7	Hans with Shinkansen station	Completed before 1995 (Fig. 11.1)
8	Hans that belong to the Pacific Ocean belt	Hans along the Pacific Ocean that are located between Tokyo and Fukuoka
9	Hans that belong to NT (2) and AIC (3)	Nic (1962) and AIC (1964) are designated to produce local employment (Fig. 11.5)
10	Hans that include war damaged city	War damaged city in which damaged building rate was more than 70 percent
11	Hans that are vulnerable to heavy snowfall	Hans along the Sea of Japan and mountain area (Fig. 11.6)
12	Hans that are excluded from national trunk railroad	Excluding the metropolitan areas
13	Hans that include rival city against regional center city	Lost regional centrality, after Meiji restoration of Kahazawa, Okayama, and Kumamoto)
14	Hans that were damaged by earthquake	Damaged area by the earthquake with more than 1,000 casualties 1995
15	Hans that include rival city against prefecture capital	Hans that have more than 150,000 koku, but without prefecture capital
16	Hans that include flood damaged zone	Damaged area by the flood in which more than 1,000 people died, before 1995. This also includes routinely flooded river junctions, such as Noubiand Yodo

(1) Category II: Classified by National Government as a domestic airport
(2) NIC: New Industrial City
(3) AIC: Area for Industrial Consolidation

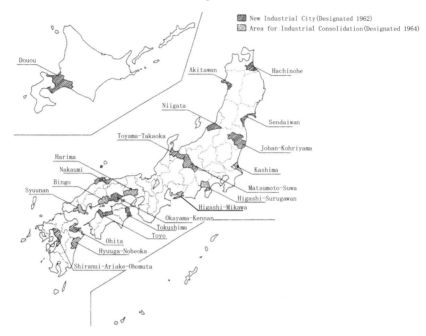

**Figure 11.5 Designation of the new industrial city and
the area for industrial consolidation**

Figure 11.6 Area that belongs to vulnerable heavy snow

Table 11.3 Model parameters for the environmental load factor

	Explanatory variable	Parameter	Standardized parameter	t-value
1	Hans that include satellite city in the metro region	285.3	0.64	8.02
2	Hans that include regional center city	129.3	0.22	3.88
3	Hans that include military cities	107.4	0.21	3.69
4	Hans that belong to the Kanto region	67.5	0.16	2.97
5	Hans with domestic airport	46.6	0.13	1.86
6	Hans with prefecture capital	41.0	0.14	1.95
7	Hans with Shinkansen station	37.2	0.12	1.82
8	Hans that belong to the Pacific Ocean belt	30.4	0.10	1.25
9	Hans that belong to NIC and AIC**	24.6	0.08	1.35
10	Hans that include war damaged city	-31.0	-0.07	-1.19
11	Hans that are vulnerable to heavy snowfall	-60.1	-0.19	-3.21
12	Hans that are excluded from national trunk railroad	-69.9	-0.20	-3.63
13	Hans that include rival cities against regional center city	-94.1	-0.12	-2.3
14	Hans that have been damaged by earthquakes	-104.1	-0.17	-3.09
15	Hans that have a rival city against prefecture capital	-120.2	-0.27	-5.05
16	Hans that include flood damaged zone	-152.8	-0.27	-4.99
	Intercept	188.0	–	11.80
Coefficient of Determination (Adjusted for the Degree of Freedom) 0.811				

Note: **NIC = New Industrial City AIC: Special Area for Industrial Consolidation.

The following findings are indicated from this model:

1. The most influential factor affecting the environmental load ratio is the existence of a satellite city in three metropolitan areas. Large populations that exceed the sustainable population are concentrated in these satellite cities.
2. Regional center cities such as Sendai, Hiroshima, and Fukuoka show a large plus parameter value. The standardized coefficient of the parameter indicates that the effect is about three times larger than that of the New Industrial City and the Special Area for Industrial Consolidation.

3. The development of a military city with divisional headquarters by the time of World War II had a large impact on the environmental load ratio.

4. Factors related to the existence of a domestic airport and a Shinkansen (high-speed rail) terminal produce a plus parameter. However, the fact that the han is not located along national trunk railroad routes leads to a minus parameter.

5. The effects of schemes for local employment development, such as the designation of a New Industrial City and a Special Area for Industrial Consolidation, are not great when compared to more pivotal urban functions.

6. War damage and natural disasters such as earthquakes and floods tend to disturb regional growth. These factors may suppress regional population to under the pre-modern sustainable population.

7. Heavy snowfall reduces the environmental load in the region.

8. If the leading city is very competitive in the region or prefecture, the second or rival city against the leading city tends to suppress its growth. In Japan, the fact that only Tokyo enjoys a complete array of urban functions is often criticized, as this causes an over-concentration of people with consequent urban problems. However, the result of this research shows that mini over-concentration problems have also occurred in many other regions and prefectures in Japan.

Conclusion

The model proposed in this study is based on a very long-term observation (330 years) of regional changes. The authors believe this represents the first attempt to build a regional model from analysis based on such an extended period of time. Obviously, it is not easy to find accurate statistical data describing conditions prevalent 330 years ago. Though it is true that this model provides only a very rough sketch of regional sustainability, it is accurate enough to fulfill the objectives of this preliminary study. Additional research is necessary to explore the impact of other variables related to environmental capacity and sustainable populations. In the past, in pre-modern times, other factors or variables may have played an important part in keeping populations sustainable and thus reducing environmental load for the region, such as the possibility that biological and socio-cultural factors may have decreased birth rates (or increased death rates) in times of low rice harvest; factors that may not be as influential at present. Hopefully, the findings and methodology of this preliminary study will lead to further exploration in this field.

The following summarizes the findings of this study:

1. The notion of sustainable population is proposed based on rice harvest data converted to a population scale. Koku data from 1664 are adopted to calculate the sustainable population, as the beginning of the Edo era was assumed to be a form of sustainable society without modern technologies.

2. The sustainable population in each region is calculated. The environmental load ratio in each region is calculated by comparing the present population and the sustainable population as calculated from the data from the past.

The distribution pattern of ratios indicates that environmental loads tend to become larger at hans along the Pacific Ocean compared to those along the Sea of Japan. The necessity of a model analysis is indicated, as the distribution pattern of ratios is complicated.

3. The multiple-regression model is used to investigate factors affecting the environmental load ratio in each region. A variety of factors including political control, infrastructure, natural disaster, and other regional characters are considered. This model is reliable as the coefficient of determination adjusted for the degrees of freedom is 0.811.

4. The model shows that there are many important factors in explaining the regional environmental load. Areas that include a satellite city, a regional center city, a military city with divisional headquarters, and a prefectural capital have a large impact on the environmental loads. Moreover, the existence of airports, Shinkansen, and industrial policies also causes environmental loads to increase, because these factors support and encourage regional population growth.

5. Natural disasters, war damage, heavy snowfall, and competition between cities tend to decrease the regional environmental load, but these factors also restrict regional growth. From these analyses, some regional conventional handicaps (such as heavy snowfall) could be interpreted as an advantage from the environmental point of view.

For further analysis, it is necessary to evaluate the influence of other crops and products on crops and products influence on α value. Such an evaluation is indispensable in order for this approach to be applicable to other countries. Research within this field is valuable in order to support efforts to articulate effective policies that embody a good balance between concepts which are at times in conflict, such as environmental protection, sustainability, and regional growth.

Acknowledgements

The authors are indebted to Ms. Yoshiko Adachi and Mr. Takumi Kiyooka for their assistance in this study. This research forms a part of the Center of Excellence Program for the 21st Century (Ministry of Education, Culture, Sports, Science and Technology, JAPAN), Strategic Solid Waste Management for Sustainable Society.

Patrick C. Smith, MUP, and Karen Cairns, EdD, both of the University of Louisville, provided valuable editorial assistance. Content, of course, remains the responsibility of the authors.

References

Beatley, T. (1995), 'Planning and Sustainability: The Elements of a New (Improved?) Paradigm', *Journal of Planning Literature*, 9:4, 383–395.

Bradshaw, K. and Bell, C. (1987), *The Capacity to Respond* (Institute of Governmental Studies: University of California at Berkeley).

Chandler, T. (1987), *Four Thousand Years of Urban Growth* (New York: Edwin Mellen Press).

Editing Committee for Japanese History (2000), *Outline of Japanese History* (Yamakawa) (in Japanese).

Government of Japan, Statistical Bureau, Management and Coordination Agency (1985), *The Complete Works of Census, Synthesis of Population Statistics* (Toyo-Keizai) (in Japanese).

Hattori, K. (1997), *Urban Geography for Education* (Kokon-shoin) (in Japanese).

Healey, S. and Shaw, T. (1993), 'Planners, Plans, and Sustainable Development', *Regional Studies*, 27:8, 769–776.

Himass, J. (1996), *Rice, Shougaku-kan* (in Japanese).

Honnma and Komuro (1987), *Rice as Healthy Food* (Cultural Association of Agriculture, Forestry, and Fisheries) (in Japanese).

International Union for Conservation of Nature and National Resources (IUCN) (1980), *World Conservation Strategy: Living resources conservation for sustainable development*.

Japan Center for a Sustainable Environment, <http://www.jacses.org/ecosp/index2.html>.

Kodama, K. (ed.) (1956), *Map of Japanese History* (in Japanese).

Komiyayama Youkaisetsu, *Original Population Estimation for 1721* (in Japanese).

Mason, R. and Caiger, J. (1997), *A History of Japan* (Tokyo: Charles E. Tuttle Company).

Murakami et al. (eds) (2000), *An Encyclopedia of Japanese Kinsei* (Tokyodo-syuppan) (in Japanese).

Roo, G. and Miller, D. (eds) (2000), *Compact Cities and Sustainable Development* (London: Ashgate Publishing).

Shin-Jinbutu-Ohoraisha (1997), *Encyclopedia of Daimyo* (in Japanese).

Shirakawabe, T. (2000), 'Research on the *Koku* System', in Murakami et al.

Takashi Bonsen Suisan, *Original Population Estimation for 1573–1614* (in Japanese).

World Commission on Environment and Development (1987), *Our Common Future* (Oxford University Press).

Chapter 12

Sustainability of Urban Transport: Common Strategies and Individual Actions

Marta Moreno and Juan Pedro Ruiz

Introduction

Air pollution caused by motor transport, traffic congestion, and related safety issues are some of the main challenges to urban sustainability. Cities worldwide must take steps towards sustainable transport systems if overall sustainability is to be achieved. The threats to environmental integrity and public health will be even greater in the future if daily private car use cannot be substantially reduced. However, from the individual's perspective reducing private car use means sacrificing the comfort, perception of personal freedom, and the time savings offered by the car and as a result is much less desirable.

In the management of environmental urban problems it is crucial to examine individual behavior in the given social context since social variables operate as relevant influences on the decisions of individuals. The characterization of these determinants of transportation behavior would provide a good basis to orientate urban policies towards a more efficient management of cities. In this chapter, the problem of urban transport has been examined in the context of the "tragedy of the commons" model through a detailed study of drivers' attitudes and behaviors in Madrid, Spain.

The classic metaphor of the "tragedy of the commons" (Hardin 1968) is useful to model private car usage. Hardin modeled the fate of common pastureland used by herders trying to maximize their private benefits. Key to this model is that the individual herders attempt to maximize their own benefit even while the common good suffers. Individual benefit achieved "rationally" and selfishly, is therefore a function of the increase of privately owned grazing heads, while the cost comes from the resultant overgrazing which is shared by the entire community. In the case of urban traffic the equivalent of the pastureland model is that the urban space and its carrying capacity are goods shared by all the citizens but are used in varying degrees by each person. The overuse of cars results in local scale sustainability problems like air pollution, noise or road congestion, along with global scale effects like climate change. In this chapter we explore the application of this model to the sustainability of urban transport from the results of a comprehensive survey carried out in Madrid, Spain.

Although Hardin's argument, based on the enclosure of the commons in Great Britain, has been shown to be historically inaccurate, its logic is valid when applied to urban situations and global scales. Its inexorability depends upon diverse factors connected with human motivation, rules of management of the commons, and the nature of the natural goods and their response to use.

Traditional cultures across the world have achieved varying degrees of success in addressing the dilemma between individual and group interests at the local level. Some well-known examples include the management of lobster fisheries in central Maine (Acheson 1975) and the pastures of Törbel in the Swiss Alps (Netting 1976). In traditional societies access restrictions and use intensity were monitored and controlled by social mechanisms that emerged in small communities. In groups where everyone knows each other survival necessity promotes cooperation (Olson 1965; Ostrom 1990; McCay 1993). Direct contact with the environment enables shepherds or fishermen to become experts in understanding local carrying capacity and in designing suitable methods to regulate the use of resources. However, daily life in large cities in developed countries is very far from the examples of traditional communal management. For the majority of citizens, survival and well being are not as clearly perceived as being based upon local natural goods, although modern societies are still dependent upon resources as basic as non polluted water and air.

The tragedy of the commons has been presented in psychosocial research as a type of social dilemma, reflecting the conflict of interests between individuals and society. Benefits from cooperative behavior will be evenly distributed unless boycotts from selfish defectors prevail, which is fairly common in real world situations. The dilemma between individual and community priorities applied to urban transport could be represented as the continuation of indiscriminate use of cars and associated threats to sustainability *versus* increasing use of public transport (Van Vugt et al., 1996; Gärling and Stanberg 1997).

It has been suggested that these scenarios of decisions are founded upon three types of values: biospheric, altruistic, and egoistic (Stern et al., 1993). Attitudes oriented towards the protection of the environment and the interest of the community can influence moderation in the use of cars, although, as is usual in the discussion of the complex interaction in attitudes and behavior, their effect may be insufficient. Factors such as the perception of time used in transportation, available alternatives, comfort, prestige, and cost all act as important influences on attitudes and behaviors. Fujii, Gärling and Kitamura (2001), for example, studied how a temporal change of the individual benefits in daily life could encourage cooperation. In their study, a highway was closed temporarily and alternative free use of public transport was offered to the drivers. Among the most interesting effects of this study was a change in the drivers' perception of travel time. Those that made at least two legs of their journey in the public system corrected their overestimation and became more prone to use it in the future.

Psychosocial research has traditionally tried to solve social dilemmas from the assumption of selfishness of the actors concerned. The main three approaches have been: cognitive, focus on the social environment, and behavioral (Lynn and Oldenquist 1986). The *cognitive* position is based on an effort to inform the public of the long term consequences of non-cooperative behavior (Stern 1976). However, there is no clear evidence of the success of informative campaigns in changing consumer habits. Studies such as those of the promotion of measures to counteract greenhouse effect have shown little effect on behaviors (Staats et al., 1999).

The strategy based on the *social environment* includes different measures, all based in the basic human tendency to behave in ways that are socially approved. One example is the promotion of social approval as an external reinforcement of cooperation (Taylor and Moghaddam 1994) trying to make the appropriate behaviors fashionable or prestigious. However, in some cases, this strategy may have a marginal effectiveness when there are so many non-cooperating individuals that they comfortably share the burden of disapproval (Jerdee and Rosen 1974). Because the sense of belonging to a community in itself positively influences caring about the environment (Komorita et al., 1980, Chavis 1990), decrease in the size of the group or increase of communication between its members are other measures adopted in this approach (Dawes et al., 1977; Mosler 1993). Mosler proposed a label of public cooperative commitment from a virtual fisheries model in a computer simulation. The label would identify in the eyes of other participants those persons more committed to cooperative behavior, acting as a means to encourage mutual trust. Cialdini (1984) has shown that the public image acted positively in the case of fuel use reduction campaigns.

The *behavioral* strategy promotes cooperation through a rewards system that reinforces cooperative behaviors and provides penalties for non cooperative ones. One difficulty involved in this strategy is that an external authority is required to decide the "general strategy of coaction" in the terms of Hardin. This, as a non-direct democratic procedure, raises issues of lack of legitimacy, loss of educational effects in stakeholders, and general effectiveness. Other inconvenient aspects of this strategy are the need for monitoring systems on the state of the resource and its use by community members, and the fact that pro-environmental behavior tends to cancel itself when incentives diminish or disappear.

To assess the degree of acceptance of these three models and to understand the social structures influences in transport behavior, we have carried out a survey of attitudes and behavior with drivers of the city of Madrid, Spain. The information collected from the survey and described in this chapter highlights ways in which individual behavior can address a more pro-social interest.

Survey

Sample and procedure

Sampling quotas according to sex and age for each of the 21 districts of the city were established from data from the Spanish Transport Administration (http://www.dgt.es), which show that that in Madrid there are 20 percent more male drivers than female. From this population, persons that use the car at least once a week, regardless of their degree of public transport use, were selected. Data characterizing the sample is presented in Table 12.1. Interviewing was performed by an independent survey company from the 2nd to the 9th of July 2002. A total of 5,459 computer-assisted telephone calls were made to get a sample of 301 valid interviews with a 10 percent quality control.

Table 12.1 Sociodemographic data of the sample

				%				
Sex	male 59.1				female 40.9			
Age	18–24 10.6	25–34 26.2	35–44 24.3		45–54 17.6	55–65 13		> 65 7.6
Studies	non formal 1	primary 17.9		high school 35.9		college 16.3		postgraduate 28.9
Occupation	unemployed 4	employed 76		retired 10.3		housewife 5.6		student 4.4
Income	< 600 € 4.3	600–1200 € 26.2		1200–1800 € 35.6		1800–2400 € 17.6		>2.400 € 16.3

Questionnaire and data processing

The questionnaire used contains 62 items structured in three blocks with Likert-style response format ranging from 1 (completely disagree) to 4 (completely agree). The first of the three blocks comprises 36 items on opinions and attitudes towards several aspects of the traffic. The second block of 17 items focuses on the use profile of public and private transports. The third block includes 9 sociodemographic variables to characterize the sample. Variables included in the three blocks appear in Table 12.2.

Table 12.2 Structure of the questionnaire

Blocks of content	No. of items	Variables
Block I*: Opinions and attitudes	46	air quality deterioration; appropriate car use; degree of trust in others acceptance of limitations to own car use; reasons for voluntary reduction of use; identification of adequate institutions to take decisions in limitations; perceived importance of different control measures
Block II: Use profile of transport	17	walking time to next bus stop or subway station; frequency of use; more frequent itineraries; estimated times of travel; reasons for traveling; advantages perceived for every kind of transport
Block III: Sociodemographic features	9	sex; age; level of studies; income; estimated social level; occupation; profession; size of the family; last vote

Note: * = A subset of this block, consisting of 10 items, includes general environmental attitudes, such as indicators of environmental concern, and more specific measures of attitudes such as pollution evaluation. Both types of atttitudes were chosen from those deemed relevant from a previous survey to the general population (Moreno 2003; Moreno, Corraliza and Ruiz 2005).

Answers to the items of the questionnaire were processed using monovariate statistical functions (anova), regression models, and multivariate analysis (principal components analysis) to provide different complementary images of the study data. In this chapter we present frequencies of individual answers to explain driving patterns and some regression models to predict driving frequency from the described blocks of items.

Results

Psychosocial structure of transport use

We start this section with some basic data from the survey to provide an image of the individual driving patterns. Following this, a general structure of transport use is approached through the regression models predicting driving behavior from the blocks of user profile, opinion, and sociodemographic variables.

30.3 percent of the interviewees do not use, or very occasionally use, public transport. Proximity to the nearest train or subway station or bus stop does not seem a determinant factor because walking distance to them is less than 5 minutes for 75.7 percent of drivers. More frequent public transport distances are between 5 to 20km and less than 5km and more frequent time category per journey is between 20 to 30 minutes. 60.5 percent of the drivers have used public transport for the daily itinerary for which they take usually the car at an equivalent hour. Time employed is longer in this case, although drivers that never have tried that possibility estimate even longer times for their journey.

More frequent driving journeys are not more than 5km (32.4 percent of the drivers) but there is also a considerable percentage (19.1 percent) that travels more than 30 km. Travel is generally used for work reasons: 62.8 percent use the car for this (40.9 percent in the case of public transport). The next reasons in order of importance are: leisure (35.5 percent), shopping (22.6 percent), and studies (7 percent), for which both types of transport are used on the same scale. The most important arguments for choosing the car are comfort (42 percent) and speed (36.5 percent), although these reasons also explain the use of public transport (34.5 percent and 26.6 percent respectively). Money savings (20.3 percent) and avoiding parking (18.6 percent) are the most frequently perceived advantages of the latter.

From this description the typical user profile of the most frequent Madrid driver includes the following features: male; 25 to 65 years old; with relatively high income; using the car for various reasons apart from saving money; driving usually for going to work, and in longer journeys. This profile is confirmed and detailed in the regression models which represent the psychosocial structure of transport use.

Variables from the user profile block are the ones that best predict drivers' behavior; they explain more variance in a global model of regression with all the variables in the survey. The attitudes and opinions block has an intermediate explanatory capacity and the sociodemographic variables block are less predictive. We follow this order to present the regression models for the three blocks of independent variables and the dependent variable driving frequency.

Table 12.3 shows the model for the user profile block. Work as a reason for the journey is the variable with the most weight in the regression model. Next, both with negative coefficients, are weekly frequency of use of public transport and work as the reason for using public transport in daily travel. The model also extracts the variable longest usual travel by car, with less absorbed variance.

Table 12.3 Multiple regression model using user profile variables to predict driving frequency

	ΔR^2	error	β	sig.
Reason for the journey using car: work	0.269	0.096	0.428	0.000
Weekly frequency of public transport use	0.122	0.036	-0.273	0.000
Reason for the journey using public transport: work	0.021	0.109	-0.173	0.001
Longest usual travel by car	0.014	0.033	0.118	0.008

$R = 0.652$; $R^2 = 0.425$; $p < 0.01$

Table 12.4 Multiple regression model using "social dilemma" variables to predict driving frequency

	ΔR^2	error	β	sig.
Willingness to stop using the car one day a week	0.085	0.065	-0.177	0.004
Motive for voluntary car reduction: money saving	0.024	0.061	-0.172	0.003
Who has to take measures: users association	0.021	0.673	0.158	0.004
Opinion: society encourages car use	0.015	0.060	0.136	0.013
Motive for voluntary car reduction: air quality	0.013	0.067	-0.129	0.036
Proposed solution: no answer	0.012	0.121	0.108	0.044

$R = 0.413$; $R^2 = 0.17$; $p < 0.05$

With regards to variables from the attitudes and opinions block (Table 12.4) frequency of driving is best explained, with a negative coefficient, by the unwillingness to stop using the car once a week. The argument offered for using the car with best predictive capacity, also with negative coefficient, is money saving. To complete the significant contributions to the model are the variables: user association as the proposed decision making agent, air quality as a motive for reduction of use (with a negative coefficient) and no answer to proposed solutions of the problems of traffic.

Table 12.5 shows the model for the sociodemographic variables block. Age is a relevant variable in the model: people older than 65 years – and young drivers from 18 to 24, according to the anova analysis of the age categories – are the least frequent drivers. Frequency of car use is also predicted by sex and, with a lower significance level, income. Women and lower-paid individuals are associated with more moderate driving.

Table 12.5 Multiple regression model using sociodemographic variables to predict driving frequency

	ΔR²	error	β	sig.
Age	0.064	0.052	-0.250	0.000
Sex	0.024	0.147	-0.163	0.017
Income	0.018	0.063	0.139	0.044

$R = 0.326$; $R^2 = 0.106$; $p < 0.05$

Perception of the problem of traffic and evaluation of the three strategies

The main objective of this chapter is to evaluate the validity in the Madrid traffic case of the main three strategies from psychosocial studies to solve social dilemmas. To test the *cognitive* hypothesis, a question was included to evaluate the interviewees' opinion of problems caused by the traffic. Local pollution is the most common answer followed by congestion/crowding, stress and health problems as respiratory harm, allergy, and noise (Table 12.6).

Table 12.6 Perceived importance of problems caused by traffic (N=301)

	%
Local pollution	50
Congestion and crowding	15
Stress	9
Respiratory and allergic problems	8.4
Noise	6.5
Global pollution and climate change	5.2
Impact on urban landscape of traffic and roads	2.5
Safety decrease and increase of accidents probability	1.7

On the role of the individual and the community in the *social environment* hypothesis we get some mixed results. 52.8 percent of the drivers do recognize that the car user obtains immediate advantages over the long term common good (the classical enunciation of the tragedy of the commons). But this also means that 46.9 percent do not agree with that statement although 79.4 percent consider that society encourages excessive car use. 54.8 percent perceive that their own personal contribution to the solutions of the problems caused by traffic would be too small, while 76.5 percent agree that Madrid pollution is primarily due to excessive car use by a part of the population. Thus a general result is that the drivers put the responsibility of traffic problems onto other people and not so much themselves (which is common in this kind of studies). There is a feeling of mistrust towards the altruistic behavior of others: 62.4 percent think that problems of traffic and pollution do not get solved because drivers are not willing to change their behavior if they do not see equivalent measures in others.

Intervention in traffic problems as a part of the *behavioral* solution includes limiting private car use. Such eventual limitation is widely rejected by drivers (53.5 percent), but if it were to be applied the majority thinks that polls or official bodies, such as the City Council or Government, should be the relevant mechanisms or bodies to take decisions (Table 12.7).

Table 12.7 Who has to make decisions on possible limitation of car use (N=301)

	%
Polls and community participation	34.2
City Council	32.2
Government	25.3
Public Administration	6.6
Independent specialists	1
Users associations	0.7

Moreover, disposition to voluntarily reduce car use is high (79.4 percent would be willing to stop using the car once a week) and is based both on selfish and altruistic motives. Percentage of agreement varies between 91 percent when the purpose is to protect individual health and 74.4 for economic reasons. Biosphere protection as in natural ecosystems conservation and air quality improvement get intermediate scores (Table 12.8).

**Table 12.8 Average degree of agreement (1–4) with motives
of voluntary reduction of car use (N=301)**

	Average	Standard deviation
Individual health	3.495	0.724
Public health	3.442	0.708
Traffic safety	3.322	0.844
Longer time of transport	3.282	0.896
Ecosystem protection	3.229	0.802
Air quality	3.076	0.930
Economy	3.093	0.944

The degree of acceptance of other control measures is higher when it implies improvement of the public transport networks and efficiency. Drivers also propose to provide information about traffic problems although other items described above show a relevant degree of concern and information. The majority is not so supportive of more compromising measures like the introduction of a label to be shown by moderate drivers or a system of increasing taxes to excessive users (Table 12.9).

**Table 12.9 Average degree of agreement (1–4) on different
measures to control traffic problems (N=301)**

	Average	Standard deviation
Improvement of efficiency of public transport	3.575	0.765
Information about traffic problems	3.040	1.012
Closing city centre to private traffic	2.525	1.173
Label of moderate use of car	2.106	1.018
System of increasing taxes with use of car	1.870	1.039

Discussion and conclusions

Characterization of behavior patterns of drivers and of their attitudes, problems perception, and proposed solutions have allowed us to explore prerequisites for sustainable socio-environmental management in the cities. We have checked the main groups of measures proposed in the literature for social dilemmas: cognitive, social environment and behavioral, and as we discuss here, none of them seems to be able to efficiently influence usual behaviors towards moderate driving when taken alone. A combination of these three measures, in the specific context of each city, could contribute more efficiently to the improvement of traffic management. We would argue that solutions to this conundrum require a global approach with the participation of the actors involved, addressing all the systems affected through an understanding of individual behavior in the social context.

Improvement of information on traffic problems, a component of the *cognitive approach*, is the measure more generally accepted by drivers after the proposition to improve public transport. However, results from the survey show that interviewees are able to identify and arrange the main environmental problems of traffic in a plausible order. Even so, this does not seem strong enough an influence to change their dependence on private cars. They seem to put the burden of responsibility on other drivers and suggest that others should be better informed.

This strategy alone does not seem to be therefore a realistic alternative: a supposed deficit of information is not apparent. Relying on policies based on this proposal could be interpreted as being only a little committed to change as excuses for not addressing costly behavioral changes. Environmental protection can work as a partial motive of the decision to use the car or not, but many others exist depending upon the personal immediate consequences, as the considerations on the employed time, the available alternatives, or the price. Irregardless, a change in the attitudes of the drivers may not be sufficient because those that do not change their habits can take advantage of the situation while the others restrict their use.

Currently several countries are developing programs to increase awareness of transport and environment issues (Environmental European Agency 2001), but these are not always successful in behavioral terms. The real value of public information would show through integration in wider strategies and, for instance, frequent coherent campaigns could be valuable in holding public's attention and promoting acceptation of other complementary measures.

Modification of the *social environment* shows some limitations due to the consideration of car driving as a prestigious conduct and the fact that the reference group, the collective of drivers, is too big and anonymous in big cities for individual contributions to be apparent and appreciated. In the survey we found that drivers clearly perceive the social encouragement of private cars and that they focus responsibility in society as an ideal entity. The majority attributes urban air pollution to overuse of cars by some people and recognizes the need for collective action, but changes in others' behaviors that would facilitate their own are not visible enough.

Large scale social dilemmas, such as the global commons or traffic in a big city, would require a kind of "community trust" which could operate in the absence of interaction with other stakeholders. This confidence is usually developed in small homogeneous groups rather than in complex present day societies and it is the basis of the traditional rules as solutions to local commons deterioration. Results of the study confirm that individual action only becomes meaningful within a common strategy, and they also indicate that the main proposed approaches have fundamental shortcomings.

In a typical manifestation of the tragedy of the commons model, individual marginal advantages are bigger than the inconveniences shared by the community thus resulting in unsustainable car use. According to Everett and Watson's (1987) hypothesis people do not spot harmful environmental behavior unless the benefits they obtain from it are cancelled.

In our study, the main advantages of car use are perceived comfort and speed, the same indicated for public transport. This, and also the proximity to public transport stops and stations, is different to Everett and Watson's study but the relative advantageous situation does not seem to influence decisively the behavior of our sample: 30 percent of the drivers never or very seldom use public transport. This is the case even if they estimate that it takes them more time to travel daily by car, although (as in the study by Fujii et al., 2001) drivers that have not had the opportunity to compare both types of transport underestimate the speed of public transport, whereas money savings and avoiding the need for parking are the main advantages of public transport.

There seems to be more than a rational evaluation of costs and benefits, even at the individual level, as social environment clearly encourages car use through prevalent values. Madrid seems to have a public transportation system offering considerable advantages which are appreciated by drivers. Even so, other perceived benefits and the prestigious image of the use of the car must be weighting more in the public's mind, as figures of the car market and statistics of daily traffic show.

As for the *behavioral* approach, we cannot expect that the process for modifying behaviors could be spontaneously started. Madrid drivers do not trust altruism to solve social problems and measures like use limitations, taxes or labels for moderate driving get little support. Although limitation of driving is widely rejected, the majority of interviewees think that the stakeholders' decision would be more appropriate in this regard than the imposition of an external authority.

This debate falls into the classic dialectics Hardin-Ostrom (Hardin 1968; Ostrom 1990) about the optimal mechanism for controlling common goods management: authority *versus* elaboration of norms by the collective through community participation. We have to take also into account traps resulting from inadequately planned limitation measures. For example, in the case of Athens, limitation of use of cars certain days of the week according to plate numbers has resulted in people widely acquiring a second car to overcome the prohibition (Ispikoudis 2004). The battle of interests of the car industry and other actors involved must be considered from a wider perspective of social and environmental protection. Thus decisions cannot be left, as opposed to some results in the survey, in the hands of drivers, but must be taken by the community as a whole and local authorities as experience in other analogous social debates, such as smoking limitations, shows.

The stated disposition to reduce own use must be taken cautiously because its supporters are mainly partial users of public transport, who already use the car less frequently. This is another important implication of the study: unequal behavior of the different users. The majority of environmental attitudes surveys indicate than younger people and women are more pro-environmental and more prone to reduce driving frequency (Meyer 1999; Matthies et al., 2002). Income level appears as a determinant factor also in car use. So we can say that the problems caused by traffic come mainly from certain categories of drivers and a change in their behavior would have a significant impact. This applies particularly to journeys for working reasons of more affluent drivers and these should be the use and users requiring most attention.

An effective solution for integrating this set of proposals would imply some degree of transformation of traffic policies to a more manageable "traditional common" situation. In market transactions, buyers pay the value of the good they acquire but not usually the externalities involved, which affect the biosphere and present and future human generations. In this sense current economic measures do not capture properly the real environmental impact of different commercial products and services. Although there is a dynamic debate on how to determine the "correct price" of goods such as clean air, biodiversity, landscape, etc. (Cropper and Oates 1992), consumption is still accounted for in economic not in environmental and social units.

For transforming these complex situations in a more solvable traditional commons problem, the assessment of the state of environmental degradation should be carried out by scientific/technical independent bodies, also paying attention at this stage to relevant community participation. This would be necessary to avoid interested, over-optimistic views on the part of drivers, which, as the study shows, are likely to occur. From the results of the study, we propose that processes of community participation –including citizens, both drivers and non-drivers, local authorities and experts– are the best candidates for substituting the external controlling authority advocated in the classical model.

To properly integrate environmental and social considerations in the formulation of transport and urbanism policies, some specific measures have been proposed and tried with different degrees of success. Between these we could mention: development and promotion of eco-efficient technologies; application of strategic environmental impact assessment at regional and national levels; coordination of land planning, urbanism and transport infrastructure administrations and actors; and, most importantly, internalization of marginal social and environmental costs through a policy of "fair and efficient prices".

From this technical diagnosis and definition of goals to achieve, a stakeholders' decision-making process would take place in the form of an open social debate for specific actions. As regards these measures it seems that the three strategies discussed above should be discussed and tried out in different steps of plans of sustainable traffic management.

This integrated participatory approach, on the scale of big cities, would also be useful for its educational value towards real world management of very complex global commons issues, such as climate change. The importance and urgency of dealing with this problem on an international scale cannot be overstated, particularly after the news of 2005 having been the year with the hottest global temperature, the lesser extension of the Artic ice chap and the highest number of tropical storms on record.

References

Acheson, J.M. (1975), 'The Lobster Fiefs: Economic and Ecological Effects of Territoriality in the Maine Lobster Industry', *Human Ecology*, 3, 183–207.

Chavis, D. (1990), 'Sense of Community in the Urban Environment: A Catalyst for Participation and Community Development', *American Journal of Community Psychology*, 18:1, 55–81.

Cialdini, R. (1984), *Influence: Science and Practice* (Glenview, IL: Scott, Foresman).

Cropper, M. and Oates, W. (1992), 'Environment Economics: A survey', *Journal of Economic Literature*, 30, 675–704.

Dawes, R., et al. (1977), 'Behavior, Communication and Assumptions about Other People's Behavior in a Commons Dilemma Situation', *Journal of Personality and Social Psychology*, 35, 1–11.

Environmental European Agency (2001), *TERM, 2001: Indicators Tracking Transport and Environment Integration in the European Union* (Luxemburg).

Everett, P. and Watson, B. (1987), 'Psychological Contributions to Transportation', in *Handbook of Environmental Psychology*, Vol. 2 (New York: John Wiley).

Fujii, S., et al. (2001), 'Changes in Drivers' Perceptions and use of Public Transport During a Freeway Closure. Effects on Temporary Structural Change on Cooperation in a Real-life Social Dilemma', *Environment and Behavior*, 33, 796–808.

Gärling, T. and Sandberg, L. (1997), 'A Commons-dilemma Approach to Household's Intentions to Change their Travel Behavior', in *Understanding Travel Behavior in an Era of Change* (Oxford: Pergamon).

Hardin, G. (1968), 'The Tragedy of the Commons', *Science*, 662, 1243–1248.

Ispikoudis, I. (2004), Personal Communication.

Jerdee, T. and Rosen, B. (1974), 'Effects of Opportunity to Communicate and Visibility of Individual Decisions on Behavior in the Common Interest', *Journal of Applied Psychology*, 59, 712–716.

Komorita, S., et al. (1980), 'Cooperative Choice in the N-person Dilemma Situation', *Journal of Personality and Social Psychology*, 38, 504–516.

Lynn, M. and Oldenquist, A. (1986), 'Egoistic and No Egoistic Motives in Social Dilemmas', *American Psychologist*, 41:5, 529–534.

Matthies, E., et al. (2002), 'Travel Mode Choice of Women. The Result of Limitation Ecological Norm, or Weak Habit', *Environment and Behavior*, 34, 163–177.

McCay, B. (1993), 'The Meeting on Property Rights and the Performance of Natural Resource Systems', *Management Regimes* (Stockholm: The Baijer Institute).

Meyer, H. (1999), *Quantitative and Qualitative Aspects of the Mobility of Women in the Example City of Zurich* (Rüegger, Switzerland: ChurZürich).

Moreno, M. (2003), *La Imagen Social de la Crisis Ecológica. Actitudes, Dilemas y Conductas Ambientales: de Internet a la Ciudad de Madrid*. PhD Dissertation, Departments of Biology and Social Psychology, Autónoma University of Madrid.

Moreno, M., et al. (2005), 'Escala de Actitudes Ambientales Hacia Problemas Específicos', *Psicothema*, 17:3, 502–508.

Mosler, H. (1993), 'Self-dissemination of Environmentally-responsible Behavior: the Influence of Trust in a Commons Dilemma Game', *Journal of Environmental Psychology*, 13, 111–123.

Netting, R. (1976), 'What Alpine Peasants have in Common: Observations on Communal Tenure in a Swiss village', *Human Ecology*, 4, 135–146.

Olson, M. (1965), *The Logic of Collective Action* (Cambridge: Harvard University Press).

Ostrom, E. (1990), *Governing the Commons: The Evolution of Institutions for Collective Action* (Cambridge: Cambridge University Press).

Stern, P. (1976), 'Effect of Incentives and Education on Resource Conservation Decisions in a Simulated Common Dilemma', *Journal of Personality and Social Psychology*, 34, 1285–1292.

Stern, P., et al. (1993), 'Value Orientations, Gender, and Environmental Concern', *Environment and Behavior*, 25, 322–348.

Staats, H.J., Midden, C.J.H. and Wit, A.P. (1999), *The Social Dilemma of the Greenhouse Effect; Strategies of Influencing the Public* (Unpublished manuscript).

Taylor, D. and Mogahaddam, F. (1994), *Theories of Intergroup Relations: International Social Psychological Perspectives* (Westport, CT: Praeger).

Van Vugt, M., et al. (1996), 'Commuting by Car or Public Transportation? A Social Dilemma Analysis of Travel Mode Judgments', *European Journal of Social Psychology*, 26, 373–395.

Chapter 13

Mobile Vendors: Persistence of Local Culture in the Changing Global Economy of Bangkok

Kasama Polakit and Davisi Boontharm

Introduction

Official urban planning in Thailand has long been seen as very loose and, in many ways, problematic. Thai urban planning practices tend to approach social and economic aspects of the city at a macro level. This results in a better economic climate for large-scale private developments as opposed to local, social, and economic activities at neighborhood levels. In Bangkok, most of these large scale urban developments are the result of global influences which help facilitate modern metropolitan lifestyles. However, the everyday reality for the city's inhabitants is the prevalence of a multiplicity of trading activities found throughout the metropolitan area in the form of traditional trade, street- and canal- based vendors. These activities best reflect the local culture of the city (Davisi 2001).

The urban ecology of Bangkok is composed of two systems, formal and informal, in both the economy and the built form.[1] Municipal bureaucracy often sees the informal trading activities as less important than the formal ones and labels them as disordered, chaotic, dirty, poor, eyesores, unwanted, or even illegal. Although these activities constitute a significant part in everyday life of the residents of Bangkok they are hardly ever counted as a legitimate component of the Thai economy, or even of society. Moreover, their important role in providing job opportunities for the poor and the disadvantaged has never been officially recognized (Chomlada 1991).[2]

This chapter is based upon research projects of the authors conducted between 1999 and 2002. Data collection included a historical study, field observations, and informal interviews with a focus on the historical background of commercial patterns and the mobile vending activities from the past to the present-day. This examination shows how mobile vending has persisted and sustained amidst the

---

1   According to ILO (International Labor Organization) informal sector is defined by these following characteristics: ease of entry, reliance on domestic natural resources, family ownership of enterprises, small scale operation, labor intensive and adaptive technology, skills acquired outside the formal school system, unregulated and competitive markets.

2   Statistic data (Chomlada 1991) show the number of vendors arrested each year, reflecting the negative attitude of the government policy towards street vending activities (see more detail in Chomlada 1991: 1–2).

evolving dynamics of a global economy that has been imposed upon the Bangkok urban environment over time. We also investigate various forms of the present-day mobile vending activities and ways in which they function in everyday urban space, in particular in relation to urban morphology of Bangkok.

The chapter is divided into four sections. The first section explains the stages of urban development of Bangkok by focusing upon the relationships between emerging patterns of commercial space and mobile vending activities and the evolution of urban form. The second section describes ways in which the typology of mobile vending corresponds to the present-day urban spatial structure of Bangkok. The patterns of social and spatial practices of mobile vending activities as revealed in everyday urban public space are discussed in the third section and finally conclusions are drawn in the fourth section.

The Patterns of Commercial Space and Evolution of Urban Form

The patterns of commercial space in Bangkok can be described through the process of urban development which involves two different trading systems: the local and regional system and the international trade system. Both systems have influenced the ways in which the commercial quarters in the city have been structured and combined, thus, in part shaping and transforming the urban morphology of Bangkok. The city's urban structure is composed of two main systems: water and land.[3] Originally, the morphology of Bangkok emerged from an intricate network of natural and constructed waterways. These waterways acted as "liquid streets". Over the latter part of the twentieth century, much of this water network has been overlaid and displaced by roads.

The process of urban development of Bangkok can be generally divided into four stages chronologically; however, each stage overlaps, and none of them has completely superseded the previous one (Cohen 1985; Kasama 2004). The first stage began in 1782 when Bangkok, a village along a waterway, was established to be the capital city of Siam (the former name of Thailand). The beginning of the second stage was marked by the shift from water-based settlement to land-based developments in 1857, when a new urban element, the "Western Street", was first introduced, and was subsequently followed by tramways and railway lines. The third stage began after WWII and accelerated in the 1960s when Bangkok primarily developed industrial activities and modern ways of living. The fourth stage has been unfolding since the 1980s, when capitalism and globalization began to saturate the capital city.

---

3   Covering around 1569km[2], with a population over 8 million, excluding transients and commuters from adjacent provinces, Bangkok is situated on a flood plain of the Chaophraya River before it enters the sea at the Gulf of Thailand, and is only 1–1.50 meter higher than the mean sea level.

1782: Bangkok as Water-based Settlements

More two hundred years ago most people in Bangkok lived an agrarian lifestyle along intricate networks of waterways. Water was their source of life. The waterways not only facilitated everyday life, agricultural activities, trading activities, and cultural and spiritual beliefs, but they also provided the primary means of transportation and communication, lacing many local communities together. Generally, these settlements were laid out densely along the waterways. Behind them were situated orchards, then rice fields followed by the open fields and, finally, the forest (Pusadee and Manop 1982). While the main water arteries played an important part as the city-wide network and regional linkages, the hierarchical sub-system of water network served the daily needs of local people, and connected their homes and agricultural land with the outside world.

Dwellings of that period could be divided into two main types, floating and fixed (Sternstein 1982). The fixed types were generally made of wood and built on stilts attached to the edge of the land; the floating habitations were a traditional Thai dwelling resting on bamboo rafts. Some of the floating types were shop-houses, a mixed use typology of residential and commercial spaces. The mobile floating types were often used for commercial purposes (Sombat 2001), while the fixed ones usually functioned as residences, with agricultural areas in the rear (Karnjanarkaphan 1997, 1999).

Trading and exchange of goods also played an important role in agrarian village life. Two main types of marketplaces in this early period of Bangkok were land markets and floating markets (Kiet et al., 1982). Because the land marketplaces relied on the waterways for conveying and loading goods, they were often arranged in the areas close to the piers and boat-landings, where the land system met the waterways. The temple grounds and the village grounds were also used as periodic land marketplaces where temporary stalls were assembled and mobile vendors gathered temporarily transforming the ground and pathways into commercial space. The floating markets were generally located at the junctions of the crisscrossed waterways. Using boats as mobile commercial spaces, canal vendors carried and sold everyday household goods, pre-industrial artisan, and agricultural products along water circuitry. When many of them gathered together at a specified time, usually very early in the morning, they transformed a waterway, which was normally used for transportation into a transitory floating market. The large floating markets generally took place at the intersection of the main water arteries where floating shop-houses would be stationed. The smaller ones were often found at the junctions of, and along the tributary waterways.

1857: From Water-based Settlements to Land-based Development

During this period, the Choaphaya River, the main river running through the heart of Bangkok and connecting the city with the sea to the south, played a crucial role as a gateway for maritime trade. The river strengthened the role of the capital city as a center of international and regional markets. For local commercial patterns the construction of the canal networks interlinked with the existing natural ones was a common traditional practice in the urban development process of Bangkok (Piyanart et al., 1982). In 1857, as a consequence of the British Bowring Treaty in 1855, the first sign of a formal land-based development had been introduced in Bangkok. It was a Western street, wide enough for vehicles and appropriate for international commercial patterns under the colonial influences, connecting the port with the city (Nid 1982). This was then followed by the construction of railway lines and tramways.

Within the city proper most streets were laid upon the existing networks of pedestrian paths which were previously narrow and often flooded (Naengnoi et al., 1991; Nid 1982). The city configuration started to evolve from one which lined the waterways towards one that lined the roads, which soon became the principal axis of urban development. Bangkok was transformed to present the modern face of Siam, and modernization through Westernization became a new language of civilization (Jumsai 1997).

Around forty years after the land-based development began at the turn of the twentieth century Bangkok began to subsume the existing water-based settlements (see Figures 13.1 and 13.2). The function of waterways as the main arteries for communication and transportation was gradually replaced by roads (Korff 1992). Boats and elephants were increasingly substituted for horse carts, rickshaws, trams, trains and, later, automobiles. At this early stage, although many new roads were constructed, the everyday life of the commoners was still based largely on water transport and local trade, mobile street and canal vendors, and traditional marketplaces. Horse carriages were used mainly by the elites, rich merchants, and Westerners whose lifestyles were based more on international trade culture than on local tradition.

Bangkok's urban environment at the turn of the century

Khlong Somtet, Bangkok (Siam).

Figure 13.1 A water-based settlement outside of the city wall
Source: Kasama Polakit's old postcard collection.

Figure 13.2 Land-based development dominated the areas inside the city wall
Source: Kasama Polakit's old postcard collection.

Another form of land-based urban structure in Bangkok was alleyways, locally called *trok*. Troks are snake-like capillary walkways with buildings on both sides and are often only wide enough for one to two people to walk. Their width varied from approximately 0.60m to 3m, and they were either through-linkages or dead ends. These pedestrian paths laced local communities together and functioned as a subsystem connecting the communities to the main routes of the city, both the water and the land networks. Usually, the alleyways were provided by the communities and often found in dense urban areas of land-based settlements. Some were concentrated around the nodal activity areas, such as local marketplaces and religion compounds. At the beginning of the 20th century, physical boundaries of local neighborhoods became more clearly defined by the cutting of the new roads, which began to encircle the old settlements (Askew 1993a). This resulted in formation of urban blocks with local neighborhood and some agricultural areas inside (see Figure 13.3). The roads were straight, and at their junctions new commercial areas sprang up in a similar way to the markets located at the crossing points of waterways (Bubpanard 1982; Tomosugi 1991). This process produced a new physical configuration, enclosed *trok* neighborhoods (Askew 1994b).

In 1861 the first generation of shop-houses in Bangkok was constructed in a reinterpreted style derived from Penang and Singapore (Naengnoi 1996; Nid 1982). The development of shop-houses, two-story row houses consisting of four-meter-wide units along the sides of new roads, soon became normal practice.

Shop-houses could be found in both strip-like and compound forms. The strip frontages of large plots of land were subdivided to accommodate new shop-houses, with four-meter-wide access to the existing houses behind. Conversely, in some cases entire plots of land were developed as a commercial compound (Naengnoi et al., 1991). Catering to a new lifestyle which was dictated by international trade, these shop-houses were occupied by new activities such as jewelry shops, banks, publishing companies, department stores, tailor shops, furniture shops, and various other types of commercial activity. Despite their growth from seeds of international influence, the shop-houses at that time fit reasonably well into the commercial purpose of the city and local ways of life. As they were small sized and multi-functional, accommodating mixed commercial and residential activities, and highly flexible for physical and functional adaptation, the new typology experienced ever-increasing popularity (Santi 1978). The shop-houses became a symbol of urban development and have characterized the urban environment of Bangkok ever since (Naengnoi et al., 1991; Santi 1978).

Towards the end of the 1920s, local marketplaces started to move from floating along the waterways to being more stabilized on land, and movable stalls become more sedentary. During the 1940s, some shop-houses combined with local marketplaces and other kinds of entertainment activities, such as theatres, thus producing the first generation of commercial centers in Bangkok (Davisi 2001).

After WWII: Bangkok as a Modern City

During the 1950s, most houseboats disappeared from the waterscapes of Bangkok as the government cleared all the waterways (Sombat 1998, 2001). However, this regulation was not fully enforced to the canal vendors and floating markets, as they remained necessary in the areas which were inaccessible to the land-based system. Waterway networks and agrarian lifestyles were increasingly perceived as something out of date, whereas roads and land-based development presented an image of modernity and progress, introducing a modern automobile-oriented way of life. During the 1960s the government policy of modernization was generally tied to large-scale development, thus cooperating with overseas capital and private funds as a powerful mechanism for "growth" (O'Connor 1989). The idea of "development" was materialized by the state through overseas aid for the construction of the city's infrastructure (Phasuk and Baker 1997). In this manner, the government acted as a conduit of private overseas capital, while private developments played a principal role in transformation of urban environment of Bangkok. The process started at a relatively slow pace in the 1950s, but accelerated markedly during the 1960s (Askew 1994a). As a result of the application of land-based transportation technology and land speculation, this rapid urban development process transformed a substantial amount of agricultural land, rice fields and orchards into suburban areas of sprawling modern shop-houses and housing estates (Askew 2002; Durand-Lasserve 1980). The existing settlements were laced together by the network of waterways, with rice fields and agricultural activities in the urban fringe, and were subsumed in the expansion of modern Bangkok driven by a culturally alien market economy.

Without strict regulations on land-use, modern Bangkok duplicated the traditional pattern of mixed-use function and lineal development along main arteries (Askew 1993b). The difference from the past, however, was the inhabitants' way of life when the development of Bangkok geared towards industrial activities and modern automobile-oriented ways of living. This change resulted in the dramatic transformation of the urban form of Bangkok. The trams, pedaled tricycles, bicycles, and mobile street vendors were perceived as traffic obstructions and they were banned from the main streets during the mid 1960s. The last tramway was removed in 1968. Figure 13.3 shows a picture of street life in a main street of Bangkok before the regulation in the use of the main streets was enforced.

**Figure 13.3 Mobile vendors were a part of the Bangkok street scene
until the 1960s**
Source: Kasama Polakit's old postcard collection.

During the 1960s the new sub-system of the road network or laneways called the *soi* appeared. Some laneways were built by the state, branching out from the main roads; others were initiated by private developments and connected with public streets. Generally, these laneways were straight and wider than the snake-like pedestrian paths as they were developed when automobiles became a part of everyday city life. Physically, some of these laneways were not different from the major roads, particularly when they functioned as contributors to the city-wide vehicular network (Cohen 1985).

Urban blocks in Bangkok enclosed by the main roads were generally laced by the network of sub-systems, laneways, and alleyways. If one travels from the old part of the city towards the urban fringe, urban blocks become larger. Very little public transport operated inside these blocks. Within a relatively large block, local systems such as minibuses operated, linking the places within the block itself and connecting them with the main streets (Cohen 1985). Along the lines and at the junctions of the laneways within the block was often found a "neighborhood business strip" usually consisting of small shops, medical services, and a market for fresh food, catering to the basic needs of the locals living in the laneway communities (Bubpanard 1982). Local marketplaces, comprised of food stalls and mobile vendors, generally took place at the mouth of the laneways, where the sub-system of the inner block joined the main streets (Kiet et al., 1982).

The development of modern shop-houses along the main streets went hand in hand with the "ribbon development" characterized by their pattern of growth (Cohen 1985) Acting as street walls, these modern shop-houses of three to four stories allowed higher density and were a mainstream mixed-use urban development which could gain a good benefit from the least amount of land (Askew 1994a). Some shop-houses replaced the old ones, some emerged as infill development, and some were developed from the big plots of land to form mixed-use compounds of shopping centers, with a core attraction such as marketplaces, cinemas, and hotels (Cohen 1985; Kiet et al., 1982). Some of these developments lined the main streets and some penetrated into neighborhoods through the sub-systems of laneways.

The transition from the 1960s to the 1970s was also seen in the change from a relatively compact city confined in a settled area, to an automobile and road-based city, displacing the former canal-based infrastructure (Askew 1993b), along with a substantial increase in the number of private cars (Sternstein 1982). Modern housing estates and department stores, affordable to the middle class, became a signifier of the modern lifestyle in Bangkok.

As the primary city of Thailand, Bangkok has attracted migrants from other parts of the country, both for job opportunities and for higher education. Nomadic vending and servicing has become the way in which life could be sustained within this big and complex city. In modern Bangkok the new roads became wider, while the lot size of the private developments became larger. The pace of change was even faster, as Bangkok became transformed into a global city through the flux and flow of global economic capital.

1980s: Bangkok as a Global City

The fourth stage of urban development in Bangkok started in the 1980s when globalization, marked by the influx of footloose overseas investment, saturated the capital city. This period could be seen as a continuation of the third stage, but in a more explosive and massive way. An attempt to become a successful Newly Industrialized Country (NIC) in the early 1990s, which focused on drawing overseas capital into the country, led Bangkok to present itself in such a way as to attract foreign investment. The economic crisis in 1997 made it easier for global investments to gain control over local businesses.

Figure 13.4 shows a picture of Silom, a major international business district, which represents an image of Bangkok as a global city, with the concentration of high-rise buildings such as corporate towers and condominiums, a series of public arts and mass transit systems, both elevated and underground. By looking closely at the street level of the area, this international district has remained localized by local culture of mobile trading activities.

Bangkok as a global city

Figure 13.4 Silom urban spectacle presenting a global face of Bangkok
Source: Photograph by Kasama Polakit, 2001.

Bangkok is now a global city. The city is becoming more homogeneous, moving towards homogenization in its appearance much like most large cities all over the globe (Korff 1996). However, globalization also has specific local effects, and should be seen as a collection of very complex and diverse processes, not a single universal one simply labeled as Westernization or Americanization (Korff 1996). An important characteristics of the urban development of Thailand is that "national integration is based on a center which itself is increasingly integrated into a global network" (Korff 1996).

At the end of the 1980s Bangkok was the epicenter of the economic boom in Thailand, and this was manifested in its urban environments. Flyovers and expressways, a number of modern skyscrapers, shopping complexes, office and apartment buildings, and gated housing estates often reflected the latest fashion in post-modern architecture (Korff 1992). In addition, the trans-national retail companies and franchise businesses marked a change in the pattern of consumption in everyday life.

Figure 13.5 Along the street of Silom: local street vendors
Source: Photograph by Kasama Polakit, 2001.

The weakness of the state in regulating development facilitated the exaggerated power of the private sector in shaping the urban environment of Bangkok (Askew 1993b). Driven by the market economy, in the early 1990s the urban development in Bangkok exploded both horizontally and vertically and has led to more spatial and social seclusion of urban space. The changes in traditional patterns of consumption, lifestyle, rhythm of urban life and the increase in development in the car-oriented suburbs encouraged convenience, or one-stop shopping (Askew 1993b). The hyper-markets, usually run by transnational companies, soon became centers of urban life, physically and socially, in particular on the urban fringe.

As these new markets offered much lower prices, the local supermarkets, including the neighborhood convenience stores, were forced to compete. Moreover, global franchised convenience stores started to flourish in highly flexible shop-houses, operating 24 hours a day, 7 days a week within the comfort of air-conditioning. They have been gradually replacing old style local neighborhood shops.

The present-day urban environment of Bangkok can be seen as co-existence of overlapping layers of different stages of urban development, in which the latter stage has never completely superseded the former one. As a consequence, the present-day commercial patterns in Bangkok are composed of diverse spaces of various scales, ranging from transnational hyper-markets, huge shopping complexes, shopping malls and department stores, supermarkets, transnational and local convenience stores, to local marketplaces, shop-houses, tiny movable stalls, and floating shop-boats. Likewise, the urban form of Bangkok also consists of various kinds of hierarchical path systems, which include the major road networks and the sub-system networks of laneways, pedestrian paths, and waterways. This hierarchical street structure, in part, regulates the forms and types of trade through accessibility. In the next section, we will investigate and illustrate various forms of the mobile vending activities found in the everyday urban space of Bangkok.

The Typology of the Present-day Bangkok Mobile Vendors

Like small boats moving along waterways in the past, the present-day mobile vendors adapt their activities to be compatible with various forms of modern transport technology and continue to move along the network of street and waterway of Bangkok. The types of mobile vending activities can be categorized by the use of different means of mobility in response to the hierarchical street structure of the city. This hierarchical street network can be divided into two main systems: the city-wide system and the neighborhood system. The city-wide networks, the main streets, and the Chaophraya River are accessible by public transports, and they contribute to large-scale urban developments driven by the global or international market economy. The use of the main streets and their sidewalks are strictly controlled by the authorities. Behind the main streets, inside the city blocks, the neighborhoods are interconnected by the sub-system of labyrinth-like laneways and alleyways, and in some areas, still surviving water networks. With a smaller scale of urban development, lack of public transport services, and less official control in the use of space, these inner block areas are where the local culture of Thai urbanism is played out. The inner blocks, with sufficient density, are the places where mobile vendors play a significant role in delivering various kinds of household goods and services in daily life, right at the people's doors. Their goods range from furniture, fresh food, cooked food, and flowers, to essential services, such as knife sharpening, beauty salon services, clothes dyeing, and buying recycled garbage. Figures 13.6 through 13.18 illustrate the typology of mobile vendors in the present-day Bangkok.

Figure 13.6 Canal vendors

Figure 13.7 Canal vendors
Source: Illustration by Davisi Boontharm, 2004; photograph by Kasama Polakit, 2001.

Canal vendors can be seen along the network of waterways, particularly the areas on the west bank of the Chaophraya River, where some parts are inaccessible to cars. Many of the canal vendors modify their rowing boats with engines, such as the long-tail boats. They sell various kinds of goods including agricultural products, cooked food, fresh foods, and coal.

Figure 13.8 Hawkers (hab-re)

Figure 13.9 Hawkers (hab-re)

Figure 13.10 Hawkers (hab-re)
Source: Illustrations by Davisi Boontharm, 2004; photographs by Kasama Polakit, 2001.

This type is a traditional form of street vending. Some vendors carry things by hands and some carry two bamboo baskets that hang on their shoulders. On foot, they mingle with pedestrian traffic on public sidewalks along the main streets. It is the easiest and smallest form of trade, which requires minimal financial investment. These street vendors are often found at the intersections of the main arteries, skillfully using the start-stop rhythm of the traffic lights, selling jasmine garlands and flowers, newspaper, and ready-to-eat fruits.

Using push-carts is prohibited on the main streets and some laneways with heavy traffic. Like mobile kitchens, most push-carts carry the whole range of utensils together with a full gas stove cooking popular street food such as noodles, grilled chicken, and papaya salad. The small carts often move along the lines of laneway and alleyway networks, while the heavy ones tend to settle at certain places. In this case they are often found at the intersection of sub-system street structure and the area in front of primary functions such as schools, office buildings and apartment complexes, waiting for their customers. Some push-carts also provide tables and chairs.

Figure 13.11 Push-cart (rod-khen)

Figure 13.12 Push-cart (rod-khen)
Source: Illustration by Davisi Boontharm, 2004; photograph by Kasama Polakit, 2001.

Figure 13.13 Bicycle vendor

Using bicycles and motorcycles, these types of mobile vendors are commonly found within the networks of laneway and alleyway.

Figure 13.14 Bicycle vendor
Source: Illustration by Davisi Boontharm; photograph by Kasama Polakit.

Figure 13.15 Tricycle vendor

Some of the tricycles are peddled and some are motorized.

Figure 13.16 Tricycle vendor
Source: Illustration by Davisi Boontharm; photograph by Kasama Polakit.

Figure 13.17 Mini pick-up trucks

Mini pick-up trucks are increasingly used as mobile convenience stores and fresh food marketplaces. Some also provide household appliances, furniture, decorated plants, and construction goods.

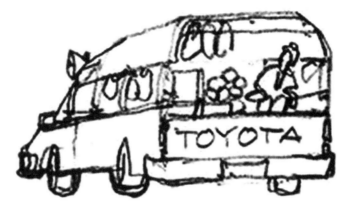

Figure 13.18 Mini pick-up trucks
Source: Illustration by Davisi Boontharm; photograph by Kasama Polakit.

These various types of mobile vendors share some similarity in their social and spatial practices, which we will discuss in the next section.

Mobile Vendors: Social and Spatial Practices

To understand how mobile street and canal vendors sustain their livelihoods and to assess how much demand for their trade exists in everyday city life, we used field observations and informal interviews. Utilizing thematic analysis to search for their common patterns of social and spatial practices, three major attributes were identified: spontaneity, fluidity, and adaptability. These three characteristics can also be regarded as indigenous practices, which are profoundly embedded in Thai culture and have persisted through time (Kasama 2004).

Spontaneity

An unplanned interaction, which we shall call "spontaneity", emerges from a chance encounter among people doing different things in their daily life. This interaction is based upon their physical co-presence in space. If we look closely at the street level to see how buildings relate to open space, what we see is "a relation of co-presence between groups doing different things" (Hillier 1996). This co-presence is a product of two-way relationships: between those within the buildings and those outside; and between those using the space outside the buildings and those passing by or moving along the line of spatial structure (Hillier 1996). This spatial structure, in part, regulates how people move and how they meet through spatial integration and permeability (Hillier 1996). Selling and at the same time moving while at some other time stabilizing at a certain spot are distinctive characteristics of mobile vending activities. Mobile vending businesses depend largely upon a chance contact between themselves and their customers. Many of these vendors use amplifiers or other selected sources of noise to catch the attention of the potential customers. Not only do they move along the spatial line seeking potential customers, they also sometimes stop at a nodal point of spatial integration where the primary functions are located, waiting for their customers at particular times, such as when schools finish, and then move on. Some street and canal vendors have developed a relationship with their customers through their service and, as a result, have created their own regular patrons.

Fluidity

Like floating markets in the past, as mentioned earlier, many canal vendors gathered at ordinary waterways normally used for transportation, thus transforming the area into a floating marketplace for periods of time. When the transactions were complete and the canal vendors moved on, the areas gradually returned to a normal everyday waterway. We shall call these phenomena "fluidity" in urban configurations. In the present-day, these phenomena are commonly experienced when ordinary sidewalks became occupied by mobile vendors at certain times, usually in the evening. Acting as mobile kitchens and lining the sidewalk, these mobile vending activities temporarily transform the area into a city public canteen, where people from different social hierarchies mingle and have food together (see Figures 13.19 and 13.20).

A phenomenon of urban trans-configuration of an everyday sidewalk in Bangkok

Figure 13.19 An ordinary sidewalk at 11am
Source: Photograph by Kasama Polakit.

Figure 13.20 The same spot at 8pm
Source: Photograph by Kasama Polakit.

Another example is found in modern housing estates where their ordinary laneways become periodic marketplaces (see Figures 13.21 and 13.22).

An ordinary laneway in a modern housing estate performs the same function as a village ground for a traditional marketplace in the past:

Such gathering of informal built forms of mobile vending activities has transformed everyday street spaces into community marketplaces every morning for more than ten years. The difference between traditional floating markets and local land markets in the past is in their physical form and means of transport, which change through time and corresponding technologies. However, what persist are the local practices, their deeply rooted patterns, and associated behaviors. In Bangkok, this persisting local practice of mobile vending can be regarded as a form of local culture.

Figure 13.21 A morning marketplace at 7am
Source: Photograph by Kasama Polakit.

Figure 13.22 The same spot at 10am
Source: Photograph by Kasama Polakit.

Adaptability

One of the most significant attributes of mobile vending activities is adaptability. Usually mobile vendors operate on a human scale. They utilize basic resources and simple technology that are easy to manage and change to cope with their everyday circumstances. This also includes modifying vehicles to fit certain types of goods, types of street networks, fashion, or even the desire of the customers. Under the pressure of the global economy imposed upon urban environments in Bangkok, local trade has to adapt in order to survive. At present, local and global commercial practices are, in fact, starting to learn from each other and are hybridizing. Global trade now comes to play at the local stage such as neighborhood shops and mobile vending (see Figure 13.23) while the local push-cart businesses selling street food now adopt entrepreneurial franchise systems (see Figure 13.24).

Global/local trade hybridity in mobile vending businesses

**Figure 13.23 Global ice-cream brand in form of local practice such
as canal vendors**
Source: Photograph by Kasama Polakit, 2001.

Figure 13.24 A local push-cart vending is, in fact, part of an entrepreneurial franchise business

Source: Photograph by Kasama Polakit, 2001.

Operating at a small scale, ongoing adaptability to different neighborhoods and their preferences, and flexible delivery services has become marketing strategies that global commerce has adopted from the local practice of mobile vending activities.

Conclusions

The emergence of global or international commerce and trading has had a significant impact on Bangkok's large scale urban developments. Mobile vending activities, which originated before the development of modern Bangkok have successfully adapted to the modern ways of life. Functioning at the grassroots level, serving some of the basic needs of the city's inhabitants, utilizing simple technologies and basic resources which include recycled material and requiring low investment, these mobile vending activities have not only persisted as a part of Bangkok's everyday life, but they also complement the "real" economy of the city. Various types of mobile vendors are formed in correspondence to the diverse hierarchical street structures of the city to deliver services to neighborhoods and individuals in areas that are hard to reach or are inaccessible to public transport systems. Their common distinctive quality is in their spontaneity, fluidity, and high adaptability, all of which are profoundly embedded local practices in Thai culture. These local practices have manifested themselves in their ability to manage and sustain themselves in an ever-changing and often unfavorable environment. The global economy is now taking part in local economic activities which were previously the exclusive domain of small scale local businesses, including mobile vending. At the same time, the local businesses mimic practices and rules of global operators, in a form of entrepreneurial franchise management. Those two trends are part of a broader push towards homogenization of mobile vending activities, which is likely to lead to more sedentary patterns, less spontaneous, less fluid, and less adaptable ways of doing local business. We also see a decrease in accessibility for disadvantaged members of society, who will be unable to sustain their lives in competition with the big business and within the system which requires higher financial investment. The role of mobile vendors in modern Bangkok is more than obvious and their contribution is valuable but the present economic climate denies a future to their activities.

All the above raises a crucial question: how can poor, mobile vendors survive, and keep on giving their necessary contributions to the everyday life of Bangkok?

References

Aasen, C. (1998), *Architecture of Siam: A Cultural History Interpretation* (Singapore: Oxford University Press).

Askew, M. (1993a), 'The Banglumphu District: A Portrait of Change in Inner Bangkok' (Bangkok, Thailand: Development Research Institute).

Askew, M. (1993b), 'The Making of Modern Bangkok: State, Market and People in the Shaping of the Thai Metropolis' (Bangkok: The 2010 Project).

Askew, M. (1994a), 'Bangkok: Transformation of the Thai City', in *Cultural Identity and Urban Change in Southeast Asia: Interpretative Essays*, Askew, M. and Logan, W.S. (eds).

Askew, M. (1994b), *Interpreting Bangkok: The Urban Question in Thai Studies* (Bangkok: Chulalongkorn University Press).

Askew, M. (2002), *Bangkok, Place, Practice and Representation* (London: Routledge).

Bubpanard, S. (1982), in *Song Satawat Rattanakosin: Kwamplienplang khong Sungkhom Thai* [Two Hundred Years of Rattana Kosin: The Transformation of Thai Society] (ed Institute, T.K.R.).

Chomlada, L. (1991), in *Faculty of Economics* (Bangkok: Thamasart University).

Cohen, E. (1985), 'A Soi in Bangkok: the Dynamics of Lateral Urban Expansion', *The Journal of the Siam Society*, 73:2, 22.

Davisi, B. (2001), *Lieux du commerce et l'évolution urbaine de Bangkok 1782–2000* (Paris: University Paris 8).

Durand-Lasserve, A. (1980), in *Thai-European Seminar on Social Change in Contemporary Thailand*.

Durand-Lasserve, A. (1982), 'The Urban Land Issue and the Balance of Power between Public and Private Sectors: Some characteristics of the process of land appropriation in Bangkok during the last three decades' (Paris: Centre d' Etudes de Georgraphie Tropicale).

Hillier, B. (1996), 'Cities as Movement Economies', *Urban Design International*, 1:1, 41–60.

Hillier, B. (1996), *Space is the Machine: A Configurational Theory of Architecture* (New York: Cambridge University Press).

Karnjanarkaphan (1999), *Dek Khlong Bangluang Lem Song* [A Child of Khlong Bangluang Volume 2] (Bangkok: Sarakadee Press).

Kasama, B. (2004), in *Faculty of Architecture, Building and Planning* (Melbourne: The University of Melbourne).

Chiwakul, K., et al. (1982), *Talad Nai Krungthep: Karn Khayaytua Lae Phattanakarn* [Markets in Bangkok: The Expansion and the Development] (Bangkok, Chulalongkorn University Press).

Korff, R. (1992), 'Markets, Trade and State: Urbanism in Bangkok' (Bielefeld: Sociology of Development Research Centre, Faculty of Sociology, University of Bielefeld).

Korff, R. (1996), 'Global and Local Spheres: The Diversity of Southeast Asian Urbanism' (Bielefeld: Faculty of Socilogy, University of Bielefeld).

Naengnoi, S. (1996), *Palaces of Bangkok: Royal Residences of the Chakri Dynasty* (Bangkok: Asia Books).

Naengnoi, S., et al. (1991), *Ong Prakob Tang Kayapab Krung Ratanakosin* [Physical Components of Ratanakosin] (Bangkok: Chulalongkorn University Press).

Nid, H. (1982), in *Ratanakosin Bicentenial Ceremony*, Vol. 1 (Chulalongkorn University).

O'Connor, R. (1989), 'From "Fertility" to "Order", Paternalism to Profits: The Thai City's Impact on the Culture-Environment Interface', in *Culture and Environment in Thailand* (Bangkok: D.K. Printing House).

Phasuk, P. and Baker, C. (1997), *Thailand: Economy and Politics* (Chiang Mai: Silkworm Books).

Piyanart, B., et al. (1982), *Khlong Nai Krungthep* [Canals in Bangkok : History, Changes and Their Impact 1782–1982] (Bangkok: Chulalongkorn University Press).

Pusadee, T. and Manop, P. (1982), *Ban Nai Krungthep* [Houses in Bangkok: Characters and Changes during the last 200 years 1782–1982 A.D.] (Bangkok: Chulalongkorn University Press).

Santi, C. (1978), in *Faculty of Architecture* (Bangkok: Chulalongkorn University).

Sombat, P. (1998), *Kerd Nai Rue* [Born in the Boat] (Bangkok: Matichon).

Sombat, P. (2001), *Chiwit Tarm Khlong* [Ways of Life Along the Canals] (Bangkok: Saitharn).

Sternstein, L. (1982), *Portrait of Bangkok* (Bankok: Bangkok Metropolitan Administration).

Sumet, J. (1997), *Naga: Cultural Origins in Siam and the West Pacific* (Bangkok: Chalermnit Press and DD Books).

Tomosugi, T. (1991), 'A Historical Perspective of Urbanism in Bangkok: From the Viewpoint of the Relationship Between Rural Villages and Bangkok', in *Rethinking*

the Substantive Economy in Southeast Asia: On the Margins between Utilities and Meanings (Tokoyo: Instutute of Oriental Culture, University of Tokyo).

Van Beek, S. (1999), *Bangkok Then and Now* (Bangkok: AB Publications)

Chapter 14

Educational Changes for Sustainable Cities: Autonomous Knowledge

Georgina Echániz Pellicer

Introduction

Empowering human society to engage in sustainable development requires improving the methods by which we gain understanding of the impact of human activities on the urban environment. This chapter addresses this issue, and proposes educational activities that contribute to an improved environmental understanding. The relationship between education and sustainable cities is discussed and the historical events that draw attention to the weaknesses of old educational paradigms are analyzed. A new constructionist theory of education is suggested and a case study describing the implementation of constructionist ideas and the use of technological tools in the environmental education learning process is presented. Finally, conclusions are suggested for how new educational methods, combined with new technology, can promote a better understanding of environmental issues and improve urban practices.

Education for Sustainable Cities

Sustainability is not a novel term; it has been used for around thirty years, and was popularized by the publication *Our Common Future* as "development that meets the needs of the present without compromising the ability of future generations to meet their own needs" (Brundtland 1987).

Therefore, when we talk about sustainable cities, we conceive a city where policy, urban planning, economics, consumption and development are congruent. In the words of United Nations Educational, Scientific and Cultural Organization (UNESCO), "sustainable development is widely understood to involve the natural sciences and economics, but it is even more fundamentally concerned with culture: with the values people hold and how they perceive their relations with others". (Mortensen 2000) Thus, moving towards sustainable cities requires new tendencies for science, regulation and even the economy, but evolution in the direction of sustainable urban practices is also deeply related to human development. This brings up our duty to contribute to make life sustainable in this planet; but how do we become aware of this responsibility, and how do we prepare ourselves to face it?

Environmental education, a means of implementation of sustainability according to Agenda 21, has been suggested as a key element to improve the capacity of the people to address environment and development issues and to promote sustainability. (UNCED 1992) Yet, one of the most empowering contributions education can bring to people is the recognition that we each have a role in the shaping of our lives, our homes, our workplaces, our communities, and hence, our world (Mortensen 2000).

The desire to include environmental education as a main element of any plan for sustainability was articulated in the 1970s and endorsed by several international documents, such as the 1972 Stockholm Conference, the 1977 Tbilisi Declaration, and, more recently, the Rio Declaration and Agenda 21. The latter recognizes that "there is still a considerable lack of awareness of the interrelated nature of all human activities and the environment due to inaccurate or insufficient information" (UNCED 1992). Although, more than a lack of information, there are two main problems with traditional environmental education models: considering education as the mere act of conveying information from the knowledgeable to the unknowledgeable and expecting the learners to solely rely upon information about the environment that is received from external sources and do not question it or try to produce their own information.

Old Paradigms and New Education Methods

If education is understood only as conveying information, then it would be acceptable to believe that people will modify their behavior by accumulating information about environmental knowledge. On the contrary, too much environmental knowledge, particularly relating to the various global crises, can be useless if a deeper learning process is not taking place (Sterling 2001), that is, if the real causes and effects of environmental problems are not understood. On the other hand, if knowledge about the environment is gained through information produced or conveyed by others, then the level of understanding about environment issues, and basic concepts, remains limited. With this narrow vision and deficient preparation, the learner might not be able to effectively respond to an environmental challenge, or may not respond at all (FCCSET 1993).

This counterproductive effect happens when education is constrained to the acquisition of biased environmental information without an adequate local context and a deeper thinking process. The lack of connection between causes and effects of local environmental issues, in addition to the "information delivery" education process, impedes people to conceive sustainability as a whole interconnected system, and generates what Seymour Papert calls *denatured knowledge* (Papert 1976). This kind of knowledge is fruitless because it is not related to other knowledge structures, impeding people to apply it to a real situation.

That is the case for cities where there are severe environmental problems and authorities take action imposing regulations and limiting citizens' activities in order to control the situation. Nevertheless, those limitations will not serve their original aims if people are not able to understand the basic reasons behind those restrictions. For example, in a city that suffers smog problems, such as Mexico City, authorities implemented the program "hoy no circula" in which people cannot drive their car once a week depending on the last number of their license plate. As citizens do not have enough information regarding the facts about why the limitations were imposed, they do not understand the relation between these activities and environmental protection in their city. The immediate results were that people ended up buying another car to drive on the forbidden day, and it usually was an old inexpensive model that polluted more.

Environmental education should not be about impositions, it has to be about understanding the causes and effects of environmental issues, and how those issues relate to current sustainability needs. If sustainability transition involves fundamental changes in society, then, education also demands a change of a similar magnitude (Sterling 2001). In order to foster critical thinking and learning about environmental issues it is necessary to work on a participatory learning environment and utilize suitable learning material to aid the process of understanding causes and effects of environmental facts (Echániz 2003).

Constructing Autonomous Knowledge

Constructionist learning is precisely about encouraging people to build their own knowledge through personal experiences, by constructing an object or a project with the support of technological tools (Harel and Papert 1991). One of the main criticisms of constructionism is that not everything can be learned autonomously. It would take too long for people to learn (e.g. complex math or physics theories), or the learning process could result in experiences that generate beliefs, which can be confused with real knowledge (Matthews 2002).

On the other hand, learning from others can bring awareness and knowledge but, attitudes and skills can only be learned by constructing a situation that makes them practical for the learner. A facilitator can guide this situation but, at the end of the day, the final project should be a product of the pupil. We might not have a problem thinking of adults creating these learning situations and producing projects and objects; however, sometimes it is hard to imagine that young people or even children can formulate and conduct this kind of activity.

It has been demonstrated that the capacity to define creative paths and structures for exploring environmental issues is present in children in primary levels. Children have the ability to design their own learning tasks and also generate and justify their own personal rules for it (Jimenez 2001). Moreover, as said by Roger Cousinet seventy years ago, children are considered as scientifically active beings; their creativity is fostered if they can work freely, more as playing and not being a recipient of content (UNESCO 1993).

Education, then, can no longer be an action of "content delivery" exercised by a master on his pupils, for such action has proved futile; environmental education should also develop critical thinking skills in order to emphasize the complexity of environmental problems, as recommended by the Tbilisi Declaration (UNESCO 1977). Furthermore, environmental education should consist of activities whereby people, specifically children, can interact with the environment and explore environmental issues to generate their own information and knowledge. This education process can evolve in an open and participatory learning environment, utilizing adequate learning material and with the guide of a facilitator who is available for guidance and advisory purposes.

Case Study[1]

This case study shows, in practice, how an open and participatory learning environment fosters people's creativity to generate their own environmental experiences and knowledge, guided by a facilitator. The case was developed in the USA, at the Fayerweather Street School in Cambridge, Massachusetts. A group of 7/8th grade students, called the Unit, was chosen to participate in the study, and was personally guided by the author through a constructionist methodology over five days, so they would have a personal project by the end of the week. This section is a summary of these experiences that exemplifies a proposal for educational change, a fresh vision of methods and an innovative application based on inexpensive technological learning material.

B. Ozone Detector

A. Electronic Board

C. Noise Sensor

Figure 14.1 Technological learning material

---

1   Taken from: Echániz Pellicer, G.; Learning Material for Constructing Environmental Understanding. Master's Thesis, Massachusetts Institute of Technology, 2003.

Suitable learning material was available during the workshop. These inexpensive technological tools (see Figure 14.1) developed at the MIT/Media Lab consisted of an electronic board with sensor ports and a memory chip. The board could also be attached to the computer to download the data registered by the sensors using a serial cable. These electronic sensors included indicators such as noise, ground level ozone, temperature and sunlight.

The education method utilized during the workshop was based on constructionist ideas; it included four basic steps that the participants undertook during the workshop. Those steps included the following: a) Choose an environmental issue to address, b) Determine a personal methodology to explore that issue, c) Interact with the physical environment, and d. Produce a concrete final project.

a. Choosing an environmental issue to address

Children were encouraged to choose any environmental issue, but given the nature of the provided tools, they formed two teams, one of them willing to address the issue of noise in the School, and the other one interested in ground ozone levels around the School. These environmental problems are present in most cities around the world; however, the fact that we were working within the school environment represented the ideal local context for the children to deeply explore the causes and effects of those issues.

During the first session, they thought noise was not an environmental problem, and they had no idea what ground level ozone is, so we first discussed the two topics. We talked about the causes of noise in the school, and they wanted to know more about ozone. Finally, we concluded that certain amount of noise could interfere with the learning process that should take place in the classroom, and that ground ozone is the product of a chemical reaction of fumes from cars and industries with sunlight.

b. Determining a personal methodology to explore environmental issues

Children were expected to define a set of steps that would allow them to explore the chosen issue, and to develop a methodology for studying that environmental topic. The team that had chosen to work with the noise sensor realized that if the students talked at the same time as the teacher, they would not understand each other, and the generated noise could actually be an environmental problem. So after discussing their methodology, they decided to measure noise levels around the school in specific areas so they could determine which classroom was the noisiest, comparing their own classroom with the kindergarten area.

The team that had chosen to work with the ground level ozone detector was not sure what methodology they would use to explore this issue. As a facilitator, I thought about suggesting that they measure ground ozone levels and compare them with sunlight levels during the day, so we could corroborate the correlation of ground ozone with sunlight. However, at the beginning of the second session, they came up with their own methodology: they decided to measure ozone levels inside the school and compare them to ozone levels outside the school. The reasoning behind this idea was that this kind of air problems is usually thought of in terms of outdoor pollution; therefore, they wanted to find out more about indoor air quality.

To foster motivation among the children to continue with their projects, as a facilitator, I asked them for a hypothesis for each of the projects. The noise team thought that the kindergarten area should be noisier than their 7/8th grade area because the kindergarten children play inside the classroom, and the 7/8th grade students are listening to the teacher and each other, and learning. For the ozone team, it was proposed that indoor ozone levels should be lower than outdoor ozone levels, since the fumes from cars and industries, as well as sunlight, are concentrated outside the school.

c. Interacting with the physical environment

Physical interaction with the contextual surroundings was essential to verify these hypotheses. In this case, the availability of the inexpensive technological tools allowed children to explore the physical places in which they were particularly interested in measuring environmental indicators. Both teams set their sensors and electronic boards in focal sites around the school so they could collect enough data to test their hypotheses.

d. Producing a concrete final project

After choosing a topic, developing a methodology and interacting with the environment, children devoted themselves to the final task, presenting their results in a concrete final project.

The noise team decided to present a map of the school showing the sites where they measured noise levels. They found that in fact, their 7/8th grade classroom was noisier than other classrooms in the school. This was an astonishing result, because they started thinking about the causes of noise during the class, and its possible effects. They concluded that this noise problem could be an environmental factor that might even prevent them from adequate learning during their class.

The ozone team decided to present the data obtained by the electronic board and sensors in the form of graphics, and explained their interpretation. Their results were extremely interesting because the outdoors' ground level ozone graph was, as expected, rising through the day up till midday; however, the indoors' graph presented a constant low level during the first hours of measurement and an abrupt rise up to outdoors' levels at 12:30pm, dropping again to low levels around 2pm. When we discussed the reasons for these results, they immediately thought that lunchtime happened during that period and the main door that separated the indoor and outdoor sensors was opened. This fortunate event drove us to the conclusion that, due to sunlight, ozone particles are mostly present in the environment at midday and that outdoors there are higher concentrations, but also that ozone can be easily spread by the wind, which is actually one of its main characteristics.

Giving people these environmental education opportunities, and providing them with flexible and adequate learning material, makes evident for them how our daily activities contribute to current environmental situations, and helps them identify the causes and effects of environmental issues. Even though the learning experience is first produced in a small local contextual scale, these scientific experiences help people understand and extrapolate basic facts behind environmental issues. For example, a girl working on the ozone project started thinking about what could be happening with ozone levels in California, because they have more sunlight year-round.

This critical thinking experience provides students, not only with awareness and knowledge about the environment, but also with the necessary skills to explore and investigate environmental issues until they are able to produce their own conclusions: autonomous, complete and reliable data to support their hypotheses or actions regarding the prevention of environmental harms and responses to environmental problems.

Conclusion: Improving Urban Practices

Sustainable cities require educated politicians, economists, planners, and developers. The kind of education they must receive in order to participate in the transition to sustainability, is one that makes them prepared, progressive and creative people. These skills evolve better when people work freely and not under someone else's rules; however, they should be grounded in awareness, knowledge, understanding and, of course, critical thinking.

People who lack this understanding and skill set might be aware of the problems but have no solutions to propose. On the other hand, new methods for learning based on educational theories such as constructionism, and aided by suitable technological learning material, can generate opportunities for people to learn within an open and participatory environment which fosters the development of critical skills. When people are aware of environmental issues and able to understand their causes, effects and basic facts, they are better prepared with the skills to critically think of ways of preventing environmental problems, or propose solutions and alternatives for currently existing environmental issues.

For people to generate their own arguments, it is important that they are critical enough to questions others´ arguments, and also creative enough to generate their own information to support those arguments. When they are able to produce this autonomous knowledge and understanding about the complex relationship between humans and nature, they are responsible enough to face the fact that the possibility to plan and act towards a sustainable city is in their own hands.

References

Brundtland, G. (1987), *Our Common Future: The World Commission on Environment and Development* (Oxford University Press).

Echániz Pellicer, G. (2003), *Learning Material for Constructing Environmental Understanding* (Master's Thesis, Massachusetts Institute of Technology).

FCCSET (Federal Coordinating Council for Science, Engineering, and CET) (1993) (Technology Committee on Education and Training), *Report of the Ad Hoc*

Working Group on Environmental Education and Training, September 17, 1993, cited in Mortensen (ed.).

Harel, I. and Papert, S. (1991), *Constructionism* (Norwood, NJ: Ablex Publishing Corporation).

Jimenez, A. and Lopez, R. (2001), 'Designing a Field Code: Environmental Values in Primary School, a Longitudinal Study', *Environmental Education Research*, 7:1, 5–22.

Matthews, M. (2002), 'Constructivism and Science Education: A Further Appraisal', *Journal of Science Education and Technology*, 11:2, 121–134.

Mortensen, L. (2000), 'Global Change Education Educational Resources for Sustainability' in *Education for Sustainable Future A Paradigm of Hope for the 21st Century* (New York: Kluwer Academic/Plenum Publishers).

Papert, S. (1976), 'Some Poetic and Social Criteria for Education Design' (Appendix to a Proposal to the National Science Foundation).

Sterling, S. (2001), 'Sustainable Education Re-visioning Learning and Change', *Schumacher Briefing* (6) (Green Books).

UNCED (1992), Report of the United Nations Conference on Environment and Development – Agenda 21 (Rio de Janeiro).

UNESCO International Bureau of Education (1993), *PROSPECTS: The Quarterly Review of Comparative Education*, 23:1/2, 221–33 (Paris).

UNESCO, in cooperation with UNEP (the UN Environment Program) (1977), Tbilisi Declaration (Tbilisi, Georgia).

Chapter 15

Educating Architects to Address Urban Problems in Building Design

Singh Intrachooto, Luke Yeung, and Yaourai Suthiranart

Overview

The growth in Thailand's urban areas has been well documented. According to the United Nations (2003) the proportion of people living in urban areas in Thailand increased from 24 to 32 percent of the overall population from 1970 to 2003. This figure has been projected to rise even further, to an estimated 47 percent of the overall population, by 2030. In terms of population size this projected growth rate will result in an increase of 15 million people settling within Thailand's urban areas in the coming years. The physical effects of this intense urbanization can be observed in Thailand's largest city – Bangkok.[1] Despite fluctuations in economic cycles, Bangkok remains the country's dominant financial, governmental, and cultural center.

Bangkok's existing and projected development has provided the basis for investigations among urban studies researchers in Thailand and abroad. A variety of large studies have been undertaken on a variety of topics that span from socio-economic issues to policy management and environmental factors. Various perspectives, both government and non-government funded, have been represented within these studies to address the complexities of Bangkok's massive growth. Invariably, these studies concur that contemporary Bangkok is unable to cope with its rate of growth with traffic congestion, unregulated land use, urban flooding, and air and water pollution emerging as the primary issues that require attention.[2]

---

1 Bangkok Metropolis or Greater Bangkok Area (GBA) covers an area of 4,717km^2 (1,821 square mile) with 8,554,751 registered inhabitants in 2003 (excluding non-registered immigrants). It includes three adjoining provinces of Nonthaburi, Patum Thani, and Samut Prakan.

2 The master planning team led by Professor Gary Hack from the Massachusetts Institute of Technology (USA) was hired in the early 90s to investigate and assess Bangkok's physical conditions. The study revealed specific urban structures such as super blocks with infrequent outlets, disconnected roadway systems and lack of open spaces as contributing factors to the city's gridlock (MIT 1996). In another survey, Setchell (1995) disclosed that 2,100 buildings of six or more stories were approved for construction in Bangkok Metropolis between 1987–1992. The Japan International Cooperation Agency (JICA 1996) found that a total of 2.61 million square meters of retail space were developed in 1995 alone and, in the process, destroyed wetlands and natural drainage of the city.

In Bangkok, the academic and professional development of architecture has been closely associated with the growth of the city. As a result, the practice of architecture is focused on developing building projects within the urban environment. Few would question that architects should be concerned with addressing urban issues in their training and practice. Beyond this general statement however, and in light of the challenges that this city faces, what specific aspects of the urban environment should architects consider for Bangkok and how can they be applied to the scale and issues of architectural and building design?

This chapter discusses how Bangkok's pressing urban issues have been adapted within the architectural studio education at Kasetsart University. While there is an abundance of data related to Bangkok's urban environment, there have been relatively few accounts on how this data can be applied at the scale of the individual building and to architectural design. The objectives of this chapter are twofold. First the chapter identifies specific issues that relate broader urban design problems to architectural education in Thailand, and second demonstrates how the issue – climate and rainfall – was realized as a framework for architectural designers to propose creative solutions.

Urbanism and Architectural Education in Thailand

In the past, issues relating to the urban environment have been a small part of architectural training in colleges and universities in Thailand. During the intermediate stages of architectural education, typically the third and fourth years of training in the five-year professional undergraduate programs, a studio project is performed that involves the design of a building within an urban area that covers one or more blocks or acres of real estate. In these architectural studios, engagement in urban issues have primarily been confined to the building scale and to the boundaries of the physical site. Students consider certain aspects relating to urban planning processes in these traditional studios including building set-backs, plot ratio, and existing land use guidelines. This delineation of the design scope within the studio closely follows the current model of practice that divides the tasks and duties between professional architects and urban designers/planners. While this may be useful to clarify the professional obligations of the two disciplines, a segregated approach does not address environmental issues that often overlap the domains of building design and urban planning.

As a result, the perceived inadequacies in the current approach, an alternative approach to architectural training was proposed to respond to some of the larger-scale environmental problems that Bangkok is currently experiencing. An important objective of the new approach was to expand beyond the professional scope and responsibilities of architectural practice in order to provide students opportunities to actively participate in urban issues beyond the boundaries of the building site.

Redefinition of Architectural Studio Program

In order to redefine the studio program to contemporaneously address urban conditions and architectural skills, the studio began focusing on how resources in urban planning and design could be developed and applied to architectural design. Navigating the considerable amount of data that urban planning encompasses (i.e. transportation, land use, environmental and settlement patterns), developing technical proficiencies beyond existing architectural skills, and understanding how specific urban infrastructures could be applied to the various scales within an architectural program (i.e. transportation, urban water runoff, and drainage) were particularly challenging for the architectural studio. The overall utilization of urban resources was also deemed vital for developing sensibilities toward environmental and urban ecology, and ultimately, the design of an individual building. These issues were developed in the course of one academic semester with the studio process organized into four incremental stages.

Stage 1: "Determining the major urban problems of Bangkok to architecture"

Water management, transportation management, air quality, and land use rank as the most pressing problems associated with the intense urbanization of Bangkok (Krongkaew 1995). After conducting preliminary research on environmental data, it was apparent that water-related issues had been the least studied in building and urban design. Although under-examined, water-related issues are fundamental to the engineering of the entire urban infrastructure and had great potential to be developed within the framework of the architectural studio investigation.

In the past, Bangkok has received as much as 400 millimeters of rainfall at the height of its rainy season. This amount of rainfall has regularly led to annual flooding (see Figure 15.1). The damage caused by the effects of rainwater to building construction has been seen in the past. For example, in 1983 flooding during the rainy season (six months of the year) caused damages to Bangkok's infrastructure and buildings estimated to be worth 6.6 billion Baht – approximately US $149 million (Mark et al., 2001). The potential for urban flooding in Bangkok occurs in regular intervals of two and three year cycles. In 1980, flooding in the city lasted for the duration of two months; in 1983, the duration of flooding increased to four months (Yoshikawa et al., 1999). Currently, individual buildings play a minimal role in mitigating water-related issues like rainwater management. Through students' surveys it was found that inadequate drainage is a leading cause of urban flooding. In addition, the existing infrastructure is insufficient for the combined amount of gray water released from buildings and rainfall during the typical four-month long monsoon season. This discovery provided a cornerstone for further research into urban drainage systems (see Part 3 of the studio process). The issue of rainfall in Bangkok presented significant opportunities for architectural design to improve the larger urban and built environment.

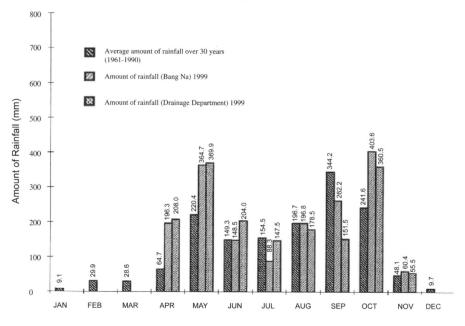

Figure 15.1 Amount of rainfall in Bangkok metropolitan area
Source: Meteorological Department of Thailand (1961–1990).

Stage 2: *"Employing urban design tools to architecture"*

It is uncommon for architects to employ Geographic Information System (GIS)[3] in their design processes. Conversely, urban planners increasingly consider this computer-based system an effective tool for understanding a place. The studio instructed architecture students to be familiar with basic GIS functions so that they could use its large database to gain a better insight into the water issues in Thailand by cross-tabulating various layers of information or by using the GIS layering technique for further site analyses.

While existing GIS data provided information on a larger urban scale, no data was available to relate rainfall levels to the scale of the individual districts or buildings in Bangkok. Given this lack of data it was necessary to further develop GIS for use in demonstrating the relationships between architecture, urban conditions, and flooding. GIS provided students with information such as open and green spaces, road patterns, topography, and general data of the area inhabitants. This data was then examined in relation to detailed information obtained from field surveys such as the heights and

---

3   A GIS is a computer-based system that organizes information about a place in layers to effectively provide a better understanding of that place. For example, GIS can help identify the best location for a new hospital, analyze environmental damage, highlight patterns of similar crimes in a city, and so forth.

dimensions of the individual buildings, specific vegetation and soil patterns found in the area, and solar conditions. The two sets of data were then integrated for the purpose of applying urban planning attributes at the scale of the building design. One example of this result is shown in Figure 15.2, correlating the amount of rainfall to the potential amount of water collected from the rainfall for individual buildings in the area if catchment devices were designed based upon the footprint and the area of the exterior surfaces of each building.

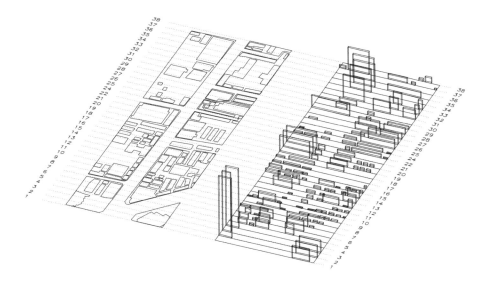

Figure 15.2 Rainfall and buildings

Stage 3: *"Water engineering and infrastructure as architecture"*

In order to develop suitable building designs, students were required to acquire knowledge of related water delivery systems commonly found in Thailand (for example, monkey cheeks,[4] pipelines, and viaducts). In addition to the conventional engineering systems, students were assigned to investigate water conveying mechanisms that are found in nature (for example leaves, tree trunks, and seeds). These natural systems provide insight into principles of water compartmentalization as well as illustrate how natural structures utilize physical form, surface characteristics of materials, and gravity to eloquently solve problems of water conveyance (see Figures 15.3, 15.4 and 15.5). Study models based on students' understanding of these natural structures were produced and reconfigured to address design and construction concerns in buildings (Figures 15.6 and 15.7).

---

4   "Monkey cheeks" is a flood prevention technique found in Thailand and refers to a large area acting as a basin or pond to temporarily detain water.

Lectures on water management and engineering were given to the students by specialists on water resource engineering and hydrological information system from Faculty members of Civil Engineering. Statistics on rainfalls, flood levels, drainage flow rates, built environment patterns, and unused spaces were integrated to support students' analyses. Actual data was crucial for students' analyses to ensure that design decisions were grounded.

Figure 15.3 Pine needles

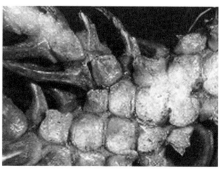

Figure 15.4 Close-up of pine needles

Figure 15.5 Graphical study of pine needles

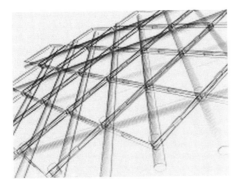

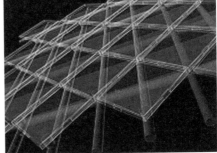

**Figure 15.6 Architectural
interpretation of pine
needles' water retaining
and delivery systems**

Figure 15.7 Water retaining façade

Stage 4: "Forming urban-architecture response"

Emphasizing complex urban contexts require numerous site visits. Students were required to examine a site on Silom Road, the main thoroughfare of Bangkok's Central Business District. An existing nine-story concrete building complex stands on the examined site and is surrounded by various modes of transportation including sky-train, underground train, buses, private vehicles, and pedestrians. Students conducting observations were encouraged to focus on specific factors that lead to the city's water overflow. Each student was not asked to analyze all site conditions and building codes but instead they were asked to focus on specific conditions in which they were concerned and/or had interest. For example, students who were interested in street activities as it relates to architecture analyzed sets of activities, but all the while, they also considered how water (such as rain, flood, etc.) affect those activities. Students who focused on hydrological systems and engineering gathered and analyzed physical conditions and control mechanisms of water systems in the Silom neighborhood and the plausible factors that could affect flow capacity. Not surprisingly, many of the drain holes were clogged with debris and with unpaved areas being few and far between the grounds were largely impervious to water. Students interested in material textures carried out their water flow experiments and recorded the specimens' water resistance characteristics (Figure 15.8). All data and analyses were shared with the entire class, stressing the interconnectivity of all aspects. This process resulted in various water retention conceptual schemes that aim to delay, store, or recycle water (see figures 15.9, 15.10, 15.11 and 15.12).

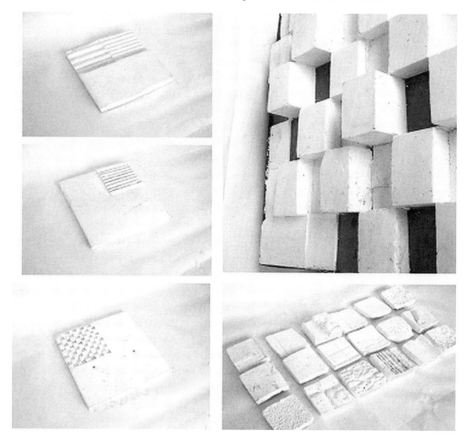

Figure 15.8 Surface texture study

Designing at both the architecture and urban scale was a challenge since design decisions are not made merely on technological reasons but also include social aspects. After students completed the examination of different water conveying mechanisms in plant materials and various other aspects of the site they moved on to formulating strategies to mitigate excessive amount of water within the densely populated area of Silom. Models of water delivery/control systems were diagrammed and built— incorporating the existing structures, open spaces, and modes of transportation into the design proposals. A "leap of concept" seemed unavoidable if architectural demands and urban problems are to be addressed in parallel. For instance, some students made the decision to focus their design on creating building envelope systems while others were re-planning roof tops of several building groups. Although these conceptual leaps focus less on conventional requirements and functionalities, the designs had to be proposed with a defined set of supporting evidence and demonstrate how their strategies could be integrated into physical structures.

Figure 15.9 Water delaying façade

Figure 15.10 A study of water retaining   **Figure 15.11 Design proposal for water**
            façade   **retaining collector**

Figure 15.12 Organic building façade

Conclusion

Architects and designers have traditionally not regarded water from rainfall as a factor in building design. This issue is a challenge to architectural training because the effect of rainfall and water is not easily visualized using typical techniques in the design process. The resulting teaching methods challenged students to justify their building design propositions and to consider architecture and urban requirements in parallel. By working in teams, more detailed analyses and research could be carried out and application of climatic data from disciplines such as water management and engineering could be made.

Addressing Bangkok's rainfall and flooding issues through analysis and research while developing a proposal for a building complex within densely populated commercial structures have generated a number of design concepts and solutions. Examples of these concepts and solutions include aspects such as water-delaying façades, organic building envelopes, and rainwater catchments systems for urban neighborhoods. These solutions naturally require development beyond the architectural studio for building application but they demonstrate the possibility for building design and engineering to mitigate annual flooding. This unconventional approach challenges today's architectural design and engineering and requires architects to expand the scope of design towards areas such as materials, mechanical systems, building enclosure, users' needs, landscape, and transportation.

The architectural studio's pedagogical approach is a continual process directed at creating architectural developments that address specific environmental and urban issues. Based on the conviction that sustainable design requires conscientious designers, the studio not only employed a student-centered approach to encourage students to take initiative and investigate independently, but also underscored an urban problem theme, i.e. urban flooding, as a critical design prerequisite. The result of this approach is the presentation of plausible strategies to address urban flooding. By integrating an urban problem into architectural studio education, could future architects provide innovative solutions that mitigate urban problems?

Acknowledgements

The authors would like to acknowledge Uruya Weesakul from the Faculty of Civil Engineering at Thammasat University and Yaianong Thimsuwan from the Faculty of Civil Engineering at Kasetsart University for their technical consultation and the students that participated in this project.

References

Bangkok Metropolitan Administration (BMA), Population Statistics in 2003, available at: <http://203.155.220.217/pipd/07Stat(Th)/Stat(th)46/01Admin/01Ad min_T/06_pop_bk&b7y.htm>, accessed January 1, 2005.

Krongkaew, M. (1995) 'The Changing Urban System in a Fast-growth City and Economy: The Case of Bangkok and Thailand' (United Nation University Press), available at: <http://www.unu.edu/unupress/unupbooks/uu11ee/uu11ee0v. htm>, accessed June 14, 2004.

Mark, O., Apirumanekul C. and Boonya Aroonnet S. (2001), 'Living with Flood Waters: The Scenario in Bangkok', *Asian Infrastructure Research Review*, 3:2.

The MIT Consulting Team and BC/BMA Project Team (1996), *The Bangkok Plan: A Vision for the BMA 1995–2005* (Bangkok, Thailand: The BMA Department of City Planning).

Pacific Consultants International (PCI) and Suuri-Keikaku Co., Ltd. (SUR) (1997), *The Study on Urban Environmental Improvement Program in Bangkok Metropolitan Area, Final Report, Volume 2: Master Plan*, for Japan International Cooperation Agency (JICA), Bangkok Metropolitan Administration (BMA), and The Government of the Kingdom of Thailand.

Setchell, C. (1995), 'The Growing Environmental Crisis in the World's Mega-Cities: The Case of Bangkok', *Third World Planning Review*, 17:1, 1–18.

The United Nations (2003), 'World Urbanization Prospects: The 2003 Revision, Department of Economics and Social Affairs, Population Division', available at: <http://www.un.org/esa/population/publications/wup2003/2003WUP.htm>.

Yoshikawa, K., et al. (1999), 'A Study of the Comprehensive Flood Damage Mitigation in Rapidly Urbanizing Watersheds', for Japan International Cooperation Agency (JICA), available at: <http://www.wrrc.dpri.kyoto-u.ac.jp/~aphw/APHW2004/proceedings/FWR/56-FWR-A783/Resubmit%2056-FWR-A783.pdf>.

Chapter 16

Education into Citizenship: Environmental Education, Participatory Democracy, and the Precautionary Principle

Karen Cairns

Introduction

Environmental education is usually seen as educating people, especially children, about "nature" and ecosystem issues like pollution. A different approach, one of education into citizenship or education for participatory democracy, would meet our current needs more directly and appropriately. Information provision is necessary for citizens to have a higher level of environmental literacy and to actively participate in environmental choices and decisions. Often citizens are at a loss as to how to make their voices heard, to change behaviors, and to affect environmental decision-making.

Environmental education includes education into citizenship: how and why to be active rather than passive about environmental issues. The Precautionary Principle (PP) offers a simple approach, easily understood by most people, echoing familiar sayings such as "Look before you leap". Beginning in Germany as "Vorsorge," which has been translated as "forecaring" (Raffensperger 2000), PP is a guideline for environmental decision-making: *When an activity raises threats of harm to human health or the environment, precautionary measures should be taken even if some cause and effect relationships are not fully established scientifically* (Raffensperger and Tickner 1999).

This approach involves careful assessment of all available alternatives, including taking no action, and takes the side of safety, even with inconclusive scientific evidence. Education about PP can help citizens understand science's role, what it can and cannot do, and highlights the importance of civic participation in the decision-making process.

Following a discussion of the rationale behind a community-based approach, two main relationships are examined in this chapter: first, environmental education and participatory democracy and, second, environmental education and PP. The chapter concludes with a short discussion of how these complement and enhance each other, ending with examples of how this approach might look in practice.

Reasons for Community-based Actions

From its inception, the field of environmental education emphasized developing educational programs about local or community issues. Environmental educators should "(F)ocus on the local environment, but do not neglect state, national, and international environmental issues" (Swan and Stapp 1974). This is an ecological approach: the small system mirrors and is connected to the larger ones; all are interdependent.

Often considered the "father of ecology," Odum specified regionalism as an important approach for uniting humans and nature. He saw watersheds as the best way to manage regional ecosystems, since these include both cultural/societal and natural systems, and called for "applied human ecology" (Odum 1971), listing 12 steps for this field. Number 12 in his list is education in ecosystem ecology.

Bioregionalism, studying ecological systems within specific "biomes," such as a watershed, is sometimes termed "ecology of place". Bioregionalism is often seen as key to increasing a sense of community (both human and other species), increasing human ability to make sustainable choices, as well as deepening our understanding of human effects upon the local environment. However, critics feel this focus may harm the ability to understand global issues and their connections with local ones (Merchant 1992). Over the past decade most environmental education programs have used a local or regional focus. Some reasons have been economic, arguing that development of local economies gives both increased control and problem-solving ability, while minimizing environmental damage (Newby 1999). Other reasons are based upon the finding that people "care" more about issues close to home and feel empowered to act upon that caring (Cairns 2001).

Students of environmental education have expressed this sentiment, stating that learning about (and acting on) local issues led to increased pride and sense of ownership. In one example, an eighth grade student reported that students "can't always do that much about places that are far away". In general, students have expressed and felt that a focus on local issues was extremely important. A local focus led to an increased sense of community, which in turn fostered increased sensitivity to others, resulting in decreased behavioral problems in schools incorporating environmental education into the curriculum (Lieberman and Hoody 1998). This sensitivity was found to affect the context of decisions and actions within both the social and ecological environments.

Most environmental education curricula specify use of local issues and concerns. In defining education for sustainable development or ESD, McKeown specifies: "ESD carries with it the inherent idea of implementing programs that are locally relevant and culturally appropriate. All sustainable development programs including ESD must take into consideration the local environmental, economic, and societal conditions" (McKeown 2000).

Langer's (1997) theory of *mindful learning*, learning that emphasizes multiple perspectives and de-emphasizes "right answers" or knowledge from experts, posits that information which is personally relevant is easiest to learn. Research in the field of psychology has shown that people tend to ignore statistics while they believe stories that are personally relevant. In *mindful learning*, knowledge only makes sense within its immediate context and with awareness of complex perspectives. With a local and regional community focus, there are a multitude of perspectives on environmental issues, as well as a citizen base with local knowledge of the pertinent social and environmental context to these issues. The theory of mindful learning puts local knowledge and input on an equal status with "expert" knowledge, supporting the use of both as a foundation for public participation in environmental decision-making.

All environmental problems have both a regional/local aspect and a global one. Air and water pollution transcend political and geographic boundaries. Global warming and ozone depletion are planetary problems with both regional and global causal factors. Seeing that some human activities might necessitate a global focus, while others would be more manageable if decentralized, Dubos (1980) famously stated, "The general formula of management for the future might be, think globally and act locally". An understanding of large and small ecosystems is necessary for both.

Dubos viewed ecology as "ethically neutral," with humans adding value judgments regarding human interactions in ecosystems. Feeling a local emphasis increased environmental protection due to innate territoriality, Hardin (1993) saw a danger in an overemphasis of global issues, stating that a global view and the premise that everything is connected, can backfire and lead to paralysis, where people are too fearful to act. In research examining factors related to motivation for environmental action, education about local issues was highly motivational. Community members spoke eloquently of being overwhelmed by the global view, but feeling empowered when given knowledge and skills to act locally (Cairns 2001).

The NASA photo of the earth from space in the 1960s increased sensitivity to the issues of the global commons, but this commons is difficult to manage. Hardin (1977) questioned the motives of "people who insist on treating nonglobal questions globally," inferring that this broad focus defuses personal responsibility. A Kentucky author and community theorist of international renown, Wendell Berry agrees that a global focus is counterproductive: "Nobody can do anything to heal a planet" and "the adjective *planetary* describes a problem in such a way that it cannot be solved" (Berry 1991).

Berry (1995) further states that a global view supports the idea that knowledge equals property and education merely means job training; he sees these beliefs as based upon a culture of consumption. Viewing these assumptions as central to today's environmental and social problems, Berry argues that humans are incapable of understanding issues on a global scale. This links his perspective with that of Ornstein and Ehrlich (1989), who posit humans as evolutionarily handicapped to see anything beyond the short-term. Working and decision-making on a small scale, in small communities, promotes sustainability because humans can then grasp the total picture and see the links between the environment, economy, spirituality, and culture (Berry 1995).

A focus on local issues does not exclude awareness of global connections to these issues. Marcuse (1996) describes the interplay between the two levels as having a global vision, but linking local culture to the context of larger issues of politics and power (racism and poverty, for instance). The developers of the Ecological Footprint program, which incorporates a local focus, found positive reactions (in the form of behavioral changes) to linking global problems to local consumption and local decisions (Wackernagel and Reese 1996).

Citizen-based government rests upon a framework of belonging to specific communities with shared values and multiple perspectives (Freyfogle 1998). This framework unites science with local knowledge, rather than relying solely upon knowledge from outside. Science becomes a tool for identifying risks, finding alternatives, and assessing them, but actual decisions involve issues of ethics and values, which are not clear-cut. Science is useful but supplies no answers. The stakeholders involved are the ones who need to participate in decision-making. In order to be competent to do so, they must be involved from the beginning, familiar with and knowledgeable about the issues. Education is necessary to facilitate citizen awareness of the role and limits of science, what it can and cannot do, so that they will be able to handle the increased responsibility involved in participatory democracy.

Participatory Democracy and Environmental Education

Citizen participation has been called a variety of terms, such as "civic environmentalism," participatory democracy, or "strong democracy". The objective is increased involvement at all decision-making and planning stages by the widest variety of stakeholders. EPA's Public Involvement Policy, drafted in 2001, made this a priority at all levels, locally and nationally. How to motivate citizens to become involved in environmental issues, and maintain participation, remains a concern.

Education is listed as a key component for many programs but often is assumed to "just happen". An unfortunate corollary to this assumption is that "anyone can teach". However, knowledge of a subject does not always translate into awareness of effective ways to transmit information into an understandable form that encourages critical thinking.

In their "Eighth Annual Report Card" of December, 1999, the National Environmental Education and Training Foundation (NEETF) gave adults in the United States an "A+" and an "A" for attitudinal measures but an "F" and a "D+" in knowledge areas. This implies that people have positive attitudes toward and are concerned about environmental issues. However, NEETF's survey found that, despite dramatic increases in the quantity of information about environmental issues, most still lack knowledge and do not understand basic concepts. Somehow a large part of the message is not getting through.

The need for education is a cry that is frequently heard when discussing both environmental issues and citizenship. William Stapp, a pioneer in the field of environmental education (EE), used this definition: "Environmental education is aimed at producing a citizenry that is knowledgeable concerning the biophysical environment and its associated problems, aware of how to help solve these problems, and motivated to work toward their solution" (Stapp et al., 1969). From its beginning, EE was perceived as a field with dual goals of knowledge and motivation to action.

Hungerford and Volk (1990) define an environmentally responsible citizen as one who possesses awareness, concern, knowledge, skills, and who becomes actively involved "at all levels" working on issues (p. 9). An environmentally responsible citizen, as defined by the 1977 Tbilisi Intergovernmental Conference on Environmental Education, is one who exhibits "citizen behavior" (Hungerford and Volk 1990).

Studying the founders of environmental education, Gough (1993) states that EE advocated participatory democracy from its inception. This original goal of encouraging an increased role in decision-making by the public is now being reexamined. Energy problems (specifically, enormous price increases when energy was privatized) in California were a "lack of democracy crisis" (Grossman 2001), rather than an "energy crisis," due to decisions being made at the corporate rather than the community or public level. Communities with locally controlled energy sources and public input into decisions did not experience extreme cost increases.

Contrary to Gough's perspective, Shutkin (2000) views traditional environmentalists as lacking democratic social vision. He and other authors (Freyfogle 2001; McCool and Guthrie 2001; Oskamp 2000; Prugh et al., 2000; Shabecoff 2000) call for education in community-based democratic process. Using a variety of terms to describe the democratic process as applied to environmental issues, like "civic environmentalism" (Shutkin 2000) or "strong democracy" (Prugh et al., 2000), this approach mandates inclusion and involvement of all stakeholders in decisions, using conflict resolution, consensus building, and problem-solving techniques to address environmental issues. Citizens have been involved in environmental issues through mounting public lawsuits and increasing numbers of volunteer community monitoring programs (Thompson 2000). However, litigious involvement is "after the fact," using an adversarial or regulatory enforcement approach, rather than citizen involvement in decision-making.

Citizen involvement in planning and decision-making processes promotes understanding of the role and value of science. A popular misconception is that science has "answers" and can supply certainty in the place of uncertainty. Orr (1996) argues that uncertainty and ignorance are part of being human. A pioneer in education, John Dewey, agreed, seeing real life as always including uncertainty.

> The distinctive characteristic of practical activity, one which is so inherent that it cannot be eliminated, is the uncertainty which attends it. Of it we are compelled to say: Act, but act at your peril ... Practical activity deals with individualized and unique situations which are never exactly duplicable and about which, accordingly, no complete assurance is possible (Dewey 1929).

Ehrenfeld's *The Arrogance of Humanism* (1981) confronts the audacious assumption that humans can solve all problems. His warning against this attitude is especially opportune now as "geoengineers" propose quick technological "fixes" for global warming. Once again, this assumes that science has the answer to the problem, rather than taking the approach of accepting the limitations of science, the uncertainty involved, and asking the question, "What then?" Connected with the assumptions that science has the answers and that the general public can just sit back and let scientists and politicians make decisions is the deep-rooted desire for speed. We want problems solved quickly and preferably by someone else.

Orr (1996) terms the rapid accumulation of new data and facts with reduced concern for meaning, responsibility, and understanding "fast knowledge". *Fast knowledge* includes the basic assumptions of a humanistic approach, such as "more is always better" and "technology can solve anything". Added are the beliefs that "only that which can be measured is true knowledge" (Orr 1996) and that there is no difference between information and knowledge. In contrast, *slow knowledge* emphasizes understanding and responsible use of knowledge, with awareness that ignorance will always be part of being human and we cannot solve everything. Orr's views of *slow* and *fast* knowledge resonate with Berry's argument against knowledge as property and education as merely job training.

There are some things we don't know; some can be learned through a scientific approach; and other things we know but are unaware we know them or don't know how to get at the knowledge. Of course, most difficult are the things we don't know that we don't know! Or when we think we know, but we don't. Since most environmental issues involve both some knowledge and much ignorance, Freyfogle (1993) proposes using values, ethics, and intuition (local knowledge and community experience) to supplement what we do know. Adding values, ethics, and intuition into the decision-making process involves public participation. Input from citizens, the public, and members of the community is necessary in order to add these to the ongoing decision-making process. How will community members learn how and when to participate?

Changing the Flow of Decision-Making Through Education for Participatory Democracy

Socrates argued that the aim of true democracy was the common good, and, therefore, the task of education is to teach citizenship (Nussbaum 1997). The founding fathers of the USA. wrote of the importance of citizens participating in the democratic process. Jefferson spoke of "education into citizenship, the heart of which was to enable people to see (and then act upon) the common good" (Kemmis 1990). This historical view of grass-roots participation as the foundation for democracy faded as more and more of our decision-making was turned over to government and corporations. Citizens may see voting or hoping for legal redress when laws are violated and environmental issues surface in their backyards as the only available avenue for democratic participation.

Tocqueville termed this "democratic despotism," the path to loss of freedom. Emphasizing the relative benevolence of this form of despotism, he saw it as a form of government that erects over its citizens "an immense protective power which is alone responsible for securing their enjoyment and watching over their fate" (quoted in Bellah et al., 1985). The path to democratic process, by contrast, combines environmental literacy and citizenship education. Education produces environmentally responsible citizens, who possess action competency skills necessary for the participatory democratic process.

The current flow of decision-making is a top-down model, with many seeing their only responsibility as voting for persons who then make decisions for them.

True democracy is a "bottom up" approach, which depends upon an involved and literate constituency. In agreement with Hardin's 1970s definition of environmental (or ecological) literacy as the ability to ask the question: "what then?" Orr (1992) views ecological literacy as the goal of environmental education. Achieving this goal involves a knowledge base of ecological systems but also a sense of wonder and kinship with natural systems. Approaching the question from an academic viewpoint, Cortese (1993) defines environmental literacy as teaching students from any field to look at the environmental ramifications of any decision before making the decision. This approach also fits Hardin's "what then?" definition.

According to Orr (1994), environmental education is education about ecosystems, including human influences and interactions, promoting actions and behaviors that support sustainability of these ecosystems. His first principle for rethinking education is that "all education is environmental" (Orr 1994). Sustainability may be defined as incorporating knowledge and behaviors that promote healthy ecosystems (animal, plant, human, and non-living systems) in the present while not compromising their future health. Sustainability is a continuous process, occurring within a context of continuous learning: learning from the past, from mistakes and problems, and using adaptive management or on-going evaluation in order to incorporate learning into new decisions. This is an ecological view of education, based upon connections and process, rather than isolated disciplines or nuggets of factual knowledge, weaving education into the warp and woof of the "vessel of community" (Orr's term). Promoting *slow knowledge* with its incorporation of values and ethics, environmental education incorporates ecological literacy with understanding of the responsibilities of citizenship and membership within the community.

Integral to this process are education (including education into citizenship), increased understanding of process and change, and the understanding that science cannot provide absolute proof, right answers, or certainty. The vessel of community unites science, education, and social issues. For many, this is an uncomfortable union. Environmental educators often struggle with the issue of advocacy versus presenting "just the facts, ma'am". However, when teaching citizenship and action skills, educators foster independence and inquiry, rather than coerce participants into one particular answer or perspective of an issue (Cairns 2002). This is education about process, rather than presentation of mere information or "facts". The educator becomes an advocate/facilitator for participation in the process, rather than for a particular answer.

Goal-setting: A Public Process

Writing extensively about the relationship between change and societal control, Fullan believes that educators should base their practice in moral purpose. He argues that we must be able to show that efforts for the common good, which are cooperative efforts, are also justified economically. Educators need to reach people on two levels. The first level is explicit knowledge, sharing data/facts/explanations, while the second level involves tacit knowledge or beliefs/myths below conscious awareness. These are usually emotion-laden. Fullan views emotions as an indispensable part of rational decision-making rather than antithetical to this process. Dispensable or indispensable, emotions are unavoidably part of our societal decisions. Emotion plays a part in our search for, and belief in, the possibility of certainty, which we wishfully hope science can provide. Fullan cites Storr's view of the desire for the "one right answer" as an appeal to the child within us who still clings to this myth (Fullan 1999).

Many people perceive science as a field that has the "the right answers," as being certain, which is why many are puzzled by the appearance of disagreements about environmental issues. Environmental education can play a part in tackling this misperception, encouraging the process of questioning and discussion. As John Dewey said, "The quest for certainty ... is an invitation to defeat" (cited in Sarason 1993). Certainty implies that if we can find the right answer, we can mandate correct action. Issues of power and locus of control are central to change and environmental education. These issues are central to any change process and part of every social system; therefore, no change effort can be successful that ignores or discounts them. Sarason defines education as including the goal of fostering critical thinking skills (differentiating it from training, which does not meet this goal), ultimately encouraging discussion and empowerment.

Process is of paramount importance. The key to empowerment is respect for the other person and for the process itself. Collaboration, based on mutual respect, is vastly different from cooperation.

> By collaboration I do not mean cooperation, which far more often than not in practice conveys a one-way street message: 'Let me tell you what you can do for me.' There is nothing wrong with that message except when the conveyor implicitly conveys the additional message: 'This is my turf so please do not intrude' (Sarason 1993).

Environmentalists sometimes fall into this trap of "Let me tell you what you can do" or "Let me tell you what you should do". This is not consistent with the goals of empowerment or environmental education. Scientists sometimes fall into the trap of "This is my turf, so please do not intrude". Increasingly specialized language often is used to mark turf and create a boundary that others who do not speak this language cannot cross, defeating the quest for increased environmental literacy and promoting feelings of resentment and powerlessness.

Citizenship education promotes empowerment through development of the skills needed to feel competent to act. Breitling and Mogensen (1999) use the term "action competency" to describe motivation and ability to act; this competency is best promoted through democratic communities of learning. Based upon democratic participation, this approach counters the traditional science-oriented approach of many environmental educators (Jensen and Schnack 1997). Competence is defined as ability plus motivation, and action defined as any problem-solving behavior done intentionally. Jensen and Schnack argue that science-oriented environmental education can overwhelm students, increasing feelings of helplessness and passivity. "Science-oriented education" is education centered on scientific "facts" or knowledge, minus social context, and without education into democratic citizenship skills. The danger is the de-emphasis on personal connections to environmental issues and ways to have impact and to participate in the environmental decision-making process.

Environmental Education and the Precautionary Principle

Many people believe that the precepts of the Precautionary Principle are already the dominant ones in our society. For about five years I attended community meetings of a group working to have their environmental complaints taken seriously. Group members had an increasing level of frustration due to the inability to *prove* that air quality in their neighborhood has *caused* health problems. Community members continue to be angered and astonished when they are, once again, told that there is no proof. They see "proof" all around them – for instance in neighbors and family members with serious respiratory problems. Some of this anger and astonishment is due to misunderstanding the different conceptual frameworks being used. One group, usually the public and community members, believes that the dominant paradigm is already the precautionary model; they believe in the folk wisdom mottos of this paradigm: "first, do no harm," "look before you leap," "err on the side of safety," and "an ounce of prevention is worth a pound of cure". The other group (whether these might be citizens from an unaffected community, industry representatives, or politicians) may believe in a different paradigm, which is that there must be proof of harm and that this proof must be linear and direct.

In qualitative research the researcher often aims for a type of verification other than the "validity" of quantitative research. Kidder terms this "face validity," describing it as "'a click of recognition' and a 'yes, of course,' instead of 'yes, but' experience" (Creswell 1998). In my experience, when I talk with people about the Precautionary Principle (PP), there is a "yes, of course" response. This response usually includes some puzzlement, and then they ask, "Isn't that what we do?" Awareness of the limitations of the scientific method in connection with human environmental health issues is lacking.

Division between the social and the biological sciences has been long-standing. Tooby and Cosmides (1992) argue that use of the Standard Social Science Model or SSM promoted this division.

> The Standard Model therefore frees those in the biological sciences to pursue their research in peace, without having to fear that they might accidentally stumble into or run afoul of highly charged social or political issues … This division of labor is, therefore, popular: Natural scientists deal with the nonhuman world and the 'physical' side of human life, while social scientists are the custodians of human minds, human behavior, and, indeed, the entire human mental, moral, political, social, and cultural world. Thus, both social scientists and natural scientists have been enlisted in what has become a common enterprise: the resurrection of a barely disguised and archaic physical/mental, matter/spirit, nature/human dualism, in place of an integrated scientific monism (Cosmides and Tooby 1992).

The precautionary principle represents an attempt to move beyond this artificial division, uniting scientific and social perspectives.

With this approach, the educational goal changes to understanding the limits of the scientific method, especially in dealing with complex situations that cannot be controlled and where relationships are anything but linear. In a truly interdisciplinary approach, education guides us by presenting use of the scientific method as a tool for one level of comprehension and adds respect for other tools, other ways of knowing, as equally valid and potentially useful for more complex levels.

Often members of "the general public" get involved with environmental issues as a result of problems which have surfaced in their backyards or communities, leading to reactive rather than proactive action, and contributing to feelings of powerlessness and frustration. In contrast, we can begin to involve people earlier, foster on-going involvement, and unite what traditionally are viewed as adversarial factions: science, politics, industry, and community stakeholders.

Adopting a precautionary approach from the outset is desirable because actions can be agreeable to all concerned parties, easier to implement, and more effective. Attempts to apply the PP retroactively are usually ineffective, precisely because implementation occurs too late. Basic characteristics of precautionary actions include prevention of ecosystem damage, precautionary restoration, and adaptive management when unexpected events happen. Hardin's idea that we learn to ask "what then?" is central to implementation of the Precautionary Principle during any stage of decision-making.

Prevention is the very reason for the existence of the Precautionary Principle, saving money and heartache in both environmental and health care fields. It requires that we pause, look around, and consider alternatives to our current approach, which often appears adversarial, offering only "lose-lose" outcomes.

What Would This Look Like?

Bardwell (1991) postulated that use of "success stories" facilitates a sense of empowerment. Environmental "success stories" are often community-based and share common features of democratic processes, giving hope that environmental education, education for citizenship, and the Precautionary Principle can become part of everyday life for all of us. The process, which is more important than specific outcomes, may be called participatory democracy, "deep democracy" (Prugh et al., 2000), or civic environmentalism (Shutkin 2000). McCool and Guthrie's (2001) study of participants in two planning projects in western Montana, where the projects were perceived as "messy" due to conflict over goals, and there was no clear cause and effect relationship established through science, concluded that the processes were successful due to an emphasis on public learning and consensus building. Learning was cited as the primary positive outcome, involving understanding of multiple perspectives, including differences in values and beliefs among stakeholders and legal and political processes, as well as knowledge about the workings of particular ecosystems involved. Public participation built relationships through informal, face-to-face meetings, establishing increased understanding and trust.

Five urban cities, including Birmingham, Alabama, and Dayton, Ohio, have demonstrated success over time using democratic process with environmental issues. Prugh, et al. (2000) reported that, while there still was not broad based citizen participation in the decision-making process, participation increased tolerance and a sense of belonging to the community and decreased conflict. City officials found participatory democracy time-consuming but with benefits substantial enough to offset this. Prugh et al. (2000) define "deep democracy" as inclusive of all stakeholders, providing a place for feelings as well as reason, and based upon cooperation. Consensus among stakeholders is not mandatory. Other examples provided include Denmark's citizen consensus conferences, Oregon's watershed councils, and New England town meetings. Shutkin (2000) terms this civic environmentalism, the key to success in community-based approaches, citing "success stories" in Boston (Massachusetts), Oakland (California), rural Colorado, and suburban New Jersey. He lists six core concepts (p. 240) for civic environmentalism:

1. democratic process
2. community and regional planning
3. education
4. environmental justice
5. industrial ecology (pollution prevention in industry)
6. place (place motivates to action).

Application of the Precautionary Principle depends upon inclusive and democratic process. Environmental education can unite education about democratic process and use of this principle, promoting dialogue about alternatives, multiple perspectives, and inclusion of the widest possible variety of disciplines and stakeholders.

An arena ripe for inclusion of the Precautionary Principle and discussion of its application is environmental education within the school system. Surveys have shown that an overwhelming majority of citizens (95 percent) within the United States favor inclusion of environmental education within public schools (National Environmental Education and Training Foundation 2001). Many states, such as Kentucky, already have strong environmental education programs within the schools. In Denmark and some other European countries, environmental educators shifted their focus to education into democratic process or environmental citizenship, rather than education about specific environmental issues, in order to successfully address environmental issues (Breitling and Mogensen 1999).

Conclusion

Orr's (1993) image of weaving "the vessel of community" combines threads of scientific information, people, local knowledge, social and ecological systems and structures. To decrease the widening gap between citizens and government/ corporations, between knowledge and attitudes, and between scientific information and public perceptions, there must be public involvement in every decision-making process as early as possible. To counteract public apathy, helplessness, frustration, hopelessness, or angry, reactive, adversarial reactions, early public involvement and a role in decision-making along the way become part of an evolving process, which grows skills and understanding over time.

This ecological approach is based upon recognition of the importance of each stakeholder in complex environmental issues. Just as each species plays an important role in an ecosystem, each human voice must be heard, respected, and involved in addressing environmental issues. Stakeholders are people at all levels within the social structure, as well as other species. All species need non-living systems (air, water, and mineral) to sustain life. Because being truly human includes a concern for one's children and one's children's children, human stakeholders include future generations.

Incorporating the Precautionary Principle into the public arena, making it an ongoing part of every planning and decision-making process, establishing a proactive rather than reactive approach, must be based upon environmental education. Environmental education, which is all education (Orr), includes education into citizenship. Education has a societal purpose beyond accumulation of facts. Education is for citizenship: local, regional, and global.

References

Bardwell, L. (1991), 'Success Stories: Imagery by Example', *The Journal of Environmental Education*, 23:1, 5–10.

Barkow H., et al. (eds), *The Adapted Mind: Evolutionary Psychology and the Generation of Culture* (New York: Oxford University Press).

Bellah, R., et al. (1985), *Habits of the Heart: Individualism and Commitment in American Life* (Berkeley: University of California Press).

Bernard, T. and Young, J. (1997), *The Ecology of Hope: Communities Collaborate for Sustainability* (Gabriola Island, BC: New Society Publishers).

Berry, W. (1991), 'The Futility of Global Thinking', in Willers (ed.).

Berry, W. (1995), 'Conserving Communities', *Orion*, Summer, 49–53.

Breitling, S. and Mogensen, F. (1999), 'Action Competence and Environmental Education', *Cambridge Journal of Education*, 29:3, 349–353.

Cairns, K. (2001), *Environmental Education with a Local Focus: The Development of Action Competency in Community Leaders Through Participation in an Environmental Leadership Program.* Dissertation (PhD), University of Louisville.

Cairns, K. (2002), 'The Legitimate Role of Advocacy in Environmental Education: How Does it Differ from Coercion?', *Ethics in Science and Environmental Politics* [online], November 2002, available at: <www.esep.de>.

Cortese, A.D. (1993), 'Building the Intellectual Capacity for a Sustainable Future: Talloires and Beyond', in Wallace et al. (eds).

Creswell, J. (1998), *Qualitative Inquiry and Research Design: Choosing Among Five Traditions* (Thousand Oaks, California: Sage Publications).

Dewey, J. (1929), *The Quest for Certainty* (New York: Minton, Balch, & Company).

Dubos, R. (1980), *The Wooing of Earth: New Perspectives on Man's Use of Nature* (New York: Charles Scribner's Sons).

Ehrenfeld, D. (1981), *The Arrogance of Humanism* (New York: Oxford University Press).

Environmental Protection Agency (2001), *Public Involvement in EPA Decisions* [online], available from: <http://www.network-democracy.org/epa-pip>.

Freyfogle, E. (1993), *Justice and the Earth: Images for Our Planetary Survival* (New York: The Free Press).

Freyfogle, E. (1997), 'Illinois Life: An Environmental Testament', *University of Illinois Law Review*, 1997:4, 1081–1108.

Freyfogle, E. (ed.) (2001), *The New Agrarianism: Land, Culture, and the Community of Life* (Washington, DC: Island Press).

Fullan, M. (1999), *Change Forces: The Sequel* (Philadelphia: Falmer Press).

Gardner, G. and Stern, P. (1996), *Environmental Problems and Human Behavior* (Boston: Alleyn and Bacon).

Gough, A. (1993), *Founders in Environmental Education* (Victoria, Australia: Deakin University Press).

Grossman, R. (2001), 'The Strategy for Electricity is Democracy', *Annals of Earth*, 19:1, 10–11.

Hardin, G. (1977), 'Denial and Disguise', in Hardin and Baden (eds).

Hardin, G. and Baden, J. (eds), *Managing the Commons* (San Francisco: W.H. Freeman and Company).

Hardin, G. (1993), *Living within Limits: Ecology, Economics, and Population Taboos* (New York: Oxford University Press).

Hungerford, H. and Volk, T. (1990), 'Changing Learner Behavior through Environmental Education', *The Journal of Environmental Education*, 2:3, 8–21.

Jensen, B. and Schnack, K. (1997), 'The Action Competence Approach in Environmental Education', *Environmental Education Research*, 3:2, 163–178.

Kemmis, D. (1990), *Community and the Politics of Place* (Norman, Oklahoma: University of Oklahoma Press).

Langer, E. (1997), *The Power of Mindful Learning* (Reading, Massachusetts: Addison-Wesley).

Lieberman, G. and Hoody, L. (1998), *Closing the Achievement Gap: Using the Environment as an Integrating Context for Learning* (Poway, California: Science Wizards).

Marcuse, A. (ed.) (1996), *Anthropology for a Small Planet: Culture and Community in a Global Environment* (NY: Brandywine Press).

McCool, S. and Guthrie, K. (2001), 'Mapping the Dimensions of Successful Public Participation in Messy Natural Resources Management Situations', *Society and Natural Resources*, 14, 309–323.

McKenzie-Mohr, D. and Smith, W. (1999), *Fostering Sustainable Behavior: An Introduction to Community-based Social Marketing* (Gabriola Island, BC: New Society Publishers).

McKeown, R. (2000), *Education for Sustainable Development Tool Kit* (Center for Geography and Environmental Education: University of Tennessee), available at: <www.esdtoolkit.org>.

Merchant, C. (1992), *Radical Ecology: The Search for a Livable World* (New York: Routledge).

National Environmental Education and Training Foundation (1999), '1999 Report Card: Environmental Readiness for the 21st Century', The Eighth Annual National Report Card on Environmental Attitudes, Knowledge, and Behavior (Washington, DC: The National Environmental Education and Training Foundation).

National Environmental Education and Training Foundation (2001), 'Lessons from the Environment: Why 95 Percent of Adult Americans Endorse Environmental

Education', The Ninth Annual Report Card on Environmental Attitudes, Knowledge, and Behavior (Washington, DC: Author).

Newby, L. (1999), 'Sustainable Local Economic Development: A New Agenda for Action?' *Local Environment*, 4:1, 67–72.

Nussbaum, M.C. (1997), *Cultivating Humanity: A Classical Defense of Reform in Liberal Education* (Cambridge, Massachusetts: The MIT Press).

Odum, E. (1971), *Fundamentals of Ecology*, 3rd edition (Philadelphia: W.B. Saunders Company).

Ornstein, R. and Ehrlich, P. (1989), *New World New Mind: Moving Toward Conscious Evolution* (New York: Simon & Schuster).

Orr, D. (1992), *Ecological Literacy: Education and the Transition to a Postmodern World* (New York: State University of New York Press).

Orr, D. (1993), 'Environmental Literacy: Education as if the Earth Mattered', Twelfth Annual E.F. Schumacher Lectures, October 31, 1992. (Stockbridge, Massachusetts: E.F. Schumacher Society).

Orr, D. (1994), *Earth in Mind: On Education, Environment, and the Human Prospect* (Washington, DC: Island Press).

Orr, D. (1996), 'Slow Knowledge', *Conservation Biology*, 10:3, 699–702.

Oskamp, S. (2000), 'Psychological Contributions to Achieving an Ecologically Sustainable Future for Humanity', *Journal of Social Issues*, 56:3, 373–390.

Prugh, T., et al. (2000), *The Local Politics of Global Sustainability* (Washington, DC: Island Press).

Sarason, S. (1993), *The Case for Change: Rethinking the Preparation of Educators* (New York: Teachers College Press).

Shabecoff, P. (2000), *Earth Rising: American Environmentalism in the 21st Century* (Washington, DC: Island Press).

Shutkin, W. (2000), *The Land that Could Be: Environmentalism and Democracy in the Twenty-first Century* (Cambridge, Massachusetts: The MIT Press).

Stapp, W., et al. (1969), 'The Concept of Environmental Education', *The Journal of Environmental Education*, 1:1, 30–31.

Swab, J. and Stapp, W. (eds) (1974), *Environmental Education: Strategies Toward a More Livable Future* (New York: Sage Publications).

Tooby, J. and Cosmides, L. (1992), 'The Psychological Foundations of Culture' in H. Barkow et al. (eds).

Thompson, B. (2000), 'The Continuing Innovation of Citizen Enforcement', *Illinois Law Review*, 2000:1, 185–235.

Wackernagel, M. and Reese, W. (1996), *Our Ecological Footprint: Reducing Human Impact on the Earth* (Gabriola Island, BC: New Society Publishers).

Wallace, B. et al. (eds) (1993), *The President's Symposium: Volume V: Environmental Literacy and Beyond* (Blacksburg, Virginia: Virginia Polytechnic Institute and State University).

Willers, B. (ed.), *Learning to Listen to the Land* (Washington, DC: Island Press).

Chapter 17

Public Participation in Achieving Sustainability in Central City Neighborhoods[1]

Ruth Yabes and David Pijawka

In the Phoenix metropolitan area, the majority of industrial facilities that contain and produce hazardous waste materials or toxic releases, or are abandoned, are located in areas where low-income families and people of color predominate (Bolin et al., 2002; Pijawka et al., 1998). In central city areas, many residential neighborhoods have raised concerns about environmental health and safety and expressed an interest in revitalizing brownfield sites and reducing environmental inequalities. In fact, the State of Arizona's Department of Environmental Quality (ADEQ) has identified children's environmental health issues, especially in urban areas, as a policy priority (Owens 2003) and has even established an environmental justice department.

Public concerns in disadvantaged and central city areas range widely. Concerns exist about the known and serious hazardous conditions (often residuals from past practices), the lack of response by governmental agencies to clean-up, and to reactions to specific toxic releases with high levels of concerns over health risks. The disproportionate burdens of hazards among the poor, often in neighborhoods of color, have resulted in an increase in social and political actions centered on environmental justice. A perception of governmental inattention to these issues has led to the growing distrust of government to mitigate environmental problems in these central cities.

As part of the growth of the Environmental Justice movement, Brownfield redevelopment in central cities and environmental health concerns many central city neighborhoods have established participation programs to seek out information and remedies to the negative environmental conditions of their neighborhoods. Central city residents frequently recognize that the industries operating in or near their neighborhoods are the source of hazards. However, many of these residents know very little about the specific details of the environmental risks or threats and the patterns of these distributions over the urban landscape. In the face of environmental decline, they often do not have enough or adequate information available to them in an understandable format to do anything about these problems.

1   The research in this chapter was supported by grants from the City of Phoenix, Arizona, the National Science Foundation, Neighborhood Partners and Arizona State University.

Environmental/hazard data may be available from government agencies, but they are not often or systematically shared with or disseminated to residents; or if provided, they are often not understood. Industrial firms in local areas do not frequently release this information to the local residents. This lack of data in the face of serious environmental degradation has led to public distrust, suspicion, and apathy toward both the industrial sector and the government agencies which are often viewed as uncaring, removed, and slow to take action – particularly in minority areas (Pijawka et al., 1998). As a result of such concerns, the US Environmental Protection Agency (EPA) established a community information program, CARE, to provide grants to neighborhood groups to help them monitor environmental contamination and disseminate the results. CARE is a unique community-based, community-driven, multimedia demonstration program designed to help communities understand and reduce risks due to toxic and environmental pollutants from all sources (EPA, CARE, n.d.). So much of the central city concerns over environmental degradation – revitalization of brownfield sites, abandoned and contaminated industries, environmental health, lack of urban amenities and political alienation – reflect a confluence of issues centered on environmental equity. Participation programs often reflect these concerns over environmental equity.

Past literature points to a typology of equity considerations that stem from concerns over distributional, process, and procedural inequities (Pijawka et al., 1998). It is these new concerns in the area of socioeconomic sustainability that are so difficult to manage through traditional planning processes and for which new participatory processes and structures are needed. Pijawka et al. (1998) argue that innovative participation programs are required to address urban inequities. Moreover, many people in urban minority areas experiencing health issues feel helpless but they lack the experience in environmental health. Central city residents in these areas may wonder why they should even bother to participate to address these problems to improve their neighborhoods. New types of environmental data affecting neighborhoods have confounded the adoption of applying typical participatory programs. In these cases, neighborhood awareness, retrieval of scientific data, and interpretation and mitigation strategies are the objectives of participation.

Recently emerging literature on participation and sustainability is useful to this analysis. Two studies in particular are noteworthy. Bernd Kasemir et al.'s book, *Public Participation in Sustainability Science* (Kasemir et al., 2003) discusses an integrated assessment approach to participation as applied to stakeholders' attitudes and strategies on climate change. Using focus groups as an input to computer climate modeling, and other tools, the project evaluates the role of public involvement in sustainability science. A second study (Kasson et al., 1998) looks at the use of collaborative design approaches, focus groups, and charrettes in establishing alternative sustainable plans for neighborhoods in the Phoenix area. The two approaches are especially relevant for this study for several reasons. First, the Kasemir study demonstrates a participatory approach involving complex science data and high levels of uncertainties. While climate change as a topic may not be directly germane to central city environmental degradation, the approaches used in citizen participation to gauge public strategies on complex environmental risk issues can be transportable to other issues at local levels. The second case demonstrates a public *citizen-based* collaborative process to design sustainable neighborhoods in central cities.

Quite a bit is known about participation in environmental resources management and the NEPA process; a bit less is addressed about participation in brownfields redevelopment and environmental justice problems, and very little is discussed on participation issues and processes directed at environmental health concerns. Participation that emphasizes social vulnerability and resilience – the two key dimensions of sustainable development in inner city America must be addressed.

Public participation in community development, design, and environmental planning are common themes in participation literature (Arnstein 1969; Barber 1981; Bickerstaff and Walker 2001; Bleiker and Bleiker 2000; Chess 2000; Crewe 2001; Hester 1999; Hibbard and Lurie 2000; International Association of Public Participation 2001a, 2001b; Palerm 2000; Sancar 1999; Sanoff 2000). Various citizen participation ladders (Arstein 1969; Connor 1988) describe steps or levels of participation. For instance, the International Association of Public Participation (IAP2) spectrum of public participation includes five stages of participation that begins with "inform" and then leads to increasing levels of public involvement impact that include "consult, involve, collaborate and empower" (IAP2 2001a). Often these participation ladders, as well as evaluation assessments based upon these public participation programs, deal with formalized or routinized participatory processes as part of official compliance requirements. What is often missing from this literature is the need for sustainable participatory practices to more effectively deal with environmental hazards in areas that have declined socially and economically. Participation is required to address strategies for building community or neighborhood resilience. Except for sporadic brownfields redevelopment projects and infrequent responses to acute toxic accidents, the participation programs are officially and publicly offered in these areas. The question is whether local governments have the capacity to establish neighborhood participation programs based on environmental justice, remediation, and environmental health considerations.

Existing participation programs are generally "top-down," based upon federal government mandates rather than emerging from local initiatives (InterAgency Working Group on Environmental Justice 1995). If neighborhood participation programs are not readily discernable, they are more difficult to maintain for the same reason they start – resources, distance from centers of political power, lack of access and control over neighborhood problems.

Participation in sustainable urban development is not a topic generally dealt with in participation literature except for discussions on participation in brownfields redevelopment (Byrne and Scattone 2000). In a recent study of sustainable development policies and techniques in US cities, a commitment to participation is not included in the list of thirty-nine sustainable development policy areas (Jepson 2004). Despite this perceived shortcoming, one effort has been accomplished on participation programs linking areas of environmental degradation with collaborative, sustainable neighborhood design in central cities (Kasson, Pijawka and Steiner 2001). This work was funded by the US Environmental Protection Agency (EPA) as part of their Sustainability Partnership Program. The study specifically addressed the use of community participation in collaborative designs for sustainable neighborhoods in Central Phoenix. In this case, over 100 members of the community were actively involved in focus groups, charrettes, interactive design sessions, and public forums (Herberger Center for Design Excellence 2000). The literature points to a paucity of information on participation in response to new demands due to sustainability practices – especially in central cities. The new demands will require interactive processes between government and stakeholder, reduction of toxic exposures, and economic revitalization.

This chapter examines the importance and new role of participation in two different neighborhoods in south/central Phoenix, each confronting serious environmental concerns as well as neighborhood degradation and decline (Table 17.1).

Table 17.1 Neighborhood characteristics

Characteristics	NFJ	QPC
Area size	6sq. miles	N/A
Total population 2000	14,874	4,305
Percent minorities	93%	98%
Households below poverty line	62.9%	38%
Percent renters	59%	36%

The first case involves a coalition of three neighborhoods whose residents are dealing with industrial hazards, noise, and acute air pollution. Participatory activities centered on the need to obtain information about their area so that residents could articulate to government officials the environmental injustices faced by their community in their search for remedial government assistance. In this case, the participation program involved a partnership with Arizona State University and local government.

The second case is located in a largely poor, African American area which has further deteriorated as a result of a toxic event. A survey of residents in this area examined participation in the community as well as the implications of a lack of participation by community members.

These two cases are distinctively different in terms of participation processes. The first case provides insights into the information necessary for participation programs in the early stage of their development and the importance of partnership building, especially between neighborhoods, universities, and non-profit organizations. The second case provides information from a neighborhood that confronted serious degradation and toxic exposure from a nearby industry. The survey demonstrates that the lack of information on environmental hazards coupled with the absence of a participation program leads to stress, alienation, miscommunication and the inability to manage or resolve conflict.

The two cases have common dimensions in terms of sustainability goals. Perhaps more than other cases of building sustainability these two experiences exemplify, in very profound ways, the issues of urban social sustainability and the application of the concept. The marginalization and deterioration of parts of central cities can be explained by social and economic processes that lead to the abandonment of stable neighborhoods, decline of environmental quality (partly due to environmental injustice), and outmigration of stabilizing firms and employment. These political ecological processes lead to unsustainable urban regions with deterioration of social capital and quality-of-life. This chapter's underlying premise is that areas that are experiencing serious social vulnerability will be more prone to, and less resilient to, degradation pressures and environmental hazards. In these areas, it is innovative participation programs that can enhance resilience, improve capacity-building measures over time, and ultimately produce sustainable development.

The establishment of *counteracting processes* through economic re-integration, investment in social capital, and mitigation of hazardous conditions are factors characterizing sustainability, if we view sustainability as the purposeful integration of economic, social, and environmental processes toward revitalization. We argue that it is through *participation* at the neighborhood level that these processes can be directed (Figure 17.1). The two cases demonstrate how participatory processes are used to enhance *community resilience*.

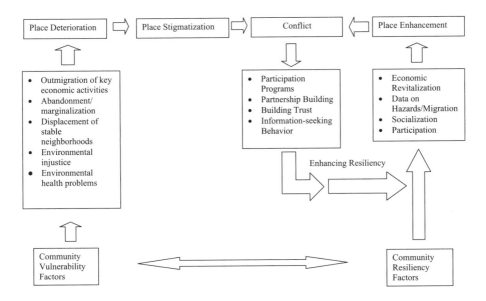

Figure 17.1 Community vulnerability and resiliency

Conceptual Framework

The framework in Figure 17.1 demonstrates the important conceptual role for considering social vulnerability and resiliency factors in sustainable community development. This conceptual framework influenced the way in which we conducted the case studies with the results pointing to the criticality of participation to enhance resiliency in advancing community sustainability. There are several entry points to the model. The typical approach taken in American cities is by entering from the "zone of conflict". The zone of conflict is characterized by reactive planning, not proactive or preventative planning. Conflicts occur between attempts to rectify declining areas or to keep places from declining further. Often these are conflicts between residents and developers or city governments over the development direction or strategies for the declining neighborhood(s). Conflict can also emerge from a lack of participatory programs, as in the two cases in Phoenix, or can directly result from participation, where demands are made of public officials or of private interests. Moving towards sustainable solutions tends to lead to conflicts that will need to be resolved. Sustainability argues for conflict resolution between the aims and objectives of equity versus economic development; environment versus community development and equity; and, environment versus economic growth. The area of governance including public participation has largely been ignored in the sustainability literature.

One participation program can result in enhanced or permanent participation programs that will address rebuilding, revitalization, and resilience. As such, it will work against place stigmatization and decline. In essence, participation in sustainability aims to reduce conflict, minimize vulnerability, and to enhance place resilience. When these processes are all working effectively and concurrently we can see the important role played by public participation in building sustainable neighborhoods in central cities.

Background and Context of the Case Studies

Phoenix has experienced two patterns of post-war industrial development. Many industrial facilities and hazardous waste-producing facilities are located along major railways and highways in central and western Phoenix (Figure 17.2) (Bolin et al., 2002). Although the second pattern of industrial location is the decentralization of electronics-manufacturing firms in suburban areas, "the majority of these polluted sites are concentrated in or near areas with significant … commercial and industrial activity, south and west of the central city," the areas in which the study sites are located (Figure 17.2) (Bolin et al., 2002: 323).

Neighborhoods for Justice (NFJ) study area

The Neighborhoods for Justice (NFJ) area in Phoenix is contained within the boundaries of Jackson St/Harrison St. to the north, the Salt River to the south, 16th St. to the east and 19th Ave. to the west, and includes three central city neighborhoods.

The three neighborhoods, Barrios Unidos, Grant Park, and Downtown Neighborhoods Southwest (DTNSW), are located immediately west of the Phoenix airport, and as such are subject to high levels of noise and air pollution and soil contamination by an old manufactured gas plant and a power substation. Additionally, a relatively large number of hazardous waste generating sites and the few hazardous waste treatment facilities in Phoenix are located here (Figure 17.2).

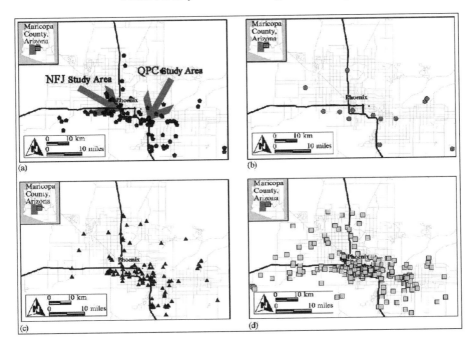

Figure 17.2 The study areas of hazardous sites in Phoenix

The impetus for forming NFJ evolved from meetings held with the non-profit organization, Neighborhood Partners, with the three different neighborhood associations. Although each group of neighborhoods suffer from problems unique to themselves, all of the three areas in NFJ were equally suffering from the expansion of the airport, noise pollution, and environmental injustice. With encouragement from Neighborhood Partners, NFJ was initially formed in 1998. Soon after NFJ began, Arizona State University, through the College of Architecture and Environmental Design and the Joint Urban Design Program, held two charrettes to assist NFJ and its leaders and residents visualize the area's assets and at the same time to address the area's challenges. Three ASU School of Planning and Landscape Architecture studio classes (1998, 2000, and 2001) also focused their class projects on items of importance to NFJ, including a history of the area, a pamphlet highlighting the services available in NFJ boundaries, and current land use maps for the three neighborhood areas. In the era of sustainability planning the role of universities embedded in a community's future and in promoting sustainable solutions through participatory mechanisms can be critical.

The NFJ's low-income minority neighborhoods are in economic and population decline. For example, in 1995 62.9 percent of households in the NFJ area were living in poverty. This compares to 13.2 percent of households living in poverty in Phoenix as a whole (US Census 1995). In 1980, 17,840 people lived within the NFJ boundaries and by 2000, only 14,874 residents still lived there, representing a 17 percent decrease in the population. This percentage decrease in residents in the

NFJ is in stark contrast to the population explosion that Phoenix experienced during the same twenty-year period – a 61 percent increase (US Census 1980, 1990, 2000; Krieps et al., 2002). Of the total NFJ population, 92.5 percent is non-white, compared to 39.7 percent non-white population in Phoenix. The Hispanic population accounts for 79 percent of the population in NFJ compared to the 34 percent in Phoenix's overall population (US Census 2000).

In 1998 the NFJ was established as a reaction to three problems. First, the three neighborhoods (Barrios Unidos, Grant Park and DSWNA), which represent a largely Hispanic population, merged in order to gather information on environmental health concerns and the environmental and health baseline conditions of the neighborhoods. Second, the City of Phoenix and Maricopa County were actively engaged in issues centered on environmental justice at the time, including controversies over permits for expanding the capacity of hazardous waste treatment facilities, airport-related relocation, and environmental clean-up. The convergence of interests among the three neighborhoods must be seen within the broader context of the environmental justice movement in the central Phoenix area. Third, the formation of a three-neighborhood partnership was the basis for political action and a participatory, communicative planning process, the first for the three neighborhoods.

Hazardous waste sites permeate within the NFJ's boundaries. In a letter to the NFJ on the status of an environmental review for the area, geologist Kathy Gerber summarized a Phase I Report prepared by Environmental First Search. The Phase I Report revealed the following results regarding the six square mile area of the NFJ: the entire six-square-mile area falls within the boundaries of two large Water Quality Assurance Revolving Fund (WQARF) sites (groundwater contamination) and two Superfund sites include portions within the NFJ boundaries – the Motorola 52nd Street OU3 on the EPA's National Priority List (NPL), and the 19th Avenue Landfill (also on EPA's NPL) (Gerber 2000). This report also identified one solid waste landfill, although four other landfills are also identified in this area on the EPA NPL. The environmental risk burden for the NFJ area also includes 113 permits for Underground Storage Tanks (UST) that store "regulated substances," while 94 sites reported Leaking Underground Storage Tanks (LUSTs). Exposure of chemicals to residents of the NFJ can be determined by the number of times that both the Arizona Department of Environmental Quality (ADEQ) Emergency Response Unit and the EPA's data base recorded chemical spills and incidents: 116 incidents occurred at 74 sites over several years (Gerber 2000). The area also has been identified as having 27 sites that are on either the EPA's NPL of confirmed or proposed Superfund Sites or the Comprehensive Environmental Response Compensation and Recovery Liability System (CERLIS). Moreover, 68 sites were on the federal listing of Resource Conservation and Recovery Information System (RCRIS) that include two known and controversial hazardous waste recycling facilities (Gerber 2000).

With respect to air quality, Particulate Matter (PM-10 and PM-2.5) is the most pressing air quality issue for Phoenix. Of the 15 sites where Maricopa County monitors PM-10 concentrations, five are near the NFJ. Four of the five sites exceeded the PM-10 24-hour standard in 2000 (Gerber 2002). The NFJ area contains two TRIs, one TSD, four LQGs and more than ten CERCLIS sites (Figure 17.2). These data demonstrate serious environmental hazards in this area with the potential for health impacts.

The Quality Printed Circuits (QPC) study area

The QPC study area lies south and east of the NFJ area and also has been an area of urban decline in central Phoenix. The area came to light over a specific environmental justice issue that lasted over a decade. Quality Printed Circuits (QPC) was the name of an electronics firm located adjacent to a disadvantaged African American neighborhood. In 1992, a fire broke out and completely destroyed the plant, leading to serious contamination in the area. The fire caused stored chemicals to ignite and disperse in a toxic smoke plume which affected a two-square mile area to the north and east of the plant. The specific equity and planning issues resulting from this case were reported by Pijawka et al. (1998).

The QPC study area consists of 11 census tracts with a population of slightly under 40,000 persons. It is unevenly distributed in residential population with old and new industrial development, significant amounts of vacant and under-utilized land, and dilapidated housing pockets. A visual survey of the area suggests neglect, under-investment, and incompatibilities between industrial activities and residential areas encouraging blight. In almost all census tracks, the mean household income was below the Phoenix average and unemployment rates were roughly double the city-wide average. Related to this statistic was the high proportion of families living below the poverty line. Census tract 1160, the area directly impacted by the toxic plume, had 38 percent of households below the poverty line in 1990 – three times the city's average. Minority residents in the 11 census tracts surrounding this incident averaged 84 percent, almost three times the City of Phoenix's percentage of minorities. Census tract 1160 had a 1990 African American population of 98 percent, and this percentage has not changed significantly in the decade since this incident.

As in the NFJ case, this study area has a higher-than-average environmental risk burden as a result of a disproportionate concentration of hazardous waste generators, abandoned sites, and toxic exposure (ADEQ 1995; Bolin et al., 2002; Pijawka et al., 1998). Pijawka et al. (1998) noted that the study area has approximately 20 percent of the state's large quantity hazardous waste generators and is the source of 39 percent of Arizona's shipments of toxic waste. Moreover, there is evidence of under-reporting of environmental problems.

Application of Public Participation in Planning for Urban Sustainable Development

The NFJ case: Participation partnerships

As the NFJ organizational name implies (Neighborhoods for Justice), its three neighborhoods have experienced loss of employment, out-migration of homeowners, a decline in neighborhood amenities, an increase in vacant properties, and an expansion of the area's hazardous waste land uses. The environmental justice issues for the three neighborhoods are pronounced. Given that NFJ is also a political coalition, community participatory activities are a natural reaction to environmental concerns in the three neighborhoods. The public participatory processes here are important to report, given these conditions and the fact that restoration – living conditions, environmental quality, and social capital – is fundamental for sustainability.

Work with the Neighborhoods for Justice Coalition in South Central Phoenix involved the efforts of two planning studios at Arizona State University (ASU) and several seminar classes that had a participation service requirement. The South Central Phoenix area suffers from a negative stigma in the City of Phoenix which, in the past, has made it difficult for NFJ residents to contact city staff and to receive information and assistance from the City of Phoenix regarding environmental conditions in their neighborhoods. After discussions with NFJ leaders and attendance at numerous NFJ and neighborhood association meetings, the instructor of the planning studios developed course syllabi and class assignments for the two studios which reflected NFJ input and suggestions. The instructor also talked with several NFJ leaders and staff from a non-profit agency about possible projects that would benefit the community while being appropriate for the skill levels of the undergraduate students for the 2001 studio class. The instructor also asked for suggestions on the scope and content of the studio. The comments and feedback from the NFJ leaders were important in the development of the course. The NFJ leaders thought the request for comments on the syllabus was "strange" because they had not been asked to do the same on other past ASU projects in the area, but this request reflected a certain level of engagement and community involvement on the part of the university that resulted in openness and communication between the residents and students.

In developing the studio assignments, South Central Phoenix leaders had a basic question: "Is it safe to continue to live in our area?" In the first studio students were asked to write short, five-page papers on a topic of interest to them taken from a long list of subjects based on the community's suggestions. Students wrote about the impacts of noise and air pollution, economic development, urban design, landscape design, property values in relation to the presence of freeways, and land use and zoning in the area. Once students had completed these papers, their topics were reviewed by community leaders and their fellow students to identify common themes and to further refine the subject matter of interest to the South Central Phoenix community.

The second undergraduate NFJ studio in 2002 combined its work with the final project of a citizen participation course. In response to the NFJ request for supplemental information on land use and zoning, the 2002 studio course focused primarily on a parcel-by-parcel land use and zoning analysis for South Central Phoenix. Information from aerial photographs, windshield surveys, ground truthing, and visits to the Maricopa County Assessor's Office were combined to create neighborhood-level land use maps that showed the distributions of residential, industrial, and vacant properties. The citizen participation course in the years 2000–2002 had a participation service component that required students to engage a community client in a participatory way that provided assistance to the community. The projects that focused on NFJ included neighborhood newsletters for the Grant Park and Downtown Southwest neighborhoods and an environmental inventory creating and renewing air quality permits for industrial firms in the NFJ area (Babu et al., 2002). The participatory process was reciprocal between NFJ and the students: community participation created knowledge to help address environmental woes in NFJ and student involvement in planning gave students important experience working directly in and with a community.

While the ASU classes were engaged with NFJ, simultaneously Jaimie Leopold of the non-profit organization Neighborhood Partners asked geologist Kathy Gerber "to sit in on some community meetings and provide volunteer environmental support for NFJ residents" (Gerber 2002). The results of Gerber's investigation provide critical and broad-based environmental information on the NFJ area in relation to emergency responses, air quality, hazardous waste facilities, landfills, Superfund sites, and other local environmental problems including brownfields and LUSTs. For example, her research on air quality demonstrated that the air quality permit process in Maricopa County provides a review process that includes public notice. The public then has thirty days to respond to the permit conditions and/or request a public hearing. Gerber emphasizes the missed opportunities for neighborhood input and participation in the permitting process:

> If the public does not respond and there is no request for modifications to the permit conditions or a public hearing is received [by ADEQ], an Air Quality Permit is issued for five years. It is important that community members learn and get involved with this permitting process because five years is a long time to get another chance to speak out about a particular facility or request a public hearing (Gerber 2002: 37).

In this case, people had just organized into the NFJ neighborhood coalition because they were seeking environmental information. Participation involved the establishment of a partnership between ASU and the three neighborhoods that was long-term and engaged residents in identifying and developing research needs. Additionally, ASU classes provided important information about environmental justice issues in the area that would lead to more participatory efforts by NFJ in seeking resolution of environmental problems from governmental agencies. This form of participation is the "inform" stage on the IAP2 public participation spectrum. The public participation goal of inform is "to provide the public with balanced and objective information to assist them in understanding the problems, alternatives and/or solutions" (IAP2 2001a).

The NFJ example is illustrative of informal participatory partnership-building involving neighborhood leadership, a non-profit organization, a community foundation, and a university. It is also an example of four institutions discovering the need for an environmental justice case to restore social and environmental capital at the neighborhood level. Through this partnership, the NFJ coalition has built up relationships with other organizations and obtained information on health risks and other environmental problems. NFJ used this information as the basis for seeking assistance on environmental problems and demanding redress from federal, state and local governmental agencies. This partnership and NFJ's participation has also strengthened NFJ's political clout and voice on environmental justice.

QPC: The importance of participation

While the NFJ case addressed participation in order to gain information and knowledge so to be able to identify and prioritize problems confronted by the communities, the QPC case illustrates community participation as a political reaction to mitigate the results of an acute toxic condition. For example, the area around the QPC fire historically had never organized politically over an environmental issue. However, one day after the fire the combination of health concerns and perceived slowness in identifying the toxics resulted in a residents' organization, Concerned Residents of South Phoenix (CRSP), and a five-year period of political and social mobilization of residents over health risks, government remediation efforts, and environmental equity. Dispute resolution was difficult due to the lack of a participatory program that would facilitate the sharing of information between the neighborhood and local government and developing mechanisms for remedial actions. To understand how perceptions of inequity stimulated the controversy and the role participation programs can play in controversies over sitings involving toxic releases, a survey of residents in the contaminated area was completed (see Lebiednik 1996).

Of the 84 completed surveys of households (Census Tract 1160), 65 percent perceived the neighborhood as having a much larger concentration of industries than any other area of Phoenix, and 74 percent felt that their area was purposely targeted as a location for industry, and that this pattern was unfair to a minority community. Significant correlations were observed between these perceptions concerning distributional inequities and perceived risks to health and safety. From a planning perspective, issues surfaced over zoning, compatible land uses, the lack of information on the processes used in local industries, inadequate emergency responses, and most importantly, the "lack of control" by community members over their own community.

The survey also measured perceptions of procedural and process equity. For example, almost 80 percent of the survey respondents felt that this area had little control over industrial location and that residents were never consulted over development in the area. Concerns were expressed over industry compliance and the lack of knowledge of hazardous materials, adequacy of permits, and inadequate communication to residents. The lack of formal participation in planning issues resulted in feelings of alienation and dissatisfaction in the political processes to help mitigate the health problems and redevelopment of the area.

Perceptions of procedural inequities stemming from the accident shook their confidence in government's enforcement abilities as well. When asked how well government worked with residents to address risk-related concerns, 77 percent indicated a response of poor or very poor. In the face of acute toxic releases, the study showed that the lack of community involvement in the past and not sharing environmental data resulted in political and social amplification over the risks, a sense of community vulnerability, and concerns over environmental justice. Process and procedural inadequacies heightened latent sensitivities to environmental problems in the area.

What did residents want as indicated on the surveys? First, they wanted strict application of compliance policies and a formal requirement for public involvement and information access. Second, the survey revealed a strong preference for public verification for new industry. Third was education and training for citizen monitoring of environmental conditions and an area involvement plan for emergencies. Lastly, because of lingering debates over health risks, there was interest expressed in establishing conflict resolution processes. Support was given to establish a citizen advisory committee for the area. These suggestions are all part of participatory processes in urban sustainability and equity practices. In fact, Lebiednik found that communication with residents was viewed as the number one strategy to reduce residents' concerns over health risks (Lebiednik 1996).

Lessons Learned

There are lessons to be learned from a case study approach that examined the role of participation in sustainable development in central cities. Overall, we found that there is a central and critical role for participation in reducing vulnerability and enhancing resilience of degraded and neglected neighborhoods. In doing so, the role of participation is to diminish the inherent conflicts among decision-makers and stakeholders about economic, social, and environmental goals. We conclude from two case studies that neighborhood participation is the vehicle to begin a process of sustainable development, however, that process must address three dimensions of neighborhood sustainability. The first is conflict negotiation and resolution along the environment-economic development, the equity-environment, and the equity-development axes. Second, participation must address the vulnerability issues in the neighborhoods. Third, participation programs need to work with other stakeholders in the community to enhance community resilience.

Table 17.2 shows the lessons learned from our two cases and the role of participation along the various sustainability dimensions. With respect to economic sustainability, participatory activities include asset and liability mapping as well as examining equity considerations. These fall within the area of assessing vulnerabilities. The development of long-term strategies for building recovery, revitalization of the economic base, and infusing social capital is viewed as economic enhancements and fall within the area of capitalizing resilience. For example, investing in brownfield redevelopment in city neighborhoods can achieve both economic and equity goals and health improvements. However, as we know from the literature, public and neighborhood participation is the requisite planning tool that can deliver sustainable development with brownfield re-development.

We discovered in these cases that participation in sustainable development is critical in central cities where many residents have given up hope, feel powerless, and have lost a sense of their role in place-making. It is therefore important to demonstrate real outcomes from neighborhood participation. We have also learned that resilience re-building and sustainable development needs to be established from a place basis and a cultural perspective. The integration of cultural sensibilities of residents within the sustainability framework will strengthen the community and give shape to the type of sustainable development that will be acceptable to the community. Without attention to culture, equity, and social well-being dimensions being central to participation objectives, sustainability will not be robust, acceptable nor provide long-term resilience.

Table 17.2 Participation and sustainability lessons

Dimensions of sustainability	Participation and sustainability lessons

Economic sustainability	• Identify assets and liabilities in the community
	• Deal directly with equity concerns and perceptions of the neighborhoods
	• Map out with community members short- and long-term strategies
	• Demonstrate to the communities real outcomes from:
	  • Neighborhood participation
	  • University participation

Social community sustainability	• Visioning is a key to inducing participation • Have the community work in terms of data collection, analysis, mapping, and making plans • Have the community do the work themselves, but have the academic planners and students also participate
Environmental/Health sustainability	• Use surveys and asset mapping to identify health issues and social impact as key participation tools
Political sustainability	• Work with neighborhood leaders, connecting them with advocacy planners in the city • Ensure longevity of university participation in the area

We also conclude that effective community visioning is an important tool for neighborhood participation. Effective visioning can and should lead to strategic plans that are bottom up from the community and likely place-based. University involvement can be at these junctures – to connect the visioning outcomes to neighborhood plan-making and urban policy. The issue of health impacts from environmental conditions in central city neighborhoods is a common problem across America as environmental justice studies have demonstrated high correlation values between contamination, hazardous facilities, spills, and toxic plumes in areas where minority populations reside. Participation by the community in this problem area is difficult for obvious reasons, even with university involvement. However, challenging health issues need to be addressed in any participatory program in building central city sustainable neighborhoods. We recommend that this is an area in which further evaluation is warranted; and, other cases around the country should be examined where health is *the* issue and locus of concern.

Governance is the key to achieving success in community – building. Participatory programs should not be terminated when low-participatory rates are the rule and when data are not available for assisting the community. We recommend that internal leadership be established in disadvantaged communities and that leadership courses should be offered by universities at the community level, if the universities are to become sustainable campuses and the drivers of sustainability thinking. Neighborhood leaders need to be connected to advocacy groups and linked to political organizations and city departments in effective ways. Longevity is the key with effective communication skills within and external to the community.

While we provide lessons learned and some recommendations there is an abundant literature on the role of participation in brownfield redevelopment that offers many more cogent recommendations for sustainable development in central cities. We have not tapped into this literature for this chapter and study. The next step is to connect the two databases and groups of literature and to examine the role of collaborative design for underserved populations. Additionally, while we have singled out each sustainable dimension and lessons learned, it is important to understand that participatory processes should consider all dimensions concurrently.

Conclusion

Urban sustainability requires addressing the environmental degradation of inner cities through clean-up, brownfield redevelopment, industrial relocation policies, and mitigation of environmental health problems. The environmental justice movement has given significant attention to these matters. This chapter addressed the role of participation in sustainable redevelopment of central cities. Outside of brownfield redevelopment, the role of participation is little known.

The chapter examined two cases of participation in Phoenix's central city. In the first case, three predominantly minority neighborhoods merged to confront concerns over industrial pollution, noise and environmental health risks. The study demonstrates that data on environmental conditions were lacking and that there is an important role for universities to play in supporting neighborhoods which require data generation and interpretation, surveys, and grant proposals. These partnerships require sustained citizen involvement, training and support from government, foundations and non-profit organizations as a first step. University engagement also requires support and commitment by the administration and a central philosophy of engagement as part of its institutional design. The sharing and distribution of information and communication are key factors in the success of start-up neighborhood organizations. University participation in community embeddedness has to be sustained as well; it cannot be a one-shot approach. Arizona State University has now established a broad-based initiative to work with urban communities that will provide faculty and student resources and incentives to engage communities. University resources will also be applied toward sustainability solutions in the city.

The second case demonstrates the enormous challenge for planners and the planning process during and after contamination events, especially in minority communities where equity issues often surface. Planners will be confronted with contemporary issues of equity in applying participation programs to sustainable development in the central city. Currently, planners are generally not up to the challenge. Therefore, equity issues will have to be at the core of education programs centered on sustainability. Environmental justice concerns and uncertainties in health risks, in addition to citizen interest in how best to participate in sustainable redevelopment of inner cities, will be central to discourse on governance and sustainability. Process and procedural equity considerations are now known to be as important as distributional issues, suggesting that the resolution of environmental risk issues will require the establishment of viable participation programs, community notification of change, cooperative decision-making, and communication exchange. Process equity goals will have to be part of sustainable policy goals in inner cities. It is clear in both case studies that participation involves an information flow between community and government which permits communities in central cities to become actively involved in environmental and land use decisions. Effective participatory programs and new governance frameworks are fundamental to achieving sustainable development in inner cities.

References

Arizona Department of Environmental Quality (ADEQ) (1995), *South Phoenix Waste Minimization Survey Project* (Phoenix, Arizona: Arizona Department of Environmental Quality).

Arnstein, S. (1969), 'A Ladder of Citizen Participation', *Journal of the American Institute of Planners*, 35:1, 216–224.

Babu, S., Nagano, A., and Wood, J. (2002), 'Neighborhoods for Justice (NFJ): Compliance and Beyond Compliance Data and Process' (PUP 510 Citizen Participation class, Professor Ruth Yabes. School of Planning and Landscape Architecture. Arizona State University).

Barber, D. (1981), *Citizen Participation in American Communities: Strategies for Success* (Dubuque, Iowa: Kendall/Hunt Publishing Co.).

Bicerstaff, K. and Walker, G. (2001), 'Participatory Local Governance and Transport Planning', *Environment and Planning A*, 33, 431–451.

Bleiker, H. and Bleiker, A. (2000), *Citizen Participation Handbook for Public Officials and Other Professionals Serving the Public* (Monterey, CA: Institute for Participatory Management and Planning (IPMP).

Bolin, B., Nelson, A., Hackett, E., Pijawka, D., Smith, S., Sadalla, E., Matranga, E., and O'Donnell, M. (2002), 'The Ecology of Technological Risk in a Sunbelt City', *Environmental and Planning A*, 34, 317–339.

Byrne, J. and Scattone, R. (2000), 'The Brownfields Challenge: Environmental Justice and Community Participation Lessons Learned from National Brownfields Pilot Projects', available at: <http://www.udel.edu/ceep/reports/brownfields/brownfields/htm>, accessed May 15, 2004.

Chess, C. (2000), 'Evaluating Environmental Public Participation: Metholodogical Questions', *Journal of Environmental Planning and Management*, 43:6, 769–784.

Connor, D. (1988), 'A New Ladder of Citizen Participation', *National Civic Review*, 77:3, 249–257.

Crewe, K. (2001), 'The Quality of Participatory Design: The Effects of Citizen Input on the Design of the Boston Southwest Corridor', *Journal of the American Planning Association*, 67:4, 437–455.

Dudley, M., Brenes-Garcia, J., Mueller, K., Tiller, J., Efird, R., Michaud, R., Aponte, R., Burns, M., Cline, K., Nam, S., Lavinsky, J., Maxwell, E., Morris, M., Ramos, C., Silentman, K., and Wollerman, G. (2001), *Neighborhoods for Justice: Our Story* (Neighborhood Planning Studio, Professor Ruth Yabes, School of Planning and Landscape Architecture, Arizona State University).

Environmental Protection Agency (n.d.), 'Community Action for a Renewed Environment (CARE) Program', R.F.P. No.: EPA-OAR-IO 06-01.

Gerber, K. (2000), Letter to Neighborhoods for Justice. Personal Communication, September 26, 2000.

Gerber, K. (2002), Environmental Review for Neighborhoods for Justice: A Compilation of Air, Soil, and Groundwater Data, and Other Environmental Information for the South Phoenix Area. Personal Communication, August 15, 2002.

Hester, R. (1999), 'A Refrain with a View', *Places*, 12:2, 12–25.

Hibbard, M. and Lurie, S. (2000), 'Saving Land but Losing Ground: Challenges to Community Planning in the Era of Participation', *Journal of Planning Education and Research*, 20, 187–195.

InterAgency Working Group on Environmental Justice, Environmental Protection Agency (1995), 'Environmental Justice Public Participation Checklist', available at: <http://www.epa.gov/epaoswer/hazwaste/permit/pubpart/appendd. pdf>, accessed on May 16, 2004.

International Association of Public Participation (IAP2) (2001a), 'IAP2 Certificate Course in Public Participation. Module 1: The IAP2 Foundations of Public Participation Student Workbook' (Alexandria, VA: IAP2).

International Association of Public Participation (IAP2) (2001b), 'IAP2 Certificate Course in Public Participation. Module 2: Designing Effective Public Participation Programs Student Workbook' (Alexandria, VA: IAP2).

Jepson, E. (2004), 'The Adoption of Sustainable Development Policies and Techniques in US Cities: How Wide, How Deep, and What Role for Planners?' *Journal of Planning Education and Research*, 23:3, 229–241.

Kasemir, B., Jäger, J., Jaeger, C. and Gardner, M. (eds) (2003), *Participation in Sustainability Science* (Cambridge: Cambridge University Press).

Kasson, W., Pijawka, D., and Steiner, F. (2001), *Sonoran Collaborations: Creating Sustainable Neighborhoods in the Sonoran Desert* (Tempe, AZ: Herberger Center for Design Excellence in association with the School of Planning and Landscape Architecture, College of Architecture and Environmental Design, Arizona State University).

Krieps, J., Allen, T., Howard, C., Storie, E., Tewaheftewa, T., Pierce, M., Di Stefano, J., Davila, A., Carr, B., Roher, M., McCabe, B., Griemsmann, N., McGeough, P., Murillo, J., Robison, M., Rehfeldt, T., and Hanson, L. (2002), *Neighborhoods for Justice: Past and Present* (Neighborhood Planning Studio, Professors Ross Cromarty and Ruth Yabes, School of Planning and Landscape Architecture, Arizona State University, Tempe, Arizona).

Lebiednik, S. (1996), 'Public Perceptions of Environmental Inequity: A Case Study of South Phoenix', Master of Environmental Planning Thesis (School of Planning and Landscape Architecture, Arizona State University).

Nasar, J. and Preiser, S. (eds) (1999), *Directions in Person-Environment Research and Practice* (Brookfield: Ashgate Publishing).

Owens, S. (2003), Presentation at Arizona State University's Workshop on Sustainability Technologies (Tempe, Arizona).

Palerm, J. (2000), 'An Empirical-Theoretical Analysis Framework for Public Participation in Environmental Impact Assessment', *Journal of Environmental Planning and Management*, 43:5, 581–600.

Pijawka, D., Blair, J., Guhathakurta, S., Lebiednik, S., and Ashur, S. (1998), 'Environmental Equity in Central Cities: Socioeconomic Dimensions and Planning Strategies', *Journal of Planning Education and Research*, 18, 113–123.

Sancar, F. (1999), 'An Integrative Approach to Public Participation and Knowledge Generation in Planning and Design', in Nasar and Preiser (eds).

Sanoff, H. (2000), *Community Participation Methods in Design and Planning* (New York: John Wiley & Sons).

Slovic, P. (2000), *Perception of Risk* (London: Earthscan).

US Census, 1980, 1990, 1995, 2000.

Chapter 18

Balancing Economic Growth and Social Equity: Less-Educated Workers in High-Tech Regions

Criseida Navarro-Díaz

Introduction

Many high-tech regions today show signs of the displacement and exclusion of low-skilled workers from the employment and wage benefits of a booming economy. Whether high-tech activities are responsible for these trends or if the *ex ante* characteristics of the region would tend to predispose its residents to this exclusion in the absence of high-tech growth are issues that scientists have left largely unexplored. Understanding what low-skilled and high-skilled workers undergo in the presence of high-tech activities and how that compares to the realities of the individuals who reside in regions where the economy is not dependent upon knowledge-intensive sectors provides an opportunity for policy makers to evaluate industry-choice decisions in the interest of economic growth and social equity in regional development. To provide that backdrop, I empirically answer the following questions in this chapter: *How are the benefits of high-tech development distributed between less- and more-educated workers? How does this distribution compare to that of regions that do not follow an education-intensive development path? Are social equity and sustained growth possible under these conditions?*

Using regression analysis across 50 regions in the United States during the 1990s, I show that shifts in regional economic-base composition towards a greater concentration of high-tech activity cannot be held, on its own, responsible for exclusionary patterns in these regions. As high-tech activity increases in a region it attracts workers of all skill levels, causing employment upsurges that are more substantial for college graduates than for high-school graduates. This shift in economic-base composition yields wage drops for low-skill workers but only when migration and cost of living are taken into consideration. Conversely, shifts in the composition of the region's workforce towards a more-educated labor pool resulting from migration flows lead to an employment-growth shrinkage for all skill groups, this adverse effect in supply being stronger on high-skill labor than on low-skill labor. As the proportion of college graduates increases, it deters other high-skill workers from entering the region, slowing down growth in their supply, their wages, and overall growth in an economy based in this input. Once cost of living and migration are taken into consideration, an increase in this proportion yields wage drops for high-school graduates and a small wage gain in college graduate wages, causing greater wage inequality between more- and less-educated workers and more- and less-educated regions.

High-Tech Growth: Road to Advancement or Exclusion?

Given the New Economy's bias towards knowledge creation and innovation, regions attempt to survive by attracting activities that are both dependent on those inputs and that can (re)produce them, under the assumption that multiplier effects will lead to not only direct, but also indirect and induced growth in employment, income, and consumption. However, empirical evidence supporting this claim in the case of knowledge-intensive economic activity is lacking, especially at the regional scale of analysis. Furthermore, the physical displacement of entire communities and the exclusion of low-skill workers and their families from opportunities of economic advancement, such as access to well-paying jobs, are noticeable today in high-tech regions in the European Union, Asia, and the United States (Lauder 2001; Schienstock 2001).

It is not evident that new jobs created directly in high-tech sectors and those resulting from any linkages to other activities are accessible to low-skill workers who are unemployed or could become unemployed due to increased skill requirements associated with an education-intensive development strategy (Brown 2001). Well-known high-tech cities, such as Boston, Massachusetts, often find that the jobs being created in the Information Technology and Biotechnology sectors, for example, are not accessible to their residents; instead, economic migrants from neighboring regions (perhaps with higher incomes, greater mobility, and capable of affording longer -interstate- commutes via car or train) come in and take those jobs, further thinning the employment-opportunity and affordable-housing pool for local residents (Boston Redevelopment Authority 2002). For instance, several states which are widely known for hosting high-tech activity, including Massachusetts, are suffering from a "growing exodus" of working families towards neighboring states as a result of skyrocketing housing prices (*The New York Times* 2003; *Hartford Courant* 2003). It is unclear whether or not high-tech regions can sustain growth under these migratory patterns, which may result in "more economically and socially stratified" regions (The Massachusetts Institute for a New Commonwealth 2003). These patterns challenge the proposition that knowledge-intensive activities could generate a trickle-down effect that could improve the level of living in a region for all to enjoy in more-or-less the same way.

Many analysts argue that these patterns reflect a demand shift, towards high-skill labor and away from low-skill workers, that is not exclusive of high-tech regions, and that wage differentials between low-skill and high-skill labor reflect a premium on higher education levels (Lash 1994; Katz et al., 1996). However, low-skill workers could be at a disadvantage, beyond the expected wage disparities that are derived from a shift in relative demand towards more-educated labor, in regions whose economic base is progressively more concentrated in sectors requiring increasingly higher levels of skill, as it is the case in high-tech regions, especially if those sectors generate or attract large gross inflows of workers from other regions. Depending upon the labor market's supply-demand balance within each region this disadvantage can take, on one hand, affect the shape of increased unemployment and underemployment when low-skill labor supply exceeds low-skill labor demand. On the other hand, clustering of high-tech firms and immigration into urban areas and the pressure they exert over land markets could decrease the net number of non-college graduates who are able to remain in the region if the prevailing low-skill wage cannot meet higher housing costs.

Migration-driven changes in workforce composition could affect the labor market outcomes of high-skill labor as well. The average regional return to education, that is, the difference between the college graduate and high-school graduate average annual income for a particular region, for an individual who resides in a region primarily dominated by a more-educated workforce can be very different from the wage differential that another with equivalent education in a region characterized by a less-educated workforce, when controlling for his/her own industry of employment and other individual and regional traits (Goetz et al., 2003). According to Goetz et al., the return to education increases with the proportion of college graduates in a region, but at a decreasing rate. As the proportion of the population that holds a college degree in his/her region of residence increases, it changes the overall composition of labor supply thus affecting the determination of relative wages and the return to migration from one region to the other.

Then net migration flows and their impact on costs-of-living could hinder a region's capacity to attract and retain labor, and, consequently, its ability to sustain long-term growth in sectors that depend of that input. Differences in the regional land markets, especially with regards to housing supply price elasticity, could be partly at fault for the exclusionary trends present in high-tech regions today. High-tech regions with few restrictions on urban growth could exhibit different housing prices and wage patterns (than regions that already are urbanized to a large extent), which would allow its residents to stay in the region and enjoy both the employment and wage benefits from economic growth in knowledge-intensive sectors.

This highlights the possibility that the concentration of a region's economic base in high-tech activities could create a society of exclusion, by reducing employment opportunities for low-skill workers, but also that the interaction between the migration flows that education-intensive activity could generate and the *ex ante* regional traits, such as the characteristics of its housing market, could exacerbate the situation by crowding out those who cannot meet price increases from the clustering of these activities, if it in fact occurs. It is possible that returns to migration into a high-tech region could decrease even for the more-educated. This could place regions in a shortage of its most important resource for education-intensive economic growth, high-skill workers. Whether or not high-tech sectors could have the potential of sustaining long-term economic growth in regions that follow that path, it is not clear that the prosperity that could come to a regional economy as a result of that choice would benefit the entire population. In this study, I seek empirical evidence of the existence or lack of this exclusionary pattern and its sources.

Cost of living, Migration, and Education-Intensive Economic Growth

Existing theoretical and empirical models of regional economies include as an assumption the presence of linkages among sectors of the economy that can be measured in terms of direct, indirect, and induced employment, income, and consumption. Several analysts have attempted to measure these impacts as generated by investment on high-tech activities. Their attempts have shown multipliers of substantial magnitude (Milken Institute 1999); however, they have failed to measure the spread of the multiplier throughout a regional population. Consequently, the assumption of these models is not backed up by sufficient empirical evidence supporting a trickling-down effect of that investment across labor groups. This deficiency stems from the fact that these models historically have concentrated on analyzing the aggregate impacts of investment or growth in one industry over other economic sectors, not their distribution across population groups. In their framework, analysts generalize and group households as one category or sector. This impedes measuring how the potential benefits of the investment could be distributed across different skill-level segments of a regional population.

In order to measure and evaluate properly the magnitude and spread of the impacts that could derive from industry-specific economic growth, I establish a theoretical framework that recognizes labor heterogeneity and the potential effect of an individual's traits and behavior on his/her outcomes. According to this model, as technology drives up the demand for high-skill labor and high-tech firms come into a region, drawn by the presence of a specialized-labor pool, suppliers, and competitors (Porter 1995), both the relative and absolute demand of high-skill workers (college graduates) are expected to go up along with their wages. (In Figure 18.1, high-skill labor demand and wages increase from D^0 to D^1 and w^0 to w^1, respectively.) In areas of relatively high labor mobility, as it is the case across the United States, high-skill labor would be inclined to migrate from regions offering lower to those offering higher returns to education (in addition to other externalities), and thus to migration (Waddington et al. 2003). Theoretically speaking, as more-educated workers come into the region, wages could continue to rise with continuous increases in demand and/or if the geographic clustering of knowledge-intensive economic activity and more-educated labor could successfully create increasing returns to scale.

Given limited availability of space in cities, a higher demand for land and housing for these workers could drive up prices and lock in or displace others who cannot afford higher housing prices to low-cost pockets across the region, in a gentrifying pattern (Milken Institute 1999). Depending on the elasticity of the housing supply (S^{0a} vs. S^{0b}), in terms of constraint for development, an increase in demand from these workers could translate into significant increases in rents or prices affecting the overall cost of living in the region. (In Figure 18.1 b, housing demand increases from D^0 to D^1 and prices can escalate from R^0 to R^{1a} in case of a highly inelastic supply or to R^{1b} in regions with greater supply elasticity.)

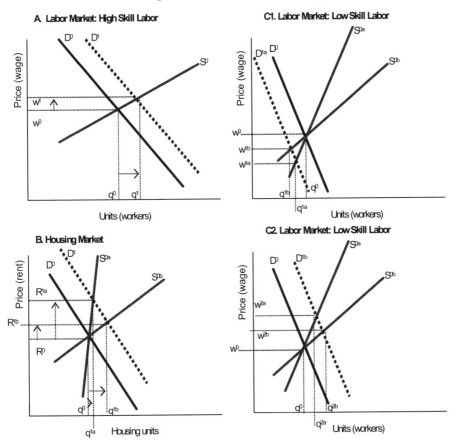

Figure 18.1 Expected behaviour of labor and housing markets in high tech regions

Notwithstanding, we know little about what happens to demand and supply of low-skill workers. First, we do not know the elasticity of their supply, that is, can they adjust by moving or do they get trapped in low-cost pockets. (Figure 18.1 c1 also illustrates a low supply response to wage changes as S^{0a} and high low-skill labor elasticity as S^{0b}). As for their demand, we expect their relative demand to drop (that is as compared to high-skill labor) but, in absolute terms, it could stay the same, go up (from D^0 to D^{1b} in Figure 18.1 -c1.) or down (from D^0 to D^{1a} in Figure 18.1 c2), depending on whether or not high-tech activities are able to generate demand for these workers in other sectors of the economy. Figure 18.1 c1 and c2 shows how alternative scenarios would yield very different results with regards to employment and wages. Whether or not the supply of low-skill labor shrinks and/or changes its elasticity due to displacement (move to another region and/or become unemployed) or skill upgrading (in order to move into the high-skill labor market) would determine how they fare as they get caught between fewer job opportunities and higher living (and particularly housing) costs. Holding low-skill supply constant, with a decrease in demand (from q^0 to q^{1a} or q^{1b} in Figure 18.1 c1), wages are likely to drop (from w^0 to w^{1a} or w^{1b} in Figure 18.1 c1), while an increase in demand (from q^0 to q^{2a} or q^{2b} in Figure 18.1 c2) would drive wages up (from w^0 to w^{2a} or w^{2b} in Figure 18.1 c2). Furthermore, the elasticity of the supply would determine the magnitude of these changes in employment and wage rate. However, with a decreasing low-skill labor supply, from migration, their pre-high-tech wages could be sustained or rise moderately.

Whether or not the concentration of education-intensive economic activity can drive up costs-of-living and/or generate migration in or out of a region could determine not only how low-skill labor fares in the short-run but also how high-skill labor could fare in the long-term in regions with those characteristics. Migration alters the overall composition of the regional workforce, which often is an important component of the region's competitive edge. In the absence of increasing returns to scale, it is possible that as the proportion of college graduates in a region rises, growth in wages could slow down until there are no differences in returns to education across regions and thus these workers have no incentive to migrate. This would slow down growth in supply and wages. Moreover, these conditions could hinder a region's capacity for growth in education-intensive economic activities.

With regard to low-skill wages in high-tech regions and how they compare to non-high-tech regions, existing labor-market models, such as those of Goetz et al. (2003) and Hanushek et al. (2000), would predict that even in the presence of larger inequality (as compared to high-skill labor), low-skill workers could earn higher wages at a high-tech region than they would otherwise (in a region with lower concentrations of high-tech activity). As demand for their labor would not automatically disappear and their supply, relative to a non-high-tech region, would be lower, they potentially could reap higher relative wages. Figure 18.2 and 18.3 illustrate higher wages for both high- and low-skill labor in high-tech regions than in non-high-tech regions).

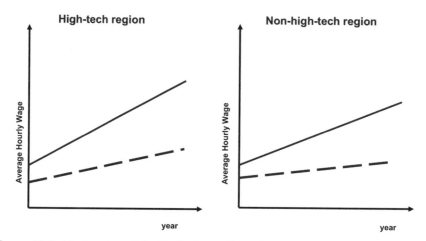

Figure 18.2 Abstract model of inflation-adjusted wage patterns

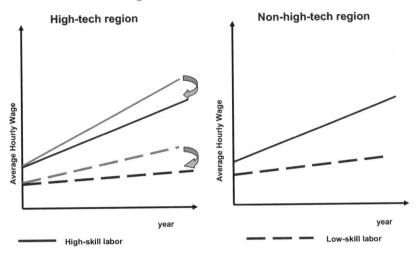

Figure 18.3 Abstract model of real wage patterns

However, those models control for inflation over time but fail to acknowledge regional cost-of-living disparities, that is, the difference in purchasing power of an individual's wage across regional jurisdictions. High-tech regions have shown higher living costs, especially with regards to land and real estate prices (ACCRA 1990, 2000). Controlling for cost-of-living differences across regions, wages reflect that the level of living that low-skill workers can afford could be very different. Their relative wages (both with regards to high-skill labor in high-tech regions and labor of equivalent levels of skill at non-high-tech regions), and subsequent purchasing power, could be substantially lower. (Figure 18.4 illustrates a drop in purchasing power when the wages in high-tech regions are adjusted for cost-of-living differences across regions.) The wages of low-skill workers in high-tech and non-high-tech regions could be equivalent in magnitude, yet the income gap between them and their skill-level counterparts could even be wider in the former, that is, that in a high-tech region low-skill workers could be in the presence of both lower wages and larger inequality. Furthermore, this difference in purchasing power, between regions that follow an education-intensive development strategy and those that do not, could affect high-skill workers also. Possibly, they could obtain lower purchasing power in a high-tech region than in a region with a more diverse economic base.

Although this research would need to test whether or not the differences in attainable wages and the costs-of-living across regions, would be sufficient to drive the migration of low-skill workers out of and high-skill workers into high-tech regions, if any divergences that derive from high-tech growth do push migration, it is possible that if these flows occur for a long enough time, wages and employment would return to their long-run equilibrium.

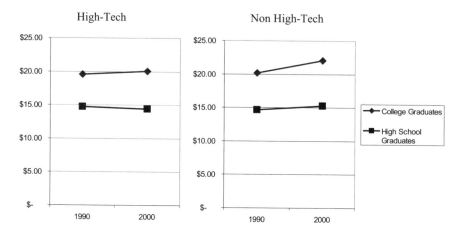

Figure 18.4 Cost-of-living adjusted average hourly wages for male workers

In the long run, whether or not the situation of the less-educated is able to improve could depend on a variety of events, including the presence or absence of a *trickling-down* effect from high-tech investment (i.e. multipliers maintaining or generating a certain level of demand for low-skill labor in other sectors and the resulting wages), the individual's ability to adapt to demand shifts through skill upgrading (higher wages in other economic sectors) or migration (lower costs-of-living and more employment opportunities elsewhere), and/or other external factors, such as public policies and programs, that may give him/her tools to bridge the gap between wages and living expenses.

Looking for Answers: Research Design and Data Sources

In order to test the null hypothesis of no effect from high-tech growth over employment, wages and migration patterns across skill groups during the 1990s and identify potential areas for policy interventions that these trends could generate, I first needed to define what I consider to be high-tech sectors and regions in this study. High-tech activities are those occurring in industries that spend an above-average proportion of their revenue on research and development and that employ an above-average number of technology-using occupations, such as scientists, engineers, mathematicians, and programmers (Milken Institute 1999). These are (along with each industry's Standard Industry Code (SIC)): Drugs (283); Computer and Office Equipment (357); Communications Equipment (366); Electronic Components and Accessories (367); Aircraft and Parts (372); Guided Missiles; Space Vehicles and Parts (376); Aeronautical Systems, Instruments and Equipment (381); Laboratory Apparatus and Instruments (382); Medical Devices (384); Telecommunications (481); Computer Programming (737); Motion Picture Production (781); Engineering and Architectural Services (871); and R&D Services (873). From this perspective, a high-tech region would be a region that exhibits above-average concentrations of firms, output, and employment in the above-indicated sectors as compared to national average values, i.e. regions with high-tech location quotients (LQ_{ht}) of value equal or greater than 1.

Then, using Weighted Least Square (WLS) Regression Analysis, I developed an empirical cross-regional model that would consider the composition of the workforce, the economic-base make-up, and a set of dummy variables to control for a region's *ex ante*, location-specific characteristics (which may include size, weather, and distance to amenities, among others) at the beginning of the decade, as potential determinants of the employment growth and wage changes that male college and high-school graduates experienced throughout the 1990s. The dependent variables of the empirical model are the 1990 to 2000 change in labor supply and wage rate for male college graduates and high-school graduates. These are further subdivided into migrant and non-migrant workers within each skill category.

In the model, the independent variables pertain to the starting point of each region with regards to the workforce and economic base composition, which determines the opportunity for employment for low-skill vis-à-vis high-skill labor, and the average hourly wage for each skill group, which determines the willingness to work for native labor and the return to migration into that region. In this framework the high-tech fraction of a regional employment pool is a measure of relative demand for high-skill and low-skill workers. The proportion of college graduates becomes a proxy for the education intensity of each region at the beginning of the decade. In addition, I created regional dummies to control for non-labor-related *ex ante* characteristics. The regional dummies follow the 1960 Census Division Code. These organize states and metropolitan areas throughout the United States into the 9 macro-regions presented in Figure 18.5. These WLS equations were weighted according to the size of the labor force at each region and were ran with and without cost of living and migration patterns taken into consideration. Other WLS regression equations were ran to explore other relationships among these variables.

I utilized five secondary data sources. To obtain the economic-base composition and location quotients, I used 1992 and 1997 Economic Census employment data for each SIC included in the high-tech sector definition. In addition, I employed individual 1990 and 2000 data from the Current Population Survey (CPS), the government's monthly household survey of employment and labor markets. The National Bureau of Economic Research (NBER) compiles and standardizes these CPS data in Merged Outgoing Rotation Group (MORG) Files that contain disaggregated data for about 30,000 individuals for selected variables. In this study, I used the MORG files to derive the employment and average hourly wage variables from information regarding an individual's hours worked, weekly earnings, highest grade completed, employment classification and industry, among others. I used the 1990 and 2000 Census of Population and its Public Use Microdata Samples to obtain aggregate and individual data regarding migration status (place of residence five years prior to the Census), as well as the income, wages, and school attainment, among others, for each migration category. Furthermore, I used the Bureau of Labor Statistics consumer price index (CPI) and the cost-of-living indices that the ACCRA-Association for Economic Development Researchers and Analysts develops to help account for inflation and regional cost-of-living differences.

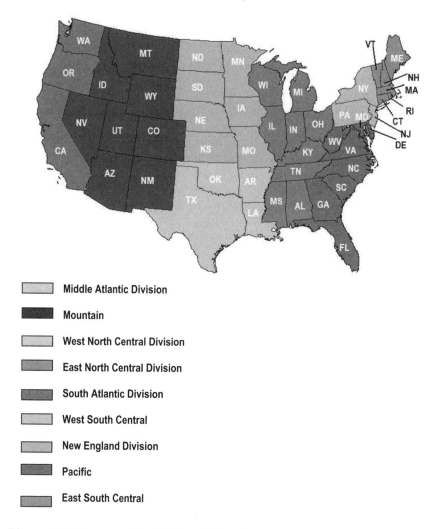

Figure 18.5 Geographic divisions defined

While the United States has hundreds of metropolitan areas as defined by each of these data sources, when taking into consideration the required variables and their availability for each region of at least two observations (i.e. 1990 and 2000 for socio-demographic variables and 1992 and 1997 for economic variables), the number of regions and level of aggregation possible for this analysis is only 50 metropolitan areas. These 50 regions are the aggregate of all metropolitan areas for each state in the country, except Wyoming which did not have any metropolitan areas in 1990. I substituted Washington, DC for Wyoming as the 50th region to include in the analysis. I hereafter label these metropolitan areas according to their state name abbreviations.

Core Findings

This research sheds light on the impact of high-tech activity on the labor market outcomes of college and high-school graduates, especially with regards to supply growth, wage rate changes and migration patterns.

Wage rate changes

The empirical model here developed does a better job at predicting the wages of college graduates than those of high-school graduates with and without cost-of-living considerations, yielding an R^2 of 0.65–0.67 for college graduates and R^2 of 0.42–0.44 (Table 18.1). It is important to recognize that, given the sample size, the model yields statistically significant coefficients only for high-skill labor. Nonetheless, the observed patterns within the sample data provide some revelations about the dynamics of the problem at least for these 50 metropolitan areas. According to this set of WLS regression results, those workers who during 1990–to–2000 resided in high-tech regions on average experienced slower growth in wages and had lower wages by 2000 than did workers who resided in regions of a low LQ_{ht}, regardless of skill level (B=-0.34 for college graduates; B=-5.55 for high-school graduates). High-tech regions started the decade with higher wages and had less space for these wages to grow, while non-high-tech regions started low and were able to catch up with them (Figure 18.6 shows patterns for sample data). While high-tech activity growth has a negative impact on wages, the concentration of educated individuals seems to have a positive effect at least on others with similar levels of skill, mainly college graduates (B=8.7, $0.20 \geq p \geq 0.10$). The proportion of college graduates in a region has a smaller effect on high-school graduate wages, especially when cost of living (COL) is controlled for (B=1.30 before, b=0.65 after COL considerations).

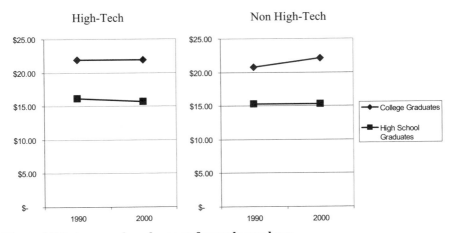

Figure 18.6 Average hourly wage for male workers

Table 18.1 Wage growth for male workers: 50 metropolitan areas in the United States, 1990–2000

Independent variables	Without cost of living consideration		Cost of living considered	
	R-square = 0.70	R-square = 0.44	R-square = 0.65	R-square = 0.42
	College graduates	High school graduates	College graduates	High school graduates
1990 Wage for skill category in region	-0.837948**	-0.852454**	-0.815357**	-0.79035**
1990 Proportion of college Graduates in region	8.760829**	1.307422	9.1575**	0.652233
1992 Fraction of high-tech jobs in region	-0.343675	-5.552301	-4.931985	-6.04812
New England (reference category for ex ante regional characteristics)				
South Atlantic	-1.184241	0.131535	1.890703	1.376602
Middle Atlantic	0.055026	0.813092	1.432249	0.896612
East North Central	0.287232	1.182805	3.025175**	2.151183
West North Central	-4.847388	0.432134	-2.29581	1.313329
East South Central	-0.517282	-0.032211	3.26506*	1.600791
West South Central	0.418892	-0.225807	4.4794**	1.518019
Mountain	0.666328	1.642536	2.532415	2.032154**
Pacific	-1.114077	1.179347	-0.897456	0.557925
(Constant)	16.42523**	12.385798**	13.466455**	10.771177*

Source: Author's calculations on 1990 and 2000 Current Population Survey Data (US Bureau of Labor Statistics).

Note: * = 0.20≥p≥0.10   ** = p≤0.10

Using 1990–2000 Census data, it has been found that an increase of 1 percent in the high-tech location quotient of a region can drive a 2 percent increase in housing prices ($0.05 \geq p \geq 0.00$). When cost-of-living differences are accounted for in the regression, the proportion of high-tech jobs has a greater negative effect on wage particularly for high-school graduates. On the other hand, the proportion of college graduates has a more positive effect on college graduates but less positive on high-school graduates. Given this relationship between high-tech growth and cost-of-living patterns, in the database, workers who reside in high-tech regions end up with smaller purchasing power than those who reside in non-high-tech regions. The situation is particularly harmful for male high-school graduates who actually suffer drops in cost-of-living-adjusted wages.

Supply growth

With regards to supply growth, while the model still has stronger explanatory power for college graduates than for high-school graduates (R^2 of 0.67 vs. 0.54, in Table 18.2), it yields statistically significant coefficients for both groups, allowing for more conclusive generalizations about the outcomes of those skill groups in high-tech regions vs. non-high-tech regions. As a matter of fact, the coefficients for high-school graduates in this model offer more statistically significance than those of college graduates. According to these WLS regression results, increases in high-tech employment share drive up supply growth for all skill groups, more markedly for college graduates than for low-skill labor (B=8,408 for college graduates vs. B=27,991 for high-school graduates). This on its own, however, does not exert an adverse effect on how workers perform across regions. As a matter of fact, the relative composition of the workforce has an opposing effect to that of economic-base composition. Regions with higher proportions of college graduates experienced smaller increases in supply for either skill level; however, the deterrence effect is larger for college graduates (B=-40,423 for college graduates vs. B=12,142 high-school graduates) who associate smaller returns to migration in the presence of greater competition in the regional workforce. According to the models, a development strategy that is centered on a more-educated labor force, i.e. relatively high proportion of college graduates, has a leveling-off effect which slows down overall supply growth. This, in turn, would limit a region's capacity to sustain growth using their more-educated labor as its competitive edge. Once cost-of-living differences are controlled for, regions with higher proportions of college graduates exert a smaller deterrence effect, yet they still grow more slowly with regards to high-skill than low-skill labor supply.

Table 18.2 Supply growth for male workers: 50 metropolitan areas in the United States, 1990–2000

Independent Variables	Without cost of living consideration		Cost of living considered	
	R-square = 0.67	R-square = 0.54	R-square = 0.67	R-square = 0.54
	College graduates	High school graduates	College graduates	High school graduates
1990 Wage for skill category in region	116.184107	-398.06264*	166.536328	-38.380894
1990 Supply of skill category in region	0.708752**	-0.140991**	0.700854**	-0.155894**
1990 Proportion of college graduates in region	-40422.66687**	-12142.0644*	-39862.76455**	-11586.58522*
1992 Fraction of high-tech jobs in region	84087.05483**	27991.2873*	80302.77625**	31346.53952**
New England (reference category for ex ante regional characteristics)				
South Atlantic	3668.904313	-2083.089359	3161.767145*	-1841.720395
Middle Atlantic	-1771.020017	-8949.713382	-1300.100511	-7028.462534
East North Central	-13164.65296*	-5405.546994	-13570.60216*	-3888.164592
West North Central	969.752711	-2578.002404*	256.560993	-1481.708984
East South Central	5218.697565	123582787	4720.762387	1166.735893
West South Central	-1600.268226	1404.433301	-2142.053398	2559.127394
Mountain	4079.997824**	2848.529579*	3657.868485**	2682.79258
Pacific	10178.678**	2727.81161*	10261.14511**	1992.750358
(Constant)	5484.566233*	9372.438832*	5024.661649	3309.234843

Source: Author's calculations on 1990 and 2000 Current Population Survey Data (US Bureau of Labor Statistics).

Note: * = 0.20≥p≥0.10   ** = p≤0.10

This would suggest that the negative impacts observable today in so-called high-tech regions do not come directly from changes in labor demand but instead from changes in the composition of the workforce throughout a decade. This factor can increase cost of living by increasing absolute labor supply (which translates into larger demand for housing). It can affect wage determination as well by determining relative supply of low-skill vis-à-vis high-skill labor.

Migration flows

When migration enters the supply model, its explanatory power changes significantly, reaching an R^2 of 0.86–0.96 for college graduate and of 0.84–0.96 for high-school graduate supply growth (Table 18.3). The R^2 for wage rate changes are also higher, 0.68–0.75 for college graduates and 0.45 for high-school graduates. In addition, nearly all coefficients have statistically significant values.

According to these WLS regression results, differences in migration patterns seem to be, at least partially, responsible for displacement observed in high-tech regions; however, this model also discerns between the impact of high-tech activity growth and that that comes from an increasing proportion of college graduates. On the one hand, increasing high-tech employment share attracts labor of all skill levels; that is, that all coefficients for migrants regardless of education level are positive. Nonetheless, while that increase raises the number of college graduates who are able to stay in the region, it reduces the number of high-school graduates who could stay in the region (while the coefficient for high-skill labor is positive, it is negative for low-skill labor). On the other hand, as the proportion of college graduates increases in a region, it not only reduces the number of workers of either skill level who are able to stay, but also deters other college graduates from entering the region, all with negative coefficients.

The clustering of more-educated workers crowds working families out of the region of both skill-levels, reducing the availability of the primary input needed for these development-path choices, which are more-educated workers. Thus, clustering could hinder the capacity of knowledge-intensive sectors to sustain growth in the long run. This clustering effect has a larger impact over low-skill workers that on college graduates, though, since high-school graduates exhibit low mobility and cannot adapt to labor-demand shocks through migration as college graduates most often are able to.

Table 18.3 Migratory patterns for male workers: 50 metropolitan areas in the United States, 1990–2000

	Without cost of living considerations			
	College graduates		High-school graduates	
	R-square = 0.86	R-square = 0.96	R-square = 0.85	R-square = 0.94
Independent variables	Migrants	Non-migrants	Migrants	Non-migrants
1990 Difference between regional and national wages for skill group in region	892.142134**	189.081882	1002.896066**	572.389733
1990 Supply for skill group in region	3.042779**	5.966701**	1.065079**	3.713496**
1990 Proportion of college graduates in region	-34317.7135*	-166567.254**	3969.532037	-32318.4389
1992 Fraction of high-tech jobs in region	37436.9366	223042.1151**	27518.1153	-22466.5441
New England (reference category for ex ante regional characteristics)				
South Atlantic	7524.39623*	-12142.6096*	10767.16345**	-26636.9782**
Middle Atlantic	-46937.0205	48726.93945	-69550.2979**	-20712.6959
East North Central	-18378.9386	10988.06126	-3051303804*	-3481.15529
West North Central	4632.44385*	-1046.73061	6086.55914**	-3426.90625
East South Central	-3922.61942	-10693.342	2281.814071	-9534.52935
West South Central	6727.06471*	2467.220237	13052.66271**	21835.36333*
Mountain	6788.73303*	4444.628629	5777.715027**	-2410.04672
Pacific	266.347044	1110.89737*	2794.545462	-10084.6091*
Constant	9969.27897	54592.73069**	-3664.65761	27495.0361**

Table 18.3 continued

	Cost of living considered			
	Male college graduates		Male high-school graduates	
	R-square = 0.86	R-square = 0.96	R-square = 0.84	R-square = 0.95
Independent variables	**Migrants**	**Non-migrants**	**Migrants**	**Non-migrants**
1990 Difference between regional and national wages for skill group in region	687.866205**	149.760649	707.268885*	459.73622
1990 Supply for skill group in region	3.00036**	5.956481**	1.065262**	3.716406**
1990 Proportion of college graduates in region	-181753654*	-165715.02**	1850.649501	-28172.046*
1992 Fraction of high-tech jobs in region	19322.3783	224345.053**	2574.67701	-19744.733
New England (reference category for ex ante regional characteristics)				
South Atlantic	8717.59135**	-12416.163*	9960.882651**	-25351.036**
Middle Atlantic	-40056.459	46775.4902	-72528.6746**	-25104.634
East North Central	-18165.722	10450.4725	-34497.7101**	-9485.3504
West North Central	2497.84826	-2036.8111	2692.317502	-5056.7732
East South Central	-4964.6109	-11588.453	-157.707693	-9955.2611
West South Central	7335.35238	1497.89187	9580.907586*	17529.178*
Mountain	6402.0252*	3572.67416	4042.153352*	-3071.3331
Pacific	3450.23675	11457.3959*	4943.192789*	-8557.7301
Constant	4963.36614	54738.2891**	-1588.67994	26123.2544**

Source: Author's calculations on 1990 and 2000 Current Population Survey Data (US Bureau of Labor Statistics).

Note: * = $0.02 \geq p \geq 0.10$ ** = $p \leq 0.10$

Table 18.4 Wage growth for male workers, controlling for migration: 50 metropolitan areas in the United States, 1990–2000

Independent variables	Without cost of living considerations		Cost of living considered	
	College graduates (R-square = 0.75)	High-school graduates (R-square = 0.45)	College graduates (R-square = 0.68)	High-school graduates (R-square = 0.45)
1985–1990 Migrant supply for skill group in region	1.53E-05**	4.91E-06	1.87E-05***	8.02E-06
1985–1990 Non-migrant supply for skill group in region	-4.47E-06*	-1.71E-06	-7.28E-06**	-3.19E-06
1990 Wage for skill group in region	-0.653428**	-0.828661**	-0.790595**	-0.77405**
1990 Proportion of college graduates in region	10.744941**	0.969825	9.794071**	0.147303
1992 Fraction of high-tech jobs in region	5.176528	-3.970048	5.426966	-3.141335
New England (reference category for ex ante regional characteristics)				
South Atlantic	-2.068227*	0.085773	0.792683	1.257864
Middle Atlantic	0.159611	1.293504	2.108498	1.836983
East North Central	0.705469	1.485663	3.622649**	2.684701**
West North Central	-4.275921**	500711	-1.796583	1.351457
East South Central	-0.105017	0.040115	3.69378**	1.615861
West South Central	-1.078203	-0.081159	3.429702**	1.763407
Mountain	0.140876	1.483501	1.606229	1.666541
Pacific	-2.818729**	1.525128	-1.276762	1.378603
(Constant)	15.180836**	12.097045**	11.990019***	10.756832**

Source: Author's Calculations on 1990 and 2000 Current Population Survey Data (US Bureau of Labor Statistics).

Note: * = $0.20 \geq p \geq 0.10$ ** = $p \leq 0.10$

When cost of living is controlled for, wages tend towards convergence and migration decreases as there is a smaller return to moving. Although high-tech activity attracts immigration of both college graduates and high-school graduates increasing their supply and affecting their wages, holding all else constant (cost of living and migration, particularly), an increase in that activity, on its own, does not result in physical displacement. Furthermore, it allowed us to confirm that migration plays an important role in determining who wins and who looses, at least on relative terms, between high- and low-skill labor, when a region follows an education-intensive economic development policy. High-school graduates not only earn lower wages in regions of high concentration of college graduates, but also are in the presence of a larger wage gap between their wage rate and that of college graduates in their region of residence (Table 18.1).

Conclusions and Policy Implications

One of the most important contributions of this research to the study of impacts of high-tech activity in regional outcomes comes from the fact that the cross-regional analysis allowed to discern between the effects of a high-tech path to development and that of an increasingly large concentration of highly educated labor, as a proxy for a broader set of economic development initiatives that depend on this labor type as their primary input. According to the employment, wage and migration model results, the 1990 regional high-tech fraction of jobs could predict how regions and their resident workers performed by the end of the decade. Increases in high-tech activity attracts both college and high-school graduates, when all else is held constant. The models also tell us that the larger the concentration of college graduates that a region had in 1990 the fewer workers it would be able to attract during the decade. The coefficient for this portion of the migration model is negative indicating that, all else constant, an increasingly high proportion of college graduates would repel workers, especially college graduates who are more mobile than high-school graduates. This suggests that striving to maintain large concentrations of a more educated labor force, first, has a stronger effect than increases in demand from high-tech growth alone, and, second, that increasing that concentration would slow down growth in this input (i.e. highly educated labor) and growth in an economy that is based in this input as a whole.

Regions that had a larger concentration of high-tech jobs not only offered higher wages for college graduates in 1990 than regions with lower concentrations of high-tech jobs but also experienced slower wage growth for that group during the decade. Regions that had a larger concentration of high-tech jobs not only offered lower wages for high-school graduates in 1990 than regions with lower concentrations of high-tech jobs but also experienced significant wage losses for that group by 2000. By the end of the decade high-school workers in regions with high high-tech fractions of jobs earned $0.75/hr less than regions of low fractions of high-tech jobs, on average.

Regions with higher proportions of college graduates offered higher college graduate wages than regions with lower proportions of college graduates throughout the decade. Nonetheless, wage growth was much slower in the former than in the latter region type. While regions with high proportions of college graduates offered higher high-school graduates wages in 1990 than regions of low proportions of college graduates, by the end of the decade the former offered lower low-skill wages than the latter because of slower growth in that indicator. When cost-of-living differences and migration patterns are considered, as a region's workforce composition becomes more-educated, it can create greater income inequality.

The estimated coefficients of these effects that I present should inform the decision of economic developers, so that they understand how are the benefits and costs of these strategies distributed between the less- and the more-educated. Furthermore, these findings also help identify potential areas of intervention in order to minimize any negative impacts that could come from growth. Given these findings I identify three areas of intervention that could better distribute the impacts from growth.

First, governments should look at the composition and diversity of their economic base and how those compare to their regional skill pool. Economic developers should keep in mind that following economic development strategies that disproportionately are based on exploiting a relatively high-concentration of college graduates could be self-limiting, especially if that region already has a relatively high cost of living, as compared to national averages, and if migration is easily possible (as it is the case in the 48 contiguous states). As the proportion of college graduates increases in a region, growth in the supply and wages of this skill group are bound to slow down, discouraging immigration of high-skill workers and thus hampering the long-term growth capacity of industry sectors that use that labor type as the primary input, as it is the case in high-tech and finance sectors, among others. Furthermore, high proportions of college graduates tend to displace native low-skill workers out of a region. These workers get trapped between fewer employment opportunities and higher cost-of-living. Thus, economic developers should foster a more diverse set of economic activities that would employ its residents at the level of skill that they possess. Activities that employ a higher level of skill become an alternative only when the educational infrastructure, that is, public and private education and training programs, can increase the skill pool of that labor force to match the needs of industry. Otherwise, immigrants would take those jobs slowing down growth and competing out any foreseeable benefits from growth.

The second area that requires attention is that of costs-of-living, particularly housing prices. In regions of relatively high cost of living, immigration within state or from other states or countries would be further discouraged not only for college graduates but also for high-school graduates. In addition, the number and proportion of workers who stay in the region (i.e. who do not migrate out of the region) would be expected to decrease significantly. Consequently, the growth capacity of the regional economic structure could be further impaired; that is, a boom in industry sectors that depend on more-educated labor would last a short time under these conditions. Regions that are expensive places to live in, even before a high-tech or a more-educated labor strategy is in place, are bound to loose in the long-run unless an aggressive affordable housing program for working families is implemented simultaneously.

The third area of intervention is migration patterns. While I have demonstrated that stabilization through migration-controls is possible (i.e. both the negative and the positive impacts are milder when migration patterns are held constant), given the boost in cost-of-living that results from increases in the economic activities of sectors that are dependent in a more-educated labor force and the limited mobility of high-school graduates, especially females, these would be bound to suffer from fewer job opportunities and lower wages (from both a decrease in demand and small increases in supply) as well as fewer living/housing options within the metropolitan core of a region. While it would be unrealistic to close the borders, so to speak, of a region, governments could require from employers in knowledge-intensive sectors a minimum proportion of jobs that must be provided to resident labor. Alternatively, local and regional governments, either through multi-state consortia or federal-level programs with support from employers, could increase the mobility of low-skill workers and women by assisting them with the economic and social costs of relocation. This assistance could vary from transportation services or subsidies, job search and job matching programs, day care, as well as orientation and financial aid for relocation.

Minimizing the negative cost-of-living and migration effects could improve the outcomes of both college graduates and low-skill workers in regions that choose to follow a development strategy that is dependent on a highly educated workforce. Furthermore, it could allow those regions to enjoy the benefits from employment and wages for a longer time before long-term migration bring these to a level of equilibrium.

References

Archibugi, D. and Lundvall, B. (eds) (2001), *The Globalizing Learning Economy* (New York: Oxford University Press).

Bartik, T. (1991), *Who Benefits From State and Local Economic Development Policies?* (Kalamazoo, Michigan: Upjohn Institute for Employment Research).

Bartik, T. (2001), *Jobs for the Poor* (Kalamazoo, Michigan: Upjohn Institute for Employment Research).

Boston Redevelopment Authority (2002), *Meeting with Research and Economic Development Staff*, including Greg Perkins and Owen Donelly.

Boston Redevelopment Authority (2003), *The Boston Economy* (Boston, Massachusetts).

Brown, P. (2001), 'Skill Formation in the Twentieth Century', in Brown, Green and Lauder (eds).

Brown, P., et al. (2001), *High Skills: Globalization Competitiveness, and Skill Formation* (New York, NY: Oxford University Press).

Castells, M. (1999) 'The Informational City is a Dual City: Can it be Reversed?' in Schor et al. (eds).

Clemetson, L. (2003), 'Poor Workers Finding Modest Housing Unaffordable, Study Says', September 9, 2003 (*The New York Times*).

Goetz, S. and Rupasingha, A. (2003), 'The Returns on Higher Education: Estimates for the 48 Contiguous States', *Economic Development Quarterly*, 17:4, 337–51.

Hanushek, E. and Kimko, D. (2000), 'Schooling, Labor-force Quality, and the Growth of Nations', *American Economic Review*, 90, 1184–1208.

Katz, L. and Goldin, C. (1996), 'Technology, Skill and the Wage Structure: Insights from the Past,' *American Economic Review*, 86, 252–257.

Lash, S. (1994), *Economies of signs and space* (Thousand Oaks, California: Sage Publications).

Lauder, H. (2001), 'Innovation, Skill Diffusion and Social Exclusion', in Brown et al. (eds).

Milken Institute (1999), *America's High-Tech Economic Growth: Growth, Development, and Risks for Metropolitan Areas* (Santa Monica, California: Milken Institute).

Porter, M. (1995), 'Global Competition and the Localization of Competitive Advantage', in *Proceedings of the Integral Strategy Collegium* (Graduate School of Business, Indiana University, Greenwich, Connecticut: JAI Press).

Schienstock, G. (2001), 'Social Exclusion in the Learning Economy', in Archibugi and Lundvall (eds).

Schor, D., et al. (1999), *High Technology and Low-Income Communities* (Cambridge, Massachusetts: MIT Press).

Swift, M. (2003), *Bay State Drain Reversed; Connecticut Sees Influx of Residents*, December 4, 2003 (The Hartford Courant).

Waddington, H. and Sabates-Wheeler, R. (2003), 'How Does Poverty Affect Migration Choice? A Review of Literature,' *Working Paper T3* (Institute of Development Studies, Sussex University's Development Research Centre on Migration, Globalization and Poverty).

Conclusion

Roles and Realities

Susan M. Opp

Man everywhere is a disturbing agent. Wherever he plants his foot, the harmonies of nature are turned to discords – George Perkins, 1864.

Many definitions and approaches to Sustainable Development exist. The most commonly used and widely recognized definition is derived from the Bruntland Report. In this report, sustainable development is defined as development that "meets the needs of the present without compromising the ability of future generations to meet their own needs," (World Commission on Environment and Development 1987). Although this report certainly helped bring the concept of sustainable development to the mainstream, it was not responsible for the creation of it. "The two words have been joined occasionally since the early 1970s, when sustainable development was actually a radical discourse for the Third World," (Dryzek 2005). However, since the Bruntland Report was first published, and as is evidenced by the geographic diversity exhibited in the chapters in this volume, global interest in sustainable development has grown significantly and is no longer considered a *radical* view.

"The decade since the United Nations Conference on Environment and Development (UNCED) has seen an extraordinary acceleration of the process globalization. The almost universal adoption of free market model of economic management, albeit with wide variations between countries, has contributed significantly to this trend" (United Nations 2002).

As economic globalization continues its acceleration, the quest for sustainable development poses a variety of roles to a very diverse set of actors. The diversity in economies, cultures, and values across the globe pose significant impediments to a more environmentally protective and sustainable future. The process of sustainable development is not an easy one and countries across the globe have tackled the issue in a variety of ways – including absolute inaction.

When taken collectively, the chapters in this volume speak to the three interlocking concepts of sustainable development – economics, community, and environment. Three good examples are in Taniguchi et al., Polakit et al., and Navarro-Díaz's chapters. More specifically, Taniguchi, Abe, and Ono's unique examination of sustainability in Japan illustrates some unique environmental concepts and methods for the measurement of sustainability. Alternatively, Polakit and Boontharm's examination of local culture persistence in the global city of Bangkok helps illustrates how community and culture is both important and impacting. Finally, Navarro-Díaz's examination of employment in high-tech regions shows some interesting economic implications, illustrating how diversity in economies exists. All of the chapters in this volume help illustrate why sustainable development is not an easy or short process.

Overall the scope of views, issues, and aspects related to the concept of sustainable development presented within this volume is striking. The diversity in these chapters illustrates the sheer volume of issues that are related to, and impact, the concept of and quest for sustainable development. They also speak to an important truth: sustainability is both a global and a local issue. Sustainability cannot begin at the global level and it cannot end at the local level. At this juncture, and in conclusion, it is important to recognize that in the face of globalizing trends the pursuit of sustainability begins at the local level – but requires both a local and a global effort. This concluding chapter offers some final remarks concerning some of the realities of roles and constraints in the quest for sustainable development.

Reframing Economic Development-First Steps

Part of the resistance and misunderstanding surrounding sustainable development is a result of a general misunderstanding of economic development. Before development can become more sustainable, a true understanding of exactly what constitutes economic development is required.

> Economic growth means more output, while economic development implies both more output and changes in the technical and institutional arrangements by which it is produced and distributed ... As with humans, to stress 'growth' involves focusing on height or weight (or GNP), while to emphasize development draws attention to changes in functional capacities – in physical coordination, for example or learning capacity (Kindleberger and Herrick 1977).

Great confusion and even debate exists across academics, practitioners, and policy makers about what constitutes economic development. In fact, much of what occurs at the local level is really just economic growth, not economic development. "The term economic development is often used to refer to what is essentially land development or physical development, frequently project based, even if these efforts are not directed at or do not increase income or employment" (Wolman and Spitzley 1996). Often, analysts seeking to study and measure economic development turn to quantitative measures such as GDP, income changes, employment changes, and unemployment statistics. Economic growth can cause increases in these quantitative measures but this economic growth does not necessary mean economic development has occurred.

The term development implies a progression. In order for a community to achieve economic development, in its real sense, a progression of the lives and economies of the community is essential – not just a change in a number. Unemployment may drop as the result of the opening of a large industrial facility in a community, but has that city actually experienced development or progression to something *better* or more efficient? Is the decrease in unemployment equal to or better than the increase in air pollution, traffic congestion, and other negative environmental and social externalities related to the location of that particular industry in the community? These types of assertions illustrate the real difference between economic growth and economic development. It is possible to have economic growth without economic development just like it is possible to have economic development without a growth in many of the traditionally used economic indicators.

The fundamental confusion over economic growth and economic development is a seriously limiting factor in achieving more *sustainable* development. If perpetual increases in standard quantitative economic indicators are what is desired and pursued – sustainability is most likely an impossible feat as this implies never-ending resources. The conventional view and goal of achieving economic growth will require reframing to one that is more focused on true *development* in order to ever achieve economic development practices that are sustainable. It has been noted that much of the confusion over the conventional viewpoint of development is rooted in several conclusions deduced from fiscal impact analysis: providing tax breaks for corporate relocations is bad, residential development only pays about 70 percent of the costs of the services provided by the local government, office and industrial development tends to pay its own way through the various taxes levied on them, and retail development almost always pays for itself if the local government shares in the distribution of sales tax revenues (Leinberger 2000). This type of view that propels typical bricks and mortar projects where policymakers are driven by *new* development opportunities is fundamentally unsustainable.

It is true that economic development does not necessarily mean *new* economic growth. It is also likely true that in some communities, economic development could be a new business or industry that provides certain needed and not internally available things. However, this does not always need to be the case, as those new employment opportunities could stem from reinvestment into the businesses that are already in the community instead of working to attract additional and new businesses. The key to economic development is that it provides an expansion, improvement, or progression in the *quality* or efficiency of a community. A major component of a more sustainable development pattern requires a look inward. That is, looking at the current state of the community and reinvesting and redeveloping the existing community can lead to development that is environmentally and economically more sustainable. This look inward can come as a result of reframing economic development and as such it should be "… a critical aspect of community planning" (Luther and Borner 1996).

Transitioning from a conventional economic growth/development pattern to one that is sustainable requires both a reframing of the traditional and conventional views of economic development and a committed collection of local, regional, and national efforts translating into a worldwide effort. Encouraging communities to embrace a different view of economic development and subsequently supporting development that is sustainable requires such an enormous global effort that progress has been extremely slow over the past few decades and has even been referred to as glacial. However, in order to become more sustainable, conventional economic development must be reframed and understood as something that emphasizes actual *development* not simply growth.

Sustainability Solution?

Fundamental cultural and economic differences that exist across the globe make the solutions to achieving sustainable development just as diverse as are the differences across the globe. There is no one size fits all in sustainable development practices. The quest to transform the conventional economic development/growth efforts into sustainable development is an immense, expensive, and politically challenging problem with no simple or short term answers. As Rosenberg so succinctly stated:

> ... this liberalization [of UN Agenda] has spurred an economic growth which has only blurred the debate further as many of the growing economies (like those of Colombia, Brazil, and Mexico) have entered the ranks of the top 20 producers of greenhouse gases. The countries of the south have always asserted their right to defer making economic sacrifices for the sake of the environment, sacrifices never made by the North during its pursuit of economic development. As the South's contributions to the problem have grown, so have the pressing human needs of their populations, thus rendering them unable to pay the price that they now demand to be paid by the developed countries: an amount estimated to be close to $125 billion a year for the underdeveloped world alone ... (Rosenberg 1994).

When faced with extreme poverty, the leaders in many developing nations are still anxiously searching for market access, technology access, investment, and financing – not necessarily future or global sustainability. It has been pointed out that many of these leaders elect for immediate satisfaction for economic demands rather than hold out for a more sustainable use of land (French 1993). For many developing nations, economic *growth* is believed to be so desperately needed that the idea of waiting or promoting a more sustainable development and environmental protection opportunity is, to them, illogical. "Sustained poverty often leads countries to engage in behaviors that exacerbate ecological deterioration. For example, billions of tons of fertile soil are lost annually as consequence of deforestation and the cultivation of steep lands, and as soil fertility declines, increased deforestation occurs for the development of new croplands" (Steel et al., 2003).

In understanding the fundamental problems associated with a collective global effort at sustainable development it is useful to draw upon other scholarly work in human needs motivations. Specifically, past scholars have pointed to theories of a hierarchy of human needs. These scholars posit that a hierarchy exists in what humans need and what actions they will embark on as a result of what level of the hierarchy they are currently on. For example, when the most basic human needs/lowest tier of the hierarchy are not being met the other levels of the hierarchy are not of concern and their actions are centered on the attainment of those basic needs (see for example Maslow 1943). One prominent human needs scholar offers a five tier hierarchy of basic human needs: Physiological, Safety, Love, Belonging, Esteem, and Self-Actualization (Maslow 1943). It is possible to draw some logical connections between Maslow's hierarchy of human needs and the quest for economic development and sustainable development.

On the lowest tier of Maslow's hierarchy are physiological needs. These physiological needs include basic human dignities and requirements such as food and water. According to Maslow, if humans do not have this basic level of need (lowest tier of hierarchy) met, all actions will be consumed with meeting this need above and beyond anything else. In many developing countries, individuals suffer extreme poverty and starvation. Following Maslow's work, it can be assumed that the drive and desire to meet these basic human needs outweighs any other option–specifically holding out for a more sustainable land use.

On the other end of the concept of a hierarchy of human needs is what is termed self-actualization. According to Maslow, self-actualizing people: embrace the facts and realities of the world as opposed to denying them or avoiding them, are spontaneous, are creative, are interested in solving problems including problems of others, and are able to see things in a non-judgmental way. Drawing lessons from this tier of the hierarchy implies that many developing countries cannot concentrate on problem identification (unsustainable economic growth and environmental degradation) and problem solving (employing the concept of sustainable development) until they reach that tier – meaning they must first meet other more basic needs. The action of meeting these basic needs generally enables them to select and encourage even the most environmentally and economically unsustainable development that can meet some of their basic needs in the short term.

Using the concept of a hierarchy of human needs illustrates one of the most fundamental problems in the path of achieving sustainable development. For many communities concentrating on a more sustainable development pattern is simply not possible due to the conditions under which they live (their position on the hierarchy of human needs). In addition to communities in the developing world, these lessons also apply to many local communities in the developing nations. With poverty and safety (tier two of Maslow's hierarchy) deficits present in many developed nations' communities, these communities are likely not able to either identify or select the sustainable development path as a result of a deficit in the current ability to meet their more basic, immediate needs. Long term environmental and economic consequences often take last place to the more immediate, noticeable, and impending issues present in many communities.

"It should come as no surprise that the environmentalist community ... would be concerned that the forces of free market capitalism and the urgency for economic development have proven to be more powerful than the regional movement towards sustainable development" (Rosenberg 1994). As Steel et al. (2003) points out, the context of environmental politics in developing countries can be summarized as follows:

- A significant proportion of the population lives in extreme poverty
- More than half the population lives in near poverty
- Well over half the working population is unable to find productive employment
- A pervasive sense of urgency about promoting industrialization, modernization, and *economic growth* is present
- Deep-seated and widespread feelings of resentment and distrust toward both the national government and postindustrial countries exist

- Low levels of appreciation for, understanding of, and concern about the natural environment characterize governmental authorities
- Very low levels of public understanding of the health risks associated with pollution are present
- Governments tend to be more interested in selling or renting the public domain than in safeguarding the public interest
- Governments tend to possess very limited revenues
- Governments tend to command only modest administrative capacity

Possessing an understanding of these contextual issues in both the developed and the developing nations points to the fact that solutions for increased acceptance and use of sustainable development concepts will require a focus upon different aspects of the environment, community, and economy across these groups. For now, a focus on simple economic *growth* will inevitably work to continue the current unsustainable development patterns. Following from the previous discussion with global economic pressures and differences in the ability of communities to meet basic human needs, it becomes apparent that local efforts must be combined with both national and global efforts, [a]s "... community activities are already interconnected with and even subsumed under regional, national and global economic systems" (Porter 2000). A strategy must encompass all the components of developing and developed nations that are impeding the ability to make the choice to develop in a more sustainable manner as opposed to the current development patterns.

Local Control

Although a reframing of what economic development actually *is* will be a necessity on the path to sustainable development as well as attention to the differences that exist in communities – another issue is also a roadblock on the quest to achieving sustainable development. This issue is that of local limitations. Many people have likely heard the phrase *Think Globally, Act Locally.* This phrase was initially coined by Rene Dubos, an advisor to the United Nations Conference on the Human Environment in 1972 (Eblen and Eblen 1994). This phrase represents and refers to the widely made argument that global environmental problems can only be addressed by considering the cultural, ecological, and economic differences that exist across the world. Although very much a cliché, this phrase has a meaning that is both relevant and powerful to the realities of sustainable development – local efforts are the starting point for solving many environmental problems. After all, global environmental problems are but a collection of local environmental problems.

Although local action is necessary and important in the quest for sustainable development, local community efforts at sustainable development are inherently limited across the globe. This limitation has some very real implications for achieving sustainable development. To be sure, local efforts at environmental protection and sustainable development are limited by what powers overhead governments' grant to them (Swanstrom 1988; Rosenbloom and Kravchuk 2005), by economic dependence and interdependence (Savitch and Vogel 1996), and by mobile capital (DeFilippis 2004). Although limited, the actual action that propels a more sustainable development practice exists at the local level. Given the limitations that local governments face in the path to sustainable development, regional and global strategies are required to enable communities to elect sustainable development over conventional, unsustainable, growth. It is very difficult, after all, to elect against development that may work to alleviate poverty in some ways and that fill a need for jobs, in favor of a higher and more sustainable use when a community is in poverty and dire need. Although the action that enables and progresses sustainable development exists at the local level- without regional and global influence and help- many localities will be both unable and unwilling to select sustainability over immediate economic growth.

The Realities of Sustainable Development

The reality of sustainable development is that it is not a process that will be easy, inexpensive, or fast. Sustainable development as a concept is plagued by confusion over the definition and confusion in the understanding of the core concepts. Even with the massive increase in awareness and support for a more sustainable development pattern across the globe, the progress towards a more sustainable future is marked with resistance, ignorance, and inaction in many parts of the world.

It is necessary to reframe the conventional economic development view to one that is not analogous to economic growth. Pure growth and industrialization is inherently unsustainable. Until the various actors assume their respective necessary roles, a sustainable future will be out of reach. Local communities cannot achieve global sustainability until the regional, national, and global communities fulfill their necessary roles in the process. For as long as the trans-national system is reliant upon material growth as the driver for economic activity, development, and new income- the future is bleak for the quest of sustainable development. The limited actions available to the local communities will not be sufficient to drive sustainable development into the future. The efforts to achieve sustainable development need to be a collaborative, global effort with roots in the local community and branches into the global community. This book concludes with a quote from Mahatma Gandhi:

> It's the action, not the fruit of the action, that's important. You have to do the right thing. It may not be in your power, may not be in your time, that there will be any fruit. But that doesn't mean you stop doing the right thing. You may never know what results come from your action. But if you do nothing, there will be no result.

References

Brewster, G. (1996), 'The Ecology of Development', *Urban Land*, June, 21–25.
DeFilippis, J. (2004), *Unmaking Goliath: Community Control in the Face of Global Capital* (New York: Routledge).
Dryzek, J.S. (2005), *The Politics of the Earth: Environmental Discourses* (Oxford: Oxford University Press).

Eblen, R. and Eblen, W. (1994), *The Encyclopedia of the Environment* (Boston: Houghton Mifflin Company).

French, H. (1993), 'Costly Tradeoffs: Reconciling Trade and the Environment', *Worldwatch Paper 113* (March) (Washington, DC: The Worldwatch Institute).

Goodland, R. (1995), 'The Concept of Environmental Sustainability', *Annual Review of Ecology and Systematics*, 26, 1–24.

Kindleberger C. and Herrick, B. (1977), *Economic Development* (International student edition) (London: McGraw-Hill).

Leinberger, C. (2000), *The Connection Between Sustainability and Economic Development*, in Porter (ed.).

Luther, J. and Borner, W. (1996), 'Planning the Sustainable Community: Indicators, Policies, and Performance Criteria Part One', *Western Planner*, January/February, 13–16.

Maslow, A. (1943), 'A Theory of Human Motivation', *Psychological Review*, 50, 370–396.

Peterson, P. (1981), *City Limits* (Chicago: University of Chicago Press).

Porter, D. (ed.) (2000), *The Practice of Sustainable Development* (Washington, DC: Urban Land Institute).

Rosenberg, R. (1994) 'Trade and the Environment: Economic Development versus Sustainable Development' *Journal of Interamerican Studies and World Affairs*, 36:3, 129–156.

Rosenbloom, D. and Kravchuk, R. (2005), *Public Administration: Understanding Management, Politics, and Law in the Public Sector* (Dushkin: McGraw-Hill).

Savitch, H. and Vogel, R. (eds) (1996), *Regional Politics* (Thousand Oaks, CA: Sage).

Steel, B., et al. (2003), *Environmental Politics and Policy: A Comparative Approach* (Boston: McGraw Hill).

Swanstrom, T. (1988) 'Semisovereign Cities: The Politics of Urban Development', *Polity*, 21:1, 83–110

United Nations Environment Programme (2002), 'From Globalization to Sustainable Development: UNEP's Work on Trade, Economics, and Sustainable Development', available at: <http://www.unep.ch/etu/wssd/BGpappc4fin.pdf>, accessed January 2, 2007.

Wolman, H. and Spitzley, D. (1996), 'The Politics of Local Economic Development', *Economic Development Quarterly*, 10:2.

World Commission on Environment and Development (1987), *Our Common Future* (New York: Oxford University Press).

Index